Python Graphics for Game Creation 3:

Working in 3 Dimensions

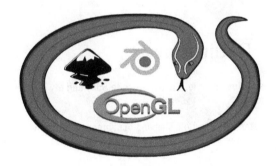

Object Creation and Animation with OpenGL and Blender.

Mike Ohlson de Fine

Python Graphics for Game Creation 3: Working in 3-Dimensions

Mike Ohlson de Fine

First published: June, 2015

Published by Mike Ohlson de Fine.
Mike.ohlsondefine@gmail.com

ISBN 978-0-620-66573-5

Dedication

I humbly dedicate this book to three people. Firstly, my wife Suzy and my son Pete. Pete I am prouder of you than you know.

Suzy for everything and for starting the whole shebang that, among other things, led to Pete. Finally I am grateful to Guido von Rossum who, with his clarity of thought gave us a pain free computer language.

Table of Contents

6

Preface and Outline

This book is for creative minds anywhere. When I wrote it I visualized young teenagers in poor countries with a burning desire to create art, create games and as a side effect, learn programming, and maybe some math and physics. I also was thinking of ways to provide engineers and scientists with some debugged code that they could use for constructing simulations and models without the need to spend weeks or months mastering programming or buying expensive software.

The art of creating games, simulations and stories on computer screens only came into existence about forty years ago.

One of the good things I hope will come out of this book series will be an awareness that mathematics and science lessons at school are a wonderful privilege if you want to become a creator of games. Be grateful to you school teachers particular the ones who teach mathematics. They are rare, special and to be appreciated. They are the givers of gifts, the value of which is boundless. Show them respect and affection. They truly deserve it.

Book Outline

This book aims to get readers quickly to the position where they can start crafting code that lets them make 3-dimensional animated images. In addition it will give the reader the tools and capability of learning to use the same techniques used in making the rich graphical worlds seen in modern video games.

It is not a text book of math although it will lean on several fields of math – some trigonometry, coordinate geometry and matrix algebra. Only the bare minimum will be used in the text; just enough to explain how the Python programs work.

This book is really a recipe cookbook of programs that illustrate many of the ideas and concepts used in the creation of computer games and simulations. The driving idea is that a young person with nothing more than a computer can become a creator of games. The book is fundamentally about the geometry used in controlling the virtual worlds of computer games.

The Python code examples presented here represent a reduced set of programs that were developed to explore the techniques discussed in this book. There was a need to keep the book to around 300 pages, which is a reasonable size. However richer and further ranging examples that complement those printed in the book can be found at https://github.com/ inside the repository "Python_3D_Graphics".

Chapter 1, *Starting with Python*: This chapter is about how to get going with Python. It attempts to answer the following questions. Why Python is the best language for creative games and graphics programming? Where can we find Python? How do we install it and how do we test that it is working?

Chapter 2, *Basic Drawing Concepts*: This chapter is a picture essay of drawing concepts, terminology, and conventions.

It includes projections as a method of representing 3D Objects. Numerical descriptions of a point in space or 3D objects. The very important perspective projections are shown.

Chapter 3, *Matrix Manipulation in 2-Dimensions*: This chapter is about transforming two-dimensional drawings by stretching them, rotating them and shifting them. The basics of matrix algebra are explained.

Chapter 4, *Matrix Manipulation in 3-Dimensions*: This chapter is about transforming three-dimensional drawings. It is the extension to three dimensions, of the same methods used in chapter 3.

Chapter 5, *Perspective Projections*: This chapter explains how perspective drawings can be controlled using a special matrix.

Chapter 6, *Object Creation Using SVG and Inkscape*: This chapter explains how to produce 2D and 3D drawings using Scaled Vector Graphics and the Open Source *Inkscape* software package.

Chapter 7, *Blender Objects*: This chapter demonstrates how to produce 3D or 2D graphic objects using the Open Source *Blender* software package.

Chapter 8, *OpenGL Graphic Shapes*: This chapter introduces the basic techniques for drawing OpenGL primitives and GLUT wireshapes.

Chapter 9, *Animation*: Here we present methods of using the OpenGL graphics standard together with Python to produce drawings and animations.

Chapter 10, *Vertex Arrays and Normals:* This chapter introduces OpenGL vertex array instructions. The importance and use of normal vectors is explained as well as a method of making normal vectors visible.

Chapter 11, *Model Construction:* This chapter presents methods of using OpenGL to assemble virtual world models from a collection of 3D objects.

Chapter 12, *OpenGL Texture:* The role of Frame and Depth buffers is introduced in the context of reducing complex multi-layer images to the showing of single pixel raster arrays.

Chapter 13, *OpenGL Fog and Transparency:* Methods of creating fog and also of controlling transparency using OpenGL with Python are demonstrated.

Chapter 14, *OpenGL Lighting:* The basic properties of light sources are demonstrated.

Attributes like light position, diffuse, ambient, emissive and specular light are shown. Spotlights are given attention by means of an extended set of examples.

Appendix 1 , *Computer Graphics Glossary*

Appendix 2 , *Program Inventory*

Appendix 3 , *The Broken Path Problem*

Appendix 4 . *Graphics Hardware and Software*

Copyrights, disclaimers and the spirit of ethical sharing.

We all learn by standing on the shoulders of others. I am indebted to thousands of talented people who have developed software and hardware. These people recognize the value of freely sharing their best work with the rest of us. In the same spirit anyone is free to use the code, ideas, and illustrations in this book. I retain the copyright of the book as an entity. Just do not lay legal claim to the code, ideas, and illustrations for yourself. That would be nasty as well as unethical.

1

Getting Started with Python

"I have the students learn Python in our undergraduate and graduate Semantic Web courses. Why? Because basically there's nothing else with the flexibility and as many web libraries," Prof. James A. Hendler, University of Maryland

"Python plays a key role in our production pipeline. Without it a project the size of Star Wars: Episode II would have been very difficult to pull off. From crowd rendering to batch processing to compositing, Python binds all things together," Tommy Burnette, Senior Technical Director, Industrial Light & Magic.

"Python enabled us to create EVE Online, a massive multiplayer game, in record time. The EVE Online server cluster runs over 50,000 simultaneous players in a shared space simulation, most of which is created in Python. The flexibilities of Python have enabled us to quickly improve the game experience based on player feedback" Hilmar Veigar Petursson of CCP Games.

Topics covered in this chapter:
- **Why Python**
- **The Shortest Python Program**
- **Python Modules**
- **The Value of Dead Tree Notebooks**

Why Python?

Python is probably the most popular computer language of the planet. I mean popular in the sense that people love it. It makes people glad when they use it and some of the reasons for this are:

- it is clear and easy to understand,
- it is easy to learn,
- it is extremely well documented and supported,
- it is fun to use,
- it is a quick, brilliant tool for rapid testing of ideas and concepts
- it is free,
- it is in very widespread use,
- it is carefully managed by very smart people.

Incorporated into Python is a graphics module called Tkinter (or tkinter if you are using Python version 3 upward). Throughout the first portion of this book we will use Tkinter to produce our drawings. It is easiest to understand concepts and principles when we draw using Tkinter. In the last few chapters we use OpenGL. OpenGL is significantly more difficult because one has to use many commands whose purpose is not obvious. OpenGL is not incorporated into Python but OpenGL commands can co-exist with Python relatively seamlessly. Certainly Python makes it easier to learn OpenGL. OpenGL, and a subset of it called OpenES, is probably poised to become the worldwide standard for producing computer graphics on most computing devices including mobile devices like cellphones and tablets.

The prerequisites for using Python and Tkinter are obviously to have both installed on our computer. Both are free and Open Source and instructions for obtaining and installing them are abundantly available on the web. Just Google phrases like "install Python" you will be spoilt for choice. "Google" is used as a verb here. I will recommend:
https://www.python.org/about/gettingstarted/
and
https://wiki.python.org/moin/BeginnersGuide/NonProgrammers

Your first task is to prove that Python and Tkinter are installed and working on your computer.

Here you are shown the simple tests you can quickly do and how to interpret the results. Most versions of Linux have both Python and Tkinter installed as part of the system tools and utilities that are part of the operating system. If you download and install Python on Windows it automatically includes Tkinter as one of the essential modules so you do not need to try to acquire and install it separately.

The Shortest Python Program

We will not be learning the fundamentals of Python programming in this book. There is an abundance of excellent learning material on the internet.
All we need now is a one line Python program that will prove that the Python interpreter is installed and working on your computer platform.

How to do it:

1. Create a folder (directory) called something like "construction_work" or "constr" for short. You will place all your experimental Python programs inside this directory. In a text editor such as *gedit* or *context* type the line below.

print ("mywereld is 'my world' in Dutch")

3. Save this as a file named ***simple_1.py***, inside the directory called *"**constr**"*

4. Open up an X terminal or a DOS window if you are using MS Windows.

5. Change to the directory ***constr*** - where ***simple_1.py*** is located.

6. Type **python simple_1.py** and your program will execute. The result should look like the screenshot shown here. In this example I have both Python 2.6 and Python 3.2 installed and evidently each works.

```
Terminal                                                    -  +  x
mikeodf@mikeodf-HP-500B-Microtower ~ $ python3 /home/mikeodf/constr/simple_1.py
mywereld is 'my world' in Dutch
mikeodf@mikeodf-HP-500B-Microtower ~ $ python2 /home/mikeodf/constr/simple_1.py
mywereld is 'my world' in Dutch
mikeodf@mikeodf-HP-500B-Microtower ~ $ ▮
```

This proves that your Python interpreter works, your editor works, and that you understand all that is needed to run all the programs in this book. Congratulations!

How it works

Any instructions you type into a Linux X terminal or DOS terminal in MS Windows are treated as operating system commands. By starting these commands from within the same directory where your Python program is stored, you do not have to tell the Python and operating system where to search for for your code. You could store the code in another directory but you would then need to precede the program name with the directory path.

Python Modules

A module is a file containing Python definitions, statements and functions. The file name is the module name with the suffix .py appended. If we wanted to use one of the functions inside a module called *wash_the_elphant.py* we add an *"import wash_the_elephant"* statement in our code before the function is called. If the particular function we needed was called *"cool_swim"* then we would call it with the statement:
wash_the_elephant. cool_swim. The same reference convention applies to accessing constants. For example if we want the constant known as *pi* from the math module we would write *math.pi.*

Frequently we will see statements like *from math import pi.* When imported this way we can leave out the *"math."* prefix and simply type *pi* whenever we want to use that constant.

What Python Modules are Available?
Many useful programs and collections of programs have been written and added to the vast standard library of programs that belong to Python and are distributed with it. To see a list of these modules go to "https://docs.python.org/2/library/" in your web browser.

In addition to the standard library, there is a growing collection of more than 47 thousand programs and collections of programs (packages) available from the "Python package index at https://pypi.python.org/pypi.

How to Test That a Needed Python Module is Present
To test if a specific module, for example a function called, *"needed_function"*, is available in the Python standard library on our local hard drive, include the statement *import needed_function* in a python program. If the program runs without issuing a *"ImportError: No module named needed_function"* error message then it is asfe to assume the module IS present as expected.

The Value of a Dead Tree Notebook

It may seem weird but an extremely valuable tool for any creative activity and software programming in particular, is a pencil or pen and a notebook made of paper. The paper is invariably manufactured from wood pulp - hence the *dead tree* reference in the heading.

Reasons for using a paper notebook:

1. You can dump incomplete and vague ideas down without inhibition. This encourages creative ideas to start flowing.

2. Your ideas can be changed, added to or dropped as your work progresses.

3. Your ideas and developments are preserved in the sequence they happened. Months and years later when you have forgotten how you did something, your notebook will bring it back to you.

4. Your ideas can grow and evolve in simple stages.

5. When your ideas are not yet clear, the act of putting them into words and sketches helps to clarify them.

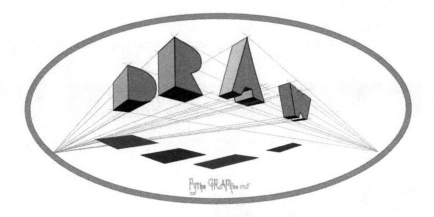

"But it is a pipe."
"No, it's not," I said. It's a drawing of a pipe. Get it? All representations of a thing are inherently abstract. It's very clever." John Green.

This chapter covers:

- **Drawings as an attempt to Capture Reality**
- **Projections Represent 3D Objects**
- **Dotted lines to Reveal Hidden Detail**
- **Shading to reveal complex Structure**
- **Numerical Description of a Point in Space**
- **The Numerical Description of 3D Objects in Computers**
- **Terminology of 3D Computer Geometry**
- **Perspective Projections**

Drawings are the closest we get to Capturing Reality

With reference to computer graphics we talk of 2D and 3D and the common understanding we all have is that these are two distinct ways of visualizing objects on a computer screen. The same can be said of drawings and photographs on sheets of paper. In every case the images are only two dimensional. Sculpture is three dimensional. A photograph of a three dimensional object like a house is still only two dimensional – the image is always on a flat sheet. But somehow when we look at images of three dimensional objects they look 3D because of the way the image is distorted when printed onto a sheet of paper.

In this chapter we discuss:
- how to represent three dimensions on two dimensional media like sheets of paper or computer screens,
- how to distort two dimensional images so that our brains visualize them as three dimensional.

The concepts in this chapter are 'discussed' using pictures mainly. Words will be kept to a minimum.

Projections as a Representation of 3D Objects

Here we show images representing an object with holes in at least four sides. Can there be another hole in one of the sides?

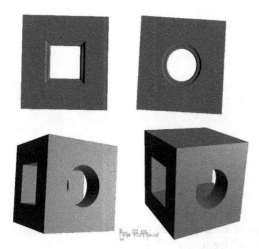

How can we Perceive the True Shape of an Object?

Do the four views shown above reveal the complete object? Can we deduce all we need, to be able to create an identical object? Is there missing information? The answer is that there is indeed missing information ; we do not have a view of the bottom surface. The bottom may have a hole in it or it may not – we cannot know. If it does then we do not know what shape the hole is. This uncertainty could have been resolved if either of the two upper views tilted the cube so we could see the underneath of the cube.

What we do in the rest of this chapter is to explore the idea of being to be able to see the complete structure of a 3-Dimensional object by means of views of the object projected onto a 2-Dimensional surface.

Two Dimensional Projections

A three dimensional object (3D) must be viewed from various angles in order to reveal its shape. For most engineering components, three projections of the object onto surfaces that are perpendicular to each other are sufficient to describe the entire shape.

Below we see an object with two or four holes. Three views projected onto plane surfaces at right angles to each other.

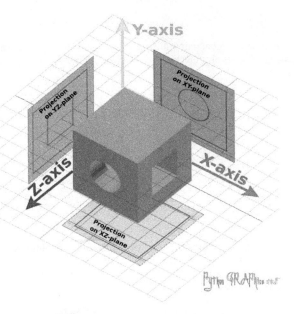

The Cartesian reference axes will be used manipulate numbers inside computers. These numbers will be controlled using the rules of trigonometry. The trigonometry is essential to preserving the shape and form of the 3D object being represented.

Below we see the three orthogonal projections. Is there sufficient information contained in the projections to re-construct the original object?

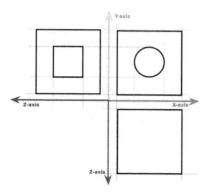

An engineering drawing is a representation containing sufficient information to completely describe the shape. An engineering drawing consists of projections of the object onto plane surfaces which are perpendicular to each other.

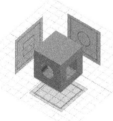

The relationship of the projections to the three dimensional object: It consists of unfolding the three orthogonal projections so that they can be shown on the same sheet of paper or computer screen. The relationship between the projections is governed by the conventions of engineering drawing.

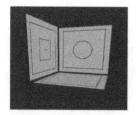 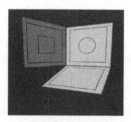 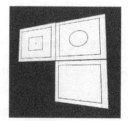

The 3D projections being folded out flat onto a 2D surface. The way the projections are positioned in relation to each other preserves the 3D information that completely describes the object.

Dotted Lines – the Convention for Revealing Hidden Internal Structure

Now we use these ideas of projections of 3D objects onto 2D surfaces to represent a complicated collection of interconnected objects where dotted lines are essential for representing surfaces that are hidden but need to be captured on the image in order for the object to be completely described. This is the basis of engineering and architectural drawing. When machine parts need to be accurately described engineering drawings are used.

How many projections are needed to represent all the details?

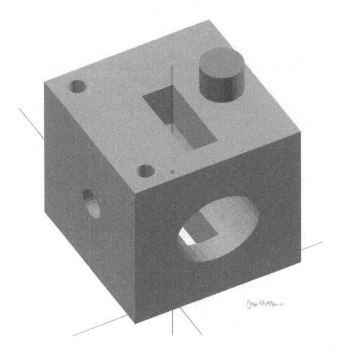

There are six sides. Each side can be represented by a projection. Features like hidden holes can be shown as dotted lines.

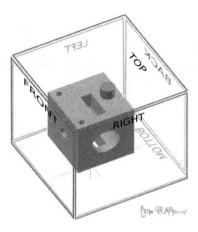

The object and the enclosing projection planes. Three of these planes will be sufficient to completely describe the object if hidden surfaces are also drawn (using dotted lines).

Below we see the projections in the process of being folded flat while still preserving their relationships to each other.

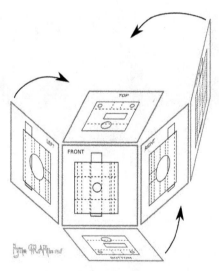

The result of folding out of the enclosing projected images. The six projected surfaces flattened out onto a single 2D surface.

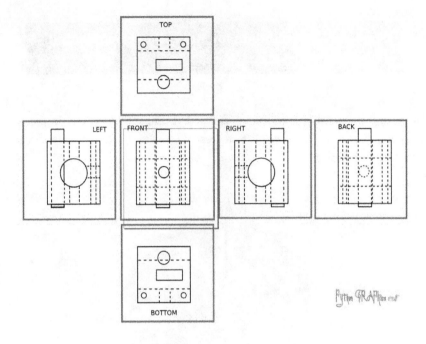

The flat 2D surface with the projections laid out in the correct relationship to each other.

Shading – a Technique for Revealing Complicated 3D Structure

An object constructed from complex surfaces that cannot be completely represented by three projections. It is not possible to represent complex 3D curved surfaces using three plane projections.

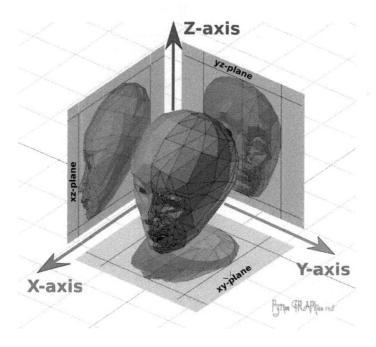

Most real world objects are too complex to be meaningfully represented by engineering drawing projections.
Complex object where simple projections and dotted lines representing hidden surfaces cannot provide a satisfactory representation. Objects with smoothly curved surfaces are only approximately represented by plane surfaces like triangles and planes.

The Numerical Description of a Point in 3D Space

The position of each point on the surface can be represented by three numbers – the shortest distance of that object to the cartesian reference planes. These are the (x-component, y-component and the z-component) that define the position of the point with reference to the yz-plane, the xz-plane and the xy-plane respectively.

A point in 3D space projected onto a 2D X-Y plane. The precise position in 3D space is not known.

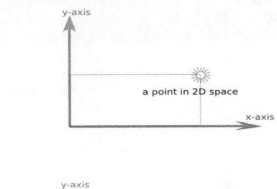

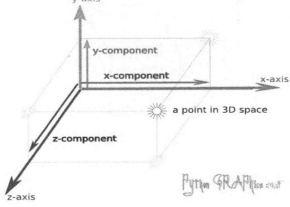

The exact position of a point in 3D space is completely known if three independent coordinates are known: the X, Y and Z coordinates.

Representation of the position of a point using a **vecto**r : a mathematical quantity that is specified by both length and direction.

Every vector in 3D space can be separated into three independent component vectors.

The three projections are shown - one on each projection plane.

The Numerical Description of 3D Objects in Computers

The position of every corner of a box is sufficient to specify the position and shape of the box. Each corner can be specified as a position vector.

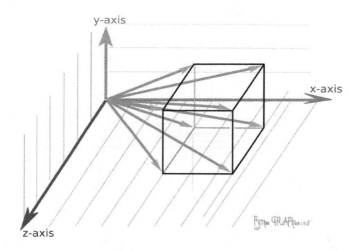

The position vectors of the eight corners of a cube. Because vectors are completely specified by their length and direction we are allowed, by the rules of vectors, to slide them around in space as long as we preserve the direction they point in. It only becomes a **position vector** if it's origin (the non-arrow end) is at the origin of the coordinate system.

This is a central idea used throughout this book to handle complex 3D objects.

Terminology of 3D Computer Geometry

The meaning of vertex, edge and face used throughout the world of 2D and 3D graphics.

Each corner is called a **vertex.**
The straight line joining two adjacent vertices on the surface are called **edges.**
The flat surface defined by having edges enclose it is called a **face.**

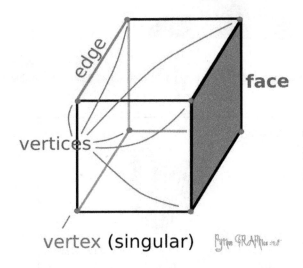

Perspective Projections

Perspective is the technique used by artists to represent distance. It is based on the obvious fact that objects that are far away from the viewer appear smaller than objects that are close.
Perspective can be handled mathematically in a way that is consistent and accurately represents what a viewer observes when looking at the real world as seen in photographs or movies.
As we shall see in Chapter 5 it is surprisingly easy to apply the rules of perspective to objects described by the 3D coordinates of points on the surface of the object.

The three-dimensional size and shape of an object require some kind of *perspective distortion* to convey the idea that parts of the object that are shrinking in size as they get further away from the viewer.

The above is an example of a central vanishing point perspective. A single vanishing point is used.

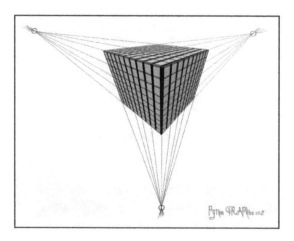

The technical value of more than one vanishing-point perspective is uncertain. A single vanishing point perspective has the same information content. However by distorting the shape along three mutually perpendicular directions, a more dramatic impression of the three-dimensional nature of an object results.

3

Matrix Image Manipulation: 2D

"He'd operated on an almost permanent adrenaline high, a byproduct of youth and proficiency, jacking into a custom cyberspace deck that projected his disembodied consciousness into the consensual hallucination that was the matrix." William Gibson.

Topics in this chapter:

- Space Shifting
- What is a Matrix?
- Two Dimensional Objects - Three Triangles
- Handling Groups of Objects as a Set
- The Conversion from Vertices to Matrices
- The Geometry Transformation using Matrices
- The Conversion from Matrices to Vertices
- Scaling Transformations - the not-so-good-way
- Scaling Transformations - the better-way
- The Sequential and Concatenated Transformations

- The Difficulty of Translation, and a Solution using Augmented Matrices
- The Augmanted Matrix for Translation
- The Other Homogeneous Transforms using Augmented Matrices

Introduction - How to Ease into Linear Algebra

Video games create and control virtual worlds using matrix multiplication. Matrix multiplication belongs to a branch of mathematics called Linear Algebra. We will not delve deeply into this theory here because it is not essential to the understanding of this chapter.

Game developers do not necessarily need to know anything about linear algebra because the software tools they use allows the linear algebra to be hidden. However, because we want to use Python to create and make prototype games it is worthwhile understanding the linear algebra operations. This kind of understanding gives the programmer more insight and freedom to innovate. Ultimately it allows us be more creative.

We want to ease into matrix transformations as painlessly as possible. So we start developing our matrix techniques in 2D (two dimensions). Extending the operations to 3D is then relatively simple. We explain what matrix multiplication is by presenting the concepts graphically. The fine detail of code that manipulates numbers inside our matrices is taken care of by the Numpy module which we use. More about Numpy later.

In this chapter we will work through the basic operations of moving and re-shaping objects in 2D space using matrix multiplication.

What we do now is to build up, one by one, some functions to eventually create 3D objects in 3D worlds. We use animation as a useful tool for debugging Python code whose purpose is to manipulate geometric objects in 2 and 3 dimensions.
The objects we create can start off as pencil drawings on paper, models made of paper, clay or wooden sticks. What we want to create are flowers, houses, castles, spacecraft, weapons, animals, humans, monsters – any object we might want to incorporate into a virtual world or a game. But we must start with the fundamentals.

Ultimately the objects we create with software are dots of light on a computer screen. The objects on the screen are symbols representing objects in real and imagined worlds. If we do a good job of object design then our created worlds and the objects they contain are easy for other people to understand and relate to. The virtual worlds become convincingly real. A player can enter the virtual world with their mind and have a diverting and engaging existence there at some level. We use dots of light to create lines and surfaces that represent the objects we are creating. This chapter builds up the tools to do this starting at square one.

We will move and control our created virtual objects by multiplying them with mathematical structures called matrices. We construct our objects from vectors. A vector represents the position of a dot of light. By multiplying the vectors with matrices we can control the light cluster inside the virtual world which will contain the objects.
We need to shift back and forth between three mathematical spaces in order to make our objects shift, expand and rotate. There is the *Cartesian space* of x, y and z coordinates. Then there is *matrix space* where the x, y and z position components are represented as vectors. In this case vectors are a particular data structure that can be multiplied by a matrix. Then in the next chapter we encounter the need to introduce a *fourth dimension* to our vector spaces in order to make shifting objects in space a simple matrix multiplication. So we end up dealing with different kinds of objects and changing from one kind of data structure to another .

In this chapter we define and use four kinds of data object. They are:
1. Two dimensional shapes. This would be the kind of thing we can draw on a piece of paper with a pencil. An example would be a drawing of a rectangle.
2. A three dimensional shapes. This would be the use of projections to represent 3D objects on a piece of paper with a pencil. A perspective drawing of a shoebox is an example.
3. A four-dimensional version of a three dimensional object (an *augmented* vector), created for the sole purpose of allowing a certain type of matrix multiplication to work properly.
4. A two dimensional version of a three-dimensional or four-dimensional object that can be shown on a computer screen. No matter how perfectly a 3D object can be represented in a computer generated 3D virtual world, it always ends up being projected onto a flat screen of some kind. Flat screens are 2D only.

We need to change one form of data to the other easily and conveniently. It can be confusing when we change from one form to another and we will try to avoid confusion by choosing labels with care. It will help if we incorporate descriptive abbreviations in the name of any collection of variables to make clear what type of object we are talking about. We use of the following descriptive cues in the names we use:
"2d" This means "Two dimensional.
"3d: means "Three dimensional.
 "4d" means four dimensional, also called *augmented*. See the note 1 below.
"mat" means a linear algebra matrix. Specifically we mean a "Numpy" matrix. See the note 2 below.
"vec" means a vector. That is, the position coordinates of a point or dot.

Note 1. Why do we need four dimensional matrices? We need them in order to make it possible to perform the shifting of objects by matrix multiplication, rather than addition. If we stick to multiplication for ALL our operations, the process of controlling a virtual world becomes surprisingly easy. More on this later.

Note 2. What is Numpy? Numpy is the name of a Python module that provides the tools of matrix algebra. We will use it mainly for matrix multiplication. We could have developed our own code for matrix multiplication but why re-invent the wheel?

What is a Matrix?

The encyclopaedia says *"A matrix is a rectangular array of mathematical objects, for which operations such as addition and multiplication are defined"*. This does not tell us much so let us try to get a visual idea of what a matrix really is.

Let us build up a picture of a matrix starting with a rectangular array of objects.

A matrix is a mathematical object organized as a rectangular grid of elements. The grid may have more than 2 dimensions.

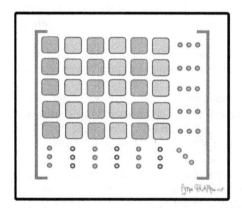

Each red rectangle is an **element** of the matrix. An element is typically just a number though it can be more complex. Each element, the contents of each red rectangle, will be a mathematical object. The particular objects we are interested in are just simple numbers. Real numbers.

Our mission is to manipulate pictures of objects in 3D virtual space. We will express the objects as vectors that indicate the positions, in three dimensional space, of the lines and dots that represent our objects.

The elements of our matrices will also include mathematical expressions incorporating addition, multiplication or trigonometric functions. This is how we can achieve shifting, rotating, shrinking or amplifying of 3D objects.

The matrix operation we use in game creation is almost always matrix multiplication. Addition and subtraction are to be avoided if possible because they can slow execution of code down (because the hardware for graphics is optimised for multiplication). Matrix multiplication is very different from ordinary multiplication. We illustrate this pictorially below.

The multiplication of two matrices requires that the number of columns of one matrix must be the same as the number of rows in the other.

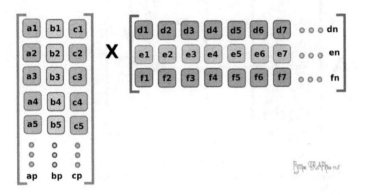

When we have the red and blue matrices shown above we can only multiply them with each other if they each have a particular shape: The rows (horizontals) of the blue matrix must have exactly the same number of entries, called elements, as the columns (verticals) of the red matrix. However the number of *rows* in the red can be different from the number of *columns* in the blue.

The actual calculation for the elements of the resulting product is the sum of products for pairs of elements as shown in the picture below.

Each element of the product is formed from the rows of one matrix and the columns of the other.

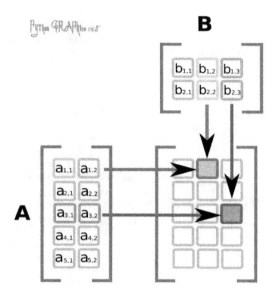

The product of two matrices A and B is illustrated below.
The intersection in the product matrix corresponds to a row of A and a column of B.

Each element of the product is the sum of the products of elements from a n appropriate row with the elements from the corresponding column.

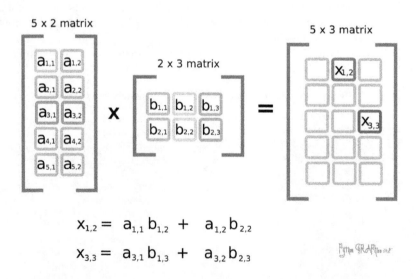

$$X_{1,2} = a_{1,1} b_{1,2} + a_{1,2} b_{2,2}$$
$$X_{3,3} = a_{3,1} b_{1,3} + a_{3,2} b_{2,3}$$

Now the good news - we do not need to be much concerned with the details of matrix multiplication because other programmers have done it for us already inside the Numpy Python module. It has been thoroughly tested and debugged. Numpy stands for "Numerical Python" and we will be using it a lot.

We use matrix multiplication to manipulate geometry. When we are working with virtual reality and game 3D worlds, the matrices we use can rotate and expand the objects inside the virtual world. Moving or shifting (the technical term being *translation*) objects by matrix **multiplication** is not possible because it requires addition instead of multiplication. However there is a way, by augmenting the matrix, to convert matrix addition into multiplication and we will do this later.

In the Python code examples in this chapter we build up a collection 2D object transformation matrices. We try to keep things simple and progress in small steps. We work on drawn objects starting with simple triangles and then use a more complex object (a human face) made up of a collection of separate parts. The need to work with collection or sets of separate parts that are components of a complete object, like the separate features of a human face, is essential and forms a key theme in this chapter and the rest of the book.

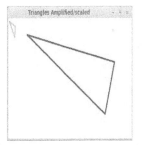

Two Dimensional Objects – Three Triangles

To start off we will develop our matrix transforms using a very simple set of shapes – three triangles. We demonstrate simple methods of drawing two dimensional shapes on a canvas.

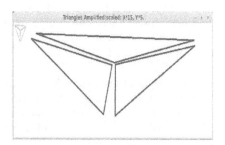

Each triangle is specified as a Python list of vertices in the form:
triangle_x = [x1,y1, x2,y2, x3,y3, x1,y1] where the first vertex is repeated at the end
so that the triangle is closed completely.

```
"""
Program name: 2d_triangles_demo_1.py
Objective: Demonstrate the display of 2D objects..

Keywords: 2d objects, display.
==============================================================================79
Comments: Three triangles are drawn. No use is made of loops.

Tested on: Python 2.6, Python 2.7, Python 3.2,
Author: Mike Ohlson de Fine
=====================================
"""

from Tkinter import *
# from tkinter import *   # Use this instead of the above for python version 3.x

root = Tk()
root.title('Trianagles')
cw = 200                         # canvas width.
ch = 200                         # canvas height.
canvas_1 = Canvas(root, width=cw, height=ch, background="white")
canvas_1.grid(row=0, column=1)
#==============================================================================
triangle_1 = [ 21.0, 40.0   ,4.1, 7.0   ,23.0, 18.3, 21.0, 40.0  ]

triangle_2 = [ 5.3 , 4.8   ,42.4, 7.5   ,23.6 , 17.4 ,5.3 , 4.8 ]

triangle_3 = [ 42.6, 10.0   ,23.7, 40.6  ,23.8, 18.2 , 42.6, 10.0   ]
#==============================================================================
canvas_1.create_line(triangle_1)
canvas_1.create_line(triangle_2)
canvas_1.create_line(triangle_3)

root.mainloop()
```

Handling Groups of Objects as a Set

The example shown below is very, very important because it shows how we can deal with complicated *collections* of graphical objects as a unit – as a single object. We use the Python loop as the basic code processing mechanism. This important code technique for dealing with groups or sets of shapes will be used many times in the future.

The basic idea is:

a) Any complex shape is represented as a basic Python list of the (x,y) vertices of the shape. Each vertex is the location of the end of a straight line segment. A segment is the smallest portion of the continuous string of line sections making up the shape.

b) Any complex shape is made up of a Python list of vertices. For instance the upper lip of the face shown above is a typical complex shape. A collection of individual complex shapes makes up a *shape-set* or group. We manipulate drawn objects like a face by processing each component part in a Python loop:

for set in range(len(triangle_group)):
  canvas_1.create_line(triangle_group[set])

Note here that the quantity **len(triangle_group)** is an integer controlling how many times the loop will be executed. The variable **set** is the counter used to control loop execution. It will always work for any number of elements in the list *triangle_group*. In the rest of this book we will form lists of different kinds of objects like 2d shapes, 3d shapes and 4d shapes so that they can be processed neatly in such loops.

Numpy arrays or matrices can also be processed in loops but we need to be careful not to confuse apples and pears – A python list (the apples) and a Numpy matrix (the pears) are completely different things and we cannot mix them together inside expressions. We have to develop methods for converting from one to the other and back again when necessary. We always need to be careful to be aware of whether we are working with a list or a matrix. Quite often we are working with a list but the elements of the list are in fact matrices so we need to keep our wits about us. Processing the elements of a matrix is very different from processing the elements of a Python list.

Processing sets or collections of objects

In the previous example we could replace the lines
canvas_1.create_line(triangle_1)
canvas_1.create_line(triangle_2)
canvas_1.create_line(triangle_3)
by a loop as outlined below. When the collections of objects becomes large this is the only sane way to go.

Three separate Triangles:

triangle_1 = [21.0, 40.0 ,4.1, 7.0 ,23.0, 18.3, 21.0, 40.0]
triangle_2 = [5.3 , 4.8 ,42.4, 7.5 ,23.6 , 17.4 ,5.3 , 4.8]
triangle_3 = [42.6, 10.0 ,23.7, 40.6 ,23.8, 18.2 , 42.6, 10.0]

Collecting the triangles into a set:

```
triangle_group = [ triangle_1, triangle_2, triangle_3 ]
```

Processing the set by means of a loop:
```
for set in range(len(triangle_group)):
    canvas_1.create_line(triangle_group[set])
```

The Conversion from Vertices to Matrices

This is a critical example because we see what a correct and useful matrix should look like.
Often when developing code something will not work and one of the first things a programmer must verify is that their data is in the correct format. For us this is especially important because we need to convert our data backwards and forwards from Python vertex lists to matrices.

In our example below the Python list of vertices is:
triangle_1 = [21.0, 40.0   ,4.1, 7.0   ,23.0, 18.3,   21.0, 40.0]

and the equivalent matrix (produced with the aid of the Numpy module) is:
triangle_1_matrix: [[21.   40.]   [4.1   7.] [23.   18.3] [21.   40.]]

We know for sure that the matrix is in the correct vector form by the fact that commas are not used to separate either individual numbers or groups of vectors in the matrix. Python will recognize the *matrices* so that correct matrix multiplication will be applied when called for by the multiplication operator symbol " * ".

```
"""
Program name: 2d_list2matrix_1.py
Objective: Convert a Python canvas shape list to numpy matrix of vertices.

Keywords: 2d canvas list, objects, convert, matrix, vertex
=================================================================================79
Comments: A triangle specified as a Python list is converted to a matrix (numpy compatible).
The rows of the numpy matrix are the x-y vertices of the triangle.

Tested on:  Python 2.7, Python 3.2,
Author: Mike Ohlson de Fine
================================
"""
import numpy

#=================================================================================
triangle_1 = [ 21.0, 40.0   ,4.1, 7.0   ,23.0, 18.3, 21.0, 40.0 ]
#=================================================================================

# Convert a Python list into a Numpy matrix of vertices.
vertex_array_1 = []
```

```
for i in range(0, len(triangle_1), 2):
    vertex_x = triangle_1[i]
    vertex_y = triangle_1[i + 1]
    vertex = [vertex_x, vertex_y]
    vertex_array_1.append(vertex)

triangle_1_matrix = numpy.matrix(vertex_array_1)
#print 'triangle_1_matrix: ' , triangle_1_matrix  # This form only works with python 2.x or lower
print ('triangle_1_matrix: ' , triangle_1_matrix)  # This form  works with python 2.x  and 3.x
''' Results
=======
triangle_1_matrix: [[ 21.    40. ]
                    [  4.1    7. ]
                    [ 23.    18.3]
                    [ 21.    40. ]]

'''
```

Be Careful with Python version 3 and integer division.

Python version 3 treats integer division as a floating point operation.
That is, 6/3 is not 2. It is 2.0, which is a floating point (a.k.a. A *float*) number so we cannot have the code:

```
for i in range(0, len(triangle_1)/2):
    vertex_x = triangle_1[2 * i]
    vertex_y = triangle_1[2 * i + 1]
    vertex = [vertex_x, vertex_y]
    vertex_array_1.append(vertex)
```

because the number of desired iterations of the loop must definitely be an integer and not a float. Python version 2.x is more forgiving and will happily execute the above loop and give the desired results.

No Need to be careful with print (…) and Python version 2.x and 3.x

Prior to version 3 of python we had to write print instructions in the form:
print 'a = ', a. With version 3 this became illegal. We now needed to write:
print ('a = ', a). The nice thing is that this also works properly with python version 2.7.
So if we always use the functional form with brackets, then we do not need different forms of the instruction for versions 2.x or 3.x.

The Geometry Transformation using Matrices

Here we use a matrix multiplication to transform the size of the triangle.

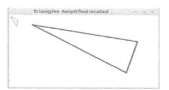

The original triangle before matrix transform is in green and the scaled-up version is in red. Note that the x-dimension (horizontal) scale factor is three times larger than the y-dimension scale factor. This elongates the shape more in the horizontal direction.

The Conversion from Matrices to Vertices

Once the matrix multiplication has taken place we need to convert the resulting amplified matrix back into a Python list of (x,y) vertices so that the shape can be drawn on the canvas. The first step is to use the **tolist()** function that takes the Numpy matrix

[[105. 320.] [20.5 56.] [115. 146.4]]

and converts it into the form:

[[105.0, 320.0], [20.5, 56.0], [115.0, 146.4]]

This form is a list of lists of vertices. It still cannot be used in a **canvas_1.create_line(...)** drawing command. To draw the shape on a canvas we need to eliminate the separating square brackets.

We solve this problem by peeling off the x and y coordinates and packing them neatly into a single list as follows:

goodlist = []
for i in range(0, len(wronglist)):
    goodlist.append(wronglist[i][0])
    goodlist.append(wronglist[i][1])

In the next example after this we use this code snippet in the form of functions.

```
"""

Program name: 2d_simple_scaling_1.py
Objective: Demonstrate the matrix scaling of 2D objects..

Keywords: 2d objects, scaling, amplification, display.
==================================================================================79
Comments: The original data must be expressed as vertices which can then be converted into matrices (by the Numpy module).
A scaling matrix is created. Simple matrix multiplication will then achieve the amplification but the result is another matrix which must finally be flattened into a simple x-y list of coordinates that tkinter "create_line()"
```

function will understand.

```
Tested on: Python 2.7, Python 3.2,
Author: Mike Ohlson de Fine
=================================
"""
from Tkinter import *
# from tkinter import *   # Use this instead of the above for python version 3.x
import numpy

root = Tk()
root.title('Triangles Amplified/scaled')
cw = 500                        # canvas width.
ch = 500                        # canvas height.
canvas_1 = Canvas(root, width=cw, height=ch, background="white")
canvas_1.grid(row=0, column=1)


#=================================================================================
triangle_1 = [ 21.0, 40.0  ,4.1, 7.0  ,23.0, 18.3, 21.0, 40.0  ]
#=================================================================================


# Size amplification factors - note horizontal is 3x more than vertical.
x_scale_factor = 15.0
y_scale_factor = 5.0

# Step 1: Construct the scaling matrix.
Scaling_Matrix  = numpy.matrix([[ x_scale_factor, 0.0], [0.0,  y_scale_factor]])

# Step 2: Transform the Python list into a list of individual vertices.
triangle_vertex_1 = [ 21.0,  40.0 ]
triangle_vertex_2 = [ 4.1,   7.0  ]
triangle_vertex_3 = [ 23.0, 18.3  ]
triangle_vertex_4 = [ 21.0,  40.0 ]

# Step 3: Combine the vertices into a list and then convert to a Numpy matrix.
triangle_shape_1 = [ triangle_vertex_1, triangle_vertex_2, triangle_vertex_3, triangle_vertex_4 ]
triangle_shape_matrix_1 = numpy.matrix(triangle_shape_1)

# Step 4: Perform the matrix multiplication that does the scaling.
# Note: The result is in the wrong format for display on a canvas.
bigger_triangle_matrix_1 = triangle_shape_matrix_1 * Scaling_Matrix
bigger_triangle_wronglist_1 = bigger_triangle_matrix_1.tolist()

# Step 5: Re-craft the resultant matrix into a nice Python list for the canvas.
bigger_triangle_goodlist_1 = []
for i in range(0, len(bigger_triangle_wronglist_1)):
    bigger_triangle_goodlist_1.append( bigger_triangle_wronglist_1[i][0] )
    bigger_triangle_goodlist_1.append(bigger_triangle_wronglist_1[i][1] )

canvas_1.create_line(triangle_1, fill ='green', width = 2)
canvas_1.create_line(bigger_triangle_goodlist_1, fill ='red', width = 3)
root.mainloop()

# Just for the record, show the various data structures.
# Note that numpy matrices have no comma separators - slightly alien creatures they are.

# Use the following 9 instructions with python 2.x and  python 3.x
```

```
print ('Scaling_Matrix: ' , Scaling_Matrix)
print (' ...............................')
print ('triangle_matrix_1: ' , triangle_shape_matrix_1)
print (' ...............................')
print ('bigger_triangle_matrix_1: ' , bigger_triangle_matrix_1)
print (' ...............................')
print ('bigger_triangle_wronglist_1: ' , bigger_triangle_wronglist_1)
print (' ...............................')
print ('bigger_triangle_goodlist_1: ' , bigger_triangle_goodlist_1 )

''' Results
    =======
Scaling_Matrix: [[ 5.  0.]
                 [ 0.  8.]]
...............................
triangle_matrix_1: [[ 21.   40. ]
                    [  4.1   7. ]
                    [ 23.   18.3]]
...............................
bigger_triangle_matrix_1: [[ 105.   320. ]
                           [  20.5   56. ]
                           [ 115.   146.4]]
...............................
bigger_triangle_wronglist_1: [[105.0, 320.0], [20.5, 56.0], [115.0, 146.4]]
...............................
bigger_triangle_goodlist_1: [105.0, 320.0, 20.5, 56.0, 115.0, 146.4]
'''
```

The Scaling Transformation of sets of Matrices: not the best way.

In the example below we do some good things as well as some not-so-good things. The good things we did were to make two useful functions: one converts a list of vertices into a Numpy matrix and the other converts a matrix back into a list of vertices. The not-so-good thing we did was to write 5 sections of repetitive and inefficient code where we do identical operation three times in a row. This is where we must get smarter about handling such activities in the form of loops acting on collections of objects. However there is a good reason for writing code inefficiently. The reason we do things inefficiently at least once is that it is easier to work on ideas that are not yet fully formed and which may be slightly flawed. This non-optimal code allows us to formulate the principles of what is required. In fact when we are creating methods and algorithms for the first time it is easier to understand what we are doing if we keep ideas as simple and explicitly obvious as possible. Long and clear is better than short and opaque. Once we have our tactics worked out and tested, then we can start introducing the use of loops and other smarter coding techniques.

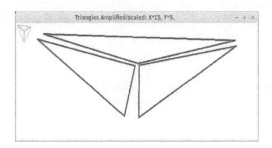

```
"""
Program name: 2d_matrix_conversion_1.py
Objective: Construct matrix converters and transforms for scaling of 2D objects.
The operators should be expressed as functions.

Keywords: 2d objects, matrix, scaling, amplification, functions,display.
========================================================================79
Commenta: The original data must be expressed as vertices which can then be converted into matrices (by the
Numpy module).
A scaling matrix is created: Scaling_Matrix  = numpy.matrix([[ x_scale_factor, 0.0], [0.0,  y_scale_factor]])
Simple matrix multiplication will then achieve the amplification but the result is another matrix which must
finally be flattened into a simple x-y list of coordinates that the tkinter "create_line()" function will understand.

Tested on: Python 2.6, Python 2.7, Python 3.2,
Author: Mike Ohlson de Fine
===================================
"""
from Tkinter import *
from tkinter import *   # Use this instead of the above for python version 3.x
import numpy

root = Tk()
root.title('Triangles Amplified/scaled: X*15, Y*5.')
cw = 700                          # canvas width.
ch = 250                          # canvas height.
canvas_1 = Canvas(root, width=cw, height=ch, background="white")
canvas_1.grid(row=0, column=1)


#=================================================================
triangle_1 = [ 21.0, 40.0  ,4.1, 7.0  ,23.0, 18.3, 21.0, 40.0 ]
triangle_2 = [ 5.3 , 4.8  ,42.4, 7.5  ,23.6 , 17.4 ,5.3 , 4.8  ]
triangle_3 = [ 42.6, 10.0  ,23.7, 40.6 ,23.8, 18.2 , 42.6, 10.0  ]
#=================================================================

# Convert a Python list into a Numpy matrix of vertices.
def list2matrix(xy_shape):
    """ Convert a Python list (xy list of a shape) into a
        Numpy matrix of vertices
    """
    vertex_array = []
    for i in range(0, len(xy_shape), 2):
        vertex_x =  xy_shape[i]
        vertex_y =  xy_shape[i + 1]
```

```
        vertex = [vertex_x, vertex_y]
        vertex_array.append(vertex)
    vertex_matrix = numpy.matrix(vertex_array)
    return  vertex_matrix

# Re-craft a 2D matrix into a nice Python list for display on the canvas.
def matrix2list(vertex_matrix):
    """ Convert Numpy matrix of vertices into a Python list (xy list of a shape)
    """
    flat_array = vertex_matrix.tolist()
    xy_list = []
    for i in range(0, len(flat_array)):
        xy_list.append( flat_array[i][0] )
        xy_list.append( flat_array[i][1] )
    return xy_list

# Size amplification factors - note horizontal is 3x more than vertical.
x_scale_factor = 15.0
y_scale_factor = 5.0

# Step 1: Construct the scaling matrix.
Scaling_Matrix  = numpy.matrix([[ x_scale_factor, 0.0], [0.0,  y_scale_factor]])

# Step 2: Transform the Python list into a list of individual vertices.
triangle_1_matrix = list2matrix(triangle_1)
triangle_2_matrix = list2matrix(triangle_2)
triangle_3_matrix = list2matrix(triangle_3)

# Step 3: Perform the matrix multiplication that does the scaling.
# Note: The result is in the wrong format for display on a canvas.
bigger_triangle_matrix_1 = triangle_1_matrix * Scaling_Matrix
bigger_triangle_matrix_2 = triangle_2_matrix * Scaling_Matrix
bigger_triangle_matrix_3 = triangle_3_matrix * Scaling_Matrix

# Step 4:Convert the scaled matrix to  Python xy-list.
bigger_triangle_1 = matrix2list(bigger_triangle_matrix_1)
bigger_triangle_2 = matrix2list(bigger_triangle_matrix_2)
bigger_triangle_3 = matrix2list(bigger_triangle_matrix_3)

# Step 5: Display the results.
canvas_1.create_line(triangle_1)
canvas_1.create_line(triangle_2)
canvas_1.create_line(triangle_3)
canvas_1.create_line(bigger_triangle_1, width = 3)
canvas_1.create_line(bigger_triangle_2, width = 3)
canvas_1.create_line(bigger_triangle_3, width = 3)

root.mainloop()
```

The Scaling Transformation of sets of Matrices: the better way

Here we fix up the weakness of the previous program by conducting the processing of the collection of shapes as a single loop:
for set in range(len(triangle_shape_set)):

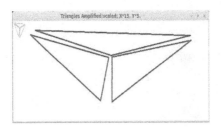

```
"""
Program name: 2d_matrix_set_operations_1.py
Objective: Construct matrix converters and transforms for scaling of 2D objects.
The operators should be expressed as functions and sets of objects processed as a single entity..

Keywords: 2d objects, matrix, scaling, amplification, functions,display.
==================================================================================79
Comments: The original data must be expressed as vertices which can then be converted into matrices (by the
Numpy module).
A scaling matrix is created. Simple matrix multiplication will then achieve the amplification but the result is
another matrix which must finally be flattened into a simple x-y list of coordinates that tkinter "create_line()"
function will understand.

Tested on: Python 2.6, Python 2.7, Python 3.2,
Author: Mike Ohlson de Fine
===========================================
"""

from Tkinter import *
#from tkinter import *   # Use this instead of the above for python version 3.x
import numpy

root = Tk()
root.title('Triangles Amplified/scaled: X*15, Y*5.')
cw = 700                        # canvas width.
ch = 250                        # canvas height.
canvas_1 = Canvas(root, width=cw, height=ch, background="white")
canvas_1.grid(row=0, column=1)


#=================================================================================
triangle_1 = [ 21.0, 40.0  ,4.1, 7.0  ,23.0, 18.3, 21.0, 40.0 ]
triangle_2 = [ 5.3 , 4.8  ,42.4, 7.5  ,23.6 , 17.4 ,5.3 , 4.8 ]
triangle_3 = [ 42.6, 10.0  ,23.7, 40.6  ,23.8, 18.2 , 42.6, 10.0  ]
#=================================================================================
# Now do everything by sets.
triangle_shape_set = [ triangle_1, triangle_2, triangle_3 ]
```

```
# Convert a Python list into a Numpy matrix of vertices.
def list2matrix(xy_shape):
    """ Convert a Python list (xy list of a shape) into a
    Numpy matrix of vertices
    """
    vertex_array = []
    for i in range(0, len(xy_shape), 2):
        vertex_x = xy_shape[ i]
        vertex_y = xy_shape[ i + 1]
        vertex = [vertex_x, vertex_y]
        vertex_array.append(vertex)
    vertex_matrix = numpy.matrix(vertex_array)
    return  vertex_matrix

# Re-craft a 2D matrix into a nice Python list for display on the canvas.
def matrix2list(vertex_matrix):
    """ Convert Numpy matrix of vertices into a Python list (xy list of a shape)
    """
    flat_array = vertex_matrix.tolist()
    xy_list = []
    for i in range(0, len(flat_array)):
        xy_list.append( flat_array[i][0] )
        xy_list.append( flat_array[i][1] )
    return xy_list

# Size amplification factors - note horizontal is 3x more than vertical.
x_scale_factor = 15.0
y_scale_factor = 5.0

# Step 1: Construct the scaling matrix.
Scaling_Matrix  = numpy.matrix([[ x_scale_factor, 0.0], [0.0,  y_scale_factor]])

for set in range(len(triangle_shape_set)):
    triangle_matrix = list2matrix(triangle_shape_set[set])          # step 2
    bigger_triangle_matrix = triangle_matrix * Scaling_Matrix       # step 3
    bigger_triangle = matrix2list(bigger_triangle_matrix)           # step 4
    canvas_1.create_line(bigger_triangle, fill = 'red', width = 3)  # step 5
    canvas_1.create_line(triangle_shape_set[set], fill = 'green')   # step 6

root.mainloop()
```

We have established the techniques we will use in applying matrix multiplication to re-shape drawn objects. Now we introduce the other main transformation matrices for reflection, shearing and rotating shapes.

The Sequential and Concatenated Transformations

We now incorporate all the transformations so far. Note that we do not include the very much needed transformation of shifting (translation) because the forms of matrix we have used so far simply cannot accommodate translation as a matrix multiplication operation. In principle shifting the location of an object only requires addition or subtraction.

In the interest of computational effectiveness we need to represent shifting (translation) as a multiplication by a matrix. Why? Because then all the transformation matrix operations can be combined as a single matrix – they can be concatenated.

In other words, if

MatrixA = MatrixB x MatrixC x MatrixD x MatrixF x MatrixG,

MatrixA ends up as a simple 2 by 2 array of numbers whose values incorporate all that went into MatrixB, MatrixC, MatrixD, MatrixF and MatrixG. So whenever the sequence of five multiplications is needed, we just use MatrixA. This turns out to be very useful and powerful as we shall see in Chaper 10.

For translation we have to change the fundamental matrix form used for translation by adding an extra dimension (augmentation) to all our matrices. But let us not get ahead of ourselves.

We shall use an object, composed of a collection or group of lines called face_set. It is contained in the face.py module as shown below:

```
# face.py
bottom_lip = [255, 291, 229, 306, 193, 317, 152, 301, 137, 290, 160, 336, 192, 348, 237, 329, 258, 289]
top_lip = [279, 276, 229, 302, 204, 313, 193, 315, 184, 313, 152, 299, 125, 280, 176, 282, 195, 295, 216, 281,
260, 278, 281, 274]
nose = [211, 121, 207, 133, 210, 194, 222, 212, 219, 228, 207, 230, 197, 236, 190, 236, 181, 230, 169, 228, 167,
212, 179, 194, 182, 133, 178, 121]
l_nostril = [170, 203, 155, 206, 150, 215, 156, 227, 169, 228]
r_nostril = [216, 201, 231, 206, 236, 215, 230, 227, 217, 228]
l_eye = [163, 115, 134, 86, 99, 82, 72, 90, 55, 103, 88, 122, 144, 126, 161, 119]
r_eye = [234, 113, 265, 88, 301, 87, 327, 98, 343, 112, 305, 129, 250, 126, 236, 118]
l_iris = [113, 86, 133, 89, 141, 100, 136, 114, 127, 124, 110, 122, 99, 110, 99, 97, 109, 86]
r_iris = [290, 89, 270, 90, 261, 100, 264, 115, 272, 125, 289, 125, 301, 115, 303, 101, 293, 89]
l_pupil = [113, 96, 109, 100, 109, 107, 113, 112, 121, 113, 127, 109, 128, 102, 126, 96, 121, 94, 116, 94]
r_pupil = [287, 99, 291, 104, 291, 110, 286, 115, 278, 115, 272, 111, 272, 104, 274, 98, 280, 97, 284, 97]
l_eyebrow = [26, 65, 52, 32, 115, 37, 176, 75, 181, 70, 183, 62, 144, 40, 111, 29, 51, 27, 27, 60]
r_eyebrow = [368, 69, 339, 29, 280, 34, 218, 75, 213, 70, 212, 62, 251, 39, 282, 25, 342, 24, 368, 63]
face_set = [ bottom_lip, top_lip, nose, l_nostril, r_nostril, l_eye, r_eye, l_iris, r_iris, l_pupil, r_pupil, l_eyebrow,
r_eyebrow ]
```

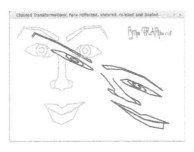

```
"""
Program name: 2d_concatenated_transforms_1.py
Objective: Demonstrate concatenated transforms.

Keywords: 2d objects, concatenated operations.
=============================================================================79
Comments: The same result is achieved in two different ways:

First - a concatenated matrix =
X_Reflect_Matrix()*Y_Reflect_Matrix()*Rotate_Matrix(3.0)*Shear_Matrix(0.5,0.7)*Scale_Matrix(1.3,0.8)
 = concatenation =  [[ 1.41540945  0.50889301]
                     [ 0.71743716  0.73554599]],
is multiplied by the vertices of the object being transformed.

Second - a series of matrix multiplications are performed, with
the result of each multiplication being fed to the subsequent one.

Tested on: Python 2.6, Python 2.7, Python 3.2,
Author: Mike Ohlson de Fine
=================================
"""
from Tkinter import *
#from tkinter import *   # Use this instead of the above for python version 3.x
import numpy
import math
import face

root = Tk()
root.title('Chained Transformations: Face reflected, sheared, rotated and Scaled.')
cw = 650                        # canvas width.
ch = 400                        # canvas height.
canvas_1 = Canvas(root, width=cw, height=ch, background="white")
canvas_1.grid(row=0, column=1)
#=============================================================================
# The scaling matrix.
def Scale_Matrix(x_scale_factor, y_scale_factor):
    """ Scaling matrix for 2D shapes. """
    scaling_matrix  = numpy.matrix([[ x_scale_factor, 0.0], [0.0,  y_scale_factor]])
    return scaling_matrix

# The x-reflection matrix (vertical reflections).
def X_Reflect_Matrix():
    """ Reflect matrix shape from the X-axis. """
    xreflect_matrix  = numpy.matrix([[-1.0, 0.0],
                                     [ 0.0, 1.0] ])
    return xreflect_matrix

# The y-reflection matrix (horizontal reflections).
def Y_Reflect_Matrix():
    """ Reflect matrix shape from the Y-axis. """
    YReflect_Matrix  = numpy.matrix([[1.0, 0.0],\
                                     [ 0.0, -1.0] ])
    return YReflect_Matrix

# The rotate in the plane matrix.
```

```python
def Rotate_Matrix(theta):
    """ Rotate points theta (radians)around the Z-axis.  """
    rotate_matrix = numpy.matrix([ [math.cos(theta),  -math.sin(theta)],\
                        [math.sin(theta),   math.cos(theta)] ])
    return rotate_matrix

# The combined x and y shear matrix.
def Shear_Matrix(shear_x, shear_y):
    """ Shear a matrix shape simultaneously in the X- and Y-directions.
    """

    shear_matrix = numpy.matrix([ [    1.0,    shear_x],
                        [shear_y,        1.0]])
    return shear_matrix

# Convert a Python list into a Numpy matrix of vertices.
def list2matrix(xy_shape):
    """ Convert a Python list (xy list of a shape) into a
        Numpy matrix of vertices
    """

    vertex_array = []
    for i in range(0, len(xy_shape), 2):
        vertex_x = xy_shape[i]
        vertex_y = xy_shape[ i + 1]
        vertex = [vertex_x, vertex_y]
        vertex_array.append(vertex)
    vertex_matrix = numpy.matrix(vertex_array)
    return  vertex_matrix

# Re-craft a 2D matrix into a nice Python list for display on the canvas.
def matrix2list(vertex_matrix):
    """ Convert Numpy matrix of vertices into a Python list (xy list of a shape)
    """

    flat_array = vertex_matrix.tolist()
    xy_list = []
    for i in range(0, len(flat_array)):
        xy_list.append( flat_array[i][0] )
        xy_list.append( flat_array[i][1] )
    return xy_list


# Series sequential transforms.
for set in range(len(face.face_set)):
    triangle_matrix = list2matrix(face.face_set[set])          # step 1
    xreflected_triangle = triangle_matrix * X_Reflect_Matrix()        # step 2
    yreflected_triangle = xreflected_triangle * Y_Reflect_Matrix()    # step 3
    rotated_triangle = yreflected_triangle * Rotate_Matrix(3.0)       # step 4
    sheared_triangle = rotated_triangle * Shear_Matrix(0.5, 0.7)      # step 5
    bigger_triangle_matrix = sheared_triangle * Scale_Matrix(1.3,0.8) # step 6
    bigger_triangle = matrix2list(bigger_triangle_matrix)             # step 7
    #canvas_1.create_line(bigger_triangle, fill = 'blue', width = 3)  # step 8

# Concatenation of matrix operations.
concatenation  = X_Reflect_Matrix() * Y_Reflect_Matrix() * Rotate_Matrix(3.0) * Shear_Matrix(0.5, 0.7) *
Scale_Matrix(1.3,0.8)
print ('concatenation: ' ,concatenation)   # For python 3.2 use this instead of the line above.
for set in range(len(face.face_set)):
    face_matrix = list2matrix(face.face_set[set])          # step 1
```

```
face_caboodle = face_matrix * concatenation          # steps 2 - 6
view_face = matrix2list(face_caboodle)               # step 7
canvas_1.create_line(view_face, fill = 'red', width = 3)   # step 8
canvas_1.create_line(face.face_set[set], fill = 'green', width = 3) # Untransformed original.
```

root.mainloop()

The constant matrix **concatenation** = [[**1.41540945 0.50889301**]
                                    [**0.71743716 0.73554599**]],
is the result of the chain of multiplications
X_Reflect_Matrix()*Y_Reflect_Matrix()*Rotate_Matrix(3.0)*Shear_Matrix(0.5,0.7)*Scale_Matrix(1.3,0.8) .
Note that *sequence* is all-important when multiplying matrices. A x B is definitely not
the same as B x A.

The Difficulty of Translation (Shifting) of Shapes, and a solution using longer Vectors and Augmented matrices

One of the most frequently used transformation operations on drawn shapes is
shifting (translation). The operations we have used up to now involve some kind of
multiplication operation on the x and y coordinate that define the shapes we are
working with. The matrix multiplications we have used so far are not able to achieve
simple addition or subtraction necessary for shifting. We could simply create
translation matrices and then remember only to use them for addition and never
multiplication. This is a bad idea for the fast graphics processing of the kind needed
for intensive animated video games because the hardware is specifically designed to
make matrix multiplication easy and quick.

The question comes down to this. Is there a form of matrix we can use that makes ALL
transformations, *including translation*, the same type of operation, namely
multiplication? And the answer is yes. We can make use of the so called *augmented
matrix* form. The augmented matrix is almost identical to the 2 row matrices we have
been using up to now. The difference is that we add a third row to the bottom and a
third column on the right of the matrix for the sole purpose of converting the addition
operation into of a matrix multiplication.

So the matrices that will perform the transformations will be 3x3 (3 rows, 3 columns)
matrices. The vectors representing the vertices of our shapes will thus have an extra
"dimension" added. They called augmented matrices.
In terms of "dimensions" we are now working with three dimensions in strict linear
algebra terminology. When we start working with true 3D objects our transformation
matrices become 4x4 (4 rows, 4 columns) and our vertex vectors will have four
elements. This will be dealt with in the next chapter.

The Augmented Matrix for Translation (Shifting)

An example of the augmented matrix for reflecting a shape around the x-axis, a
vertical flip, is the matrix x_reflect = [[-1.0   0.0   0.0]
                                          [0.0   1.0   0.0]
                                          [0.0   0.0   1.0]]

The unaugmented form of the same matrix is,
xreflect = [[-1.0   0.0]
           [0.0   1.0]]

For the translation or shifting of shapes, the matrix that would be multiplied with the
vectors of vertices would be:
shift = [[-1.0   0.0   0.0]
         [0.0   1.0   0.0]
         [shift_x   shift_y   1.0]]

Do we need to change the vectors of shape vertices?
Yes indeed we do. Where the non-homogeneous form of a vertex matrix for a point (x1,
y1) would have been vertex_1 = [[x1   y1]   ]

The homogeneous matrix for the same vertex is:
homogeneous_vertex_1 =   [[x1   y1   1.0]   ]

Translation (Shift) by Multiplication with the Augmented Matrix

shifted = numpy.matrix([[1.0,   0.0,   1.0],
                        [0.0,   1.0,   1.0],
                        [shift_x,   shift_y ,   1.0]])

and the result of applying this shift three times in succession is shown here.

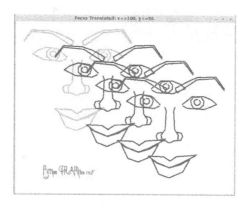

"""

Program name: 2d_augmented_translation_matrix_1.py
Objective: Demonstration translation (shifting) using the augmented matrix.

Keywords: 2d objects, augmented matrix, translation, shift functions.
===79
Comments: To support the translation (shifting sideways and up or down), we need to work with augmented matrices.
When the vertices of 2D shapes are extended by one "dimension", then objects can be shifted
by multiplication with the aaugmented matrix.

The original data must be expressed as vertices which can then be converted into matrices (by the Numpy module).
Simple matrix multiplication will then achieve the translation but the result is another matrix which must finally
be flattened into a simple x-y list of coordinates that tkinter "create_line()" function will understand.

Tested on: Python 2.7, Python 3.2,
Author: Mike Ohlson de Fine
====================================
"""

```python
from Tkinter import *
# from tkinter import *    # Use this instead of the above for python version 3.x
import numpy
import math
import faces

root = Tk()
root.title('Faces Translated: x+=100, y+=50.')
cw = 700                        # canvas width.
ch = 550                        # canvas height.
canvas_1 = Canvas(root, width=cw, height=ch, background="white")
canvas_1.grid(row=0, column=1)


#==================================================================
# Convert a Python list into a homogeneous Numpy matrix ( 2D/3D) of vertices.
# This form is necessary to support translation matrices.
def list2matrix_homog(xy_shape):
    """ Convert a Python list (xy list of a shape) into a
        Numpy matrix of vertices
    """
```

```
    vertex_array = []
    for i in range(0, len(xy_shape), 2):
        vertex_x = xy_shape[ i]
        vertex_y = xy_shape[i + 1]
        extra_element = 1.0
        vertex = [vertex_x, vertex_y, extra_element]
        vertex_array.append(vertex)
    vertex_matrix = numpy.matrix(vertex_array)
    return vertex_matrix

# Re-craft a 2D matrix into a nice Python list for display on the canvas.
def matrix2list(vertex_matrix):
    """ Convert Numpy matrix of vertices into a Python list (xy list of a shape)
    """

    flat_array = vertex_matrix.tolist()
    xy_list = []
    for i in range(0, len(flat_array)):
        xy_list.append( flat_array[i][0] )
        xy_list.append( flat_array[i][1] )
    return xy_list


def Translate(shift_x, shift_y):
    """ Shift the shape in the x-direction and y-direction by shift_x and shift_y respectively.\
    """

    shifted = numpy.matrix([[1.0,        0.0,    1.0 ],
                            [0.0,        1.0,    1.0 ],
                            [shift_x,   shift_y , 1.0 ]])
    return shifted

# Translation variables.
x_shift = 100.0
y_shift = 50.0

# View the original face.
for set in range(len(faces.face_set)):
    face_matrix = list2matrix_homog(faces.face_set[set])        # step 1
    canvas_1.create_line(faces.face_set[set], fill = 'green', width = 3)  # Original

# Translate and view faces.
for i in range(3):
    for set in range(len(faces.face_set)):
        face_matrix = list2matrix_homog(faces.face_set[set])             # step 1
        shifted_face_matrix = face_matrix * Translate(x_shift, y_shift)   # step 2
        xylist_shifted_face = matrix2list(shifted_face_matrix)            # step 3
        canvas_1.create_line(xylist_shifted_face, fill = 'red', width = 3)  # step 4
    x_shift += 100
    y_shift += 50

root.mainloop()
```

The Other Homogeneous Transforms using Augmented Matrices

Can we make all our transformation matrices into augmented matrices so that we may perform identical matrix multiplication to achieve any transformation? The answer is yes and the augmented matrices are shown here:

X-axis reflection (vertical flip). The augmented matrix for reflecting a shape around the x-axis, a vertical flip, is the matrix:

xreflect_matrix = numpy.matrix([[-1.0, 0.0, 0.0],
                                 [0.0, 1.0, 0.0],
                                 [0.0, 0.0, 1.0]])

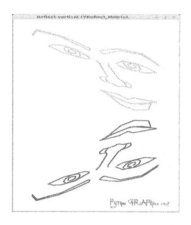

Y-axis reflection (horizontal flip). The augmented matrix for reflecting a shape around the y-axis, a horizontal flip, is the matrix:

yreflect_matrix = numpy.matrix([[1.0, 0.0, 0.0],\
                                 [0.0, -1.0, 0.0],\
                                 [0.0, 0.0, 1.0]])

Shear (skewing).
The augmented matrix for skewing a shape in both the y-axis and x-axis directions, is the matrix:

```
shear_matrix = numpy.matrix([[ 1.0,     x_shear,   0.0 ],
                             [ y_shear,  1.0,       0.0 ],
                             [ 0.0,      0.0,       1.0 ] ])
```

In the three figures below, the first shows shear on the Y-axis, the second shows shear on the X-axis while the third shows shear on both axes.

Rotation.

The augmented matrix for rotating a shape around the origin, is the matrix:

```
shear_matrix = numpy.matrix([[ math.cos(theta),   -math.sin(theta),   0.0 ],
                             [ math.sin(theta),    math.cos(theta),    0.0 ],
                             [ 0.0,                0.0,                1.0 ] ])
```

Note that because we are using the trigonometry functions sine and cosine, which are contained in the math module, the math module must be imported using "import math" ahead of the definition of the rotation function.

Scaling (Expanding and Shrinking).

The augmented matrix for scaling a shape in either or both the y-axis and x-axis directions, is the matrix:

```
scaling_matrix = numpy.matrix([[ x_scale,    0.0,   0.0 ],
                               [ 0.0,     y_scale,   0.0 ],
                               [ 0.0,        0.0,   1.0 ] ])
```

4

Matrix Image Transformation: 3D

"Have you ever had a dream, Neo, that you were so sure was real? What if you were unable to wake from that dream? How would you know the difference between the dream world and the real world? "

"This is your last chance. After this, there is no turning back. You take the blue pill - the story ends, you wake up in your bed and believe whatever you want to believe. You take the red pill - you stay in Wonderland and I show you how deep the rabbit-hole goes." Morpheus, The Matrix.

This chapter covers:
- Working in 3D is Similar to Working in 2D
- Naming Conventions Used Here
- Convert a single 2D Shape into a 4D Vector Matrix
- Amplification, Translation and Rotation by Matrix Multiplication
- Rotate the Shape about the X, Y and Z axes
- Working with Shape Sets (Groups of Shapes)
- Rotate Complex Sets of Shapes about the X, Y and Z axes
- 3D Rotation around the x-axis
- Combining Matrix Operations
- Organize the Geometry Transforms as a Python Module

Working in 3D is Similar to Working in 2D

It is pleasant surprise to discover that working with three dimensional objects is very, very similar to working in two dimensions. To move and manipulate objects we use the identical matrix multiplication methods and Python loop code. The difference with 3D is that the vertices of objects have an extra dimension – the position in the z-direction. To date, the best and simplest methods for controlling virtual 3D environments is by exclusive use of matrix multiplication. Graphics processing hardware is designed to do matrix multiplication very fast and efficiently. In this chapter we will work through the basic operations of moving objects around in 3D space using matrix multiplication.

In computer graphics we work in two dimensions and, surprisingly, four dimensions. This comes as a surprise to most of us who expect 2D and 3D, but why 4D? The simple answer is that a fourth dimension is an trick needed to allow us to move objects around using the matrix multiplication operation of linear algebra. In three dimensions we can use matrix multiplication to change the size of objects, rotate them, distort their shape (shear) or reflect them, but we cannot simply move them in a chosen direction (called *translation*). To be able to achieve translation by matrix multiplication we need the help of a fourth dimension in our description of the geometric transformations in three dimensions. The translation operators reside in the artificial fourth dimension. This is the only reason we use a fourth dimension – just to make the algebra convenient. There are alternative ways to achieve translation operations but using a fourth dimension in our algebra is just very convenient and it fits in with the way Graphics Processing Units (GPUs) work. GPUs are add-on computer procesors designed for rapid production of moving images from computed geometry .

We focus on two things in this chapter:
1. How to manipulate two dimensional shapes in three dimensions, and
2. How to move three dimensional shapes in their 3D space.

We start off by carefully describing the conventions and methods we use manipulate two-dimensional and three-dimensional objects. All moving, rotating and size-changing operations are achieved through the miraculous convenience of matrix multiplication. This turns out to be easy and convenient *as well as* computationally fast by using the Python module **Numpy** for the matrix multiplication. To use this convenience we just need to make sure the shapes we create are converted into matrices by numpy. This is simple to do: we just take our Python vectors and convert them with one line of code such as:

my_shapes_4d_numpy_matrix = numpy.matrix(my_python_shapes)

In what follows here we go through this process step-by-step using numerical examples.

The first two examples here are intended to be as simple as possible. They are "canonoical" which, in mathematics, means simplified and standardized.

I, the author, ask your forgiveness in advance for what appear to be over-explicit variable names and what are intended to be self-explanatory function names. This was done for the sole purpose of long term clarity. We will find ourselves moving rapidly in our minds between two-dimensions, three-dimensions and of course four dimensions. The explicit variable names are there to help us keep track of which particular space we are working with. I wrestled for months to find a consistent and clear way of naming things to avoid getting lost and disoriented. So the conventions here are my best effort so far. It is far from perfect and for that I most humbly apologise.

Naming Conventions Used Here

A simple shape. A shape is a single line, in a two-dimensional plane. The line can be long and and convoluted, but it is one unbroken chain of *segments*. Each segment is the straight piece leading from one position to the next. The point where two segments meet is called a *vertex*.
The python code for the shape of a simple fish would be:
fish_1 = [169.2,161.6 , 309.2,102.3 , 360.0,139.5 , 316.4,160.9 , 180.0,118.7]
where the pairs of numbers like 169.2,161.6 are the x and y coordinated of a position on our computer screen.

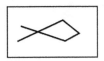

A complex shape or shape set. This is a group of shapes composed of separate lines where the entire group should be treated as a unit. An example would be a drawing of a fish where the outline, the eyes, mouth and fins would be drawn using separate lines. In the Python programs we develop in this book, shape sets are handled as lists of graphic objects that can be manipulated and animated using program loop techniques.

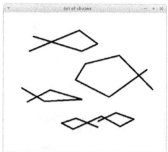

A 4D matrix. We use four dimensional vectors and matrices of four dimensional vectors to represent the *vertices* (plural of vertex) of three dimensional objects. There is a good reason for representing 3D vertices as 4D vectors. Specifically our 4D matrices represent the x, y and z coordinates of positions in the 3D space used to describe geometric objects. These geometric objects are the drawings we will show on the monitor screens of our computers.

The 4D vectors of each x-y point (vertex) of the fish shape given above would be:
fish_1_vertex1 = [169.2, 161.6, 0, 1]
fish_1_vertex2 = [309.2, 102.3, 0, 1]
fish_1_vertex3 = [360.0, 139.5, 0, 1]
fish_1_vertex4 = [316.4, 160.9, 0, 1]
fish_1_vertex5 = [180.0, 118.7, 0, 1]

The vertices above are grouped together as a two-index python array:
fish_1_4d_shape = [*fish_1_vertex1, fish_1_vertex2, fish_1_vertex3, fish_1_vertex4, fish_1_vertex5*]

Finally, for matrix multiplication we need to convert the python array *fish_1_4d_shape* into a proper numpy matrix:
fish_1_4d_shape_matrix = ***numpy.matrix**(fish_1_4d_shape)*

Convert a Single 2D Shape into a 4D Vector Matrix

Here we take a simple shape of a fish, composed of 5 vertices, and convert it into a 4D numpy matrix so that it can be transformed in a three dimensional cartesian space.

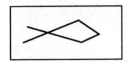

```
"""
Program name: 3d_shape_convert_2Dto4D_1.py
Objective: Convert a 2D planar shape into a list of 4D vertex vectors.

"canonical" (definition): A mathematical expression in the simplest or standard form.

Keywords: 3d shape, 2d shapes, conversion function.
===========================================================================79
Comments: 2d shape vertices are converted to lists of 4d (homogeneous) matrix/vectors.
Each vector is the location of a vertex in 3d (homogeneous) space.

A 'shape' is a 2d planar line of arbtrary number of segments.
The final list corresponds to a shape object in 3 dimensions.
The shape object is a Python list of 4D vertices.

Tested on: Python 2.6, Python 2.7.3, Python 3.2.3
Author:  Mike Ohlson de Fine
===============================
"""

import numpy

# 2D SHAPE - A simple fish shape in the x-y plane
fish_1 = [ 169.2,161.6 ,  309.2,102.3 ,  360.0,139.5 ,  316.4,160.9 ,  180.0,118.7 ]

#=====================================================
# CONVERSION OF A 2D LIST TO A MATRIX OF 4D VERTICES.
#=====================================================
def twod_shape_2_homogeneous_matrix(twod_shape):
    """ Convert a 2D shape list into a homogeneous 4D matrix (numpy form).
    The z coordinate is zero. ie. z = 0.
    """

    homogenous_4d_array = []
    for i in range(0, len(twod_shape), 2):
        new_x =  twod_shape[2 * i]
        new_y =  twod_shape[2 * i + 1]
        new_z =  0.0
        new_w = 1
        new_vertex = [new_x, new_y, new_z, new_w]
        homogenous_4d_array.append(new_vertex)

    homogenous_4d_mat = numpy.matrix(homogenous_4d_array)
    return homogenous_4d_mat

#=====================================================
# CONVERT 2D SHAPES TO 4D MATRICES (NUMPY FORM)
#=====================================================
fish_1_2d24d_mat = twod_shape_2_homogeneous_matrix(fish_1)
print ('fish_1_2d24d_mat:', fish_1_2d24d_mat) # Use instead of the above for Python 3.x.

''' RESULT
fish_1_2d24d_mat:
```

```
[[ 169.2  161.6   0.   1. ]
 [ 309.2  102.3   0.   1. ]
 [ 360.   139.5   0.   1. ]
 [ 316.4  160.9   0.   1. ]
 [ 180.   118.7   0.   1. ]]
"""
```

Amplification, Translation and Rotation by Matrix Multiplication

Shape Rotation

To achieve the rotation of a vertex vector by an angle of *theta* radians we use the following rotation transform matrices:

a) Rotation around the X-axis

```
def T_rotx(theta):
    """ Rotate points theta (radians)around the X-axis.
    """
    T = np.matrix([[1.0,           0.0,              0.0,           0.0],
                   [0.0,   math.cos(theta),  -math.sin(theta),     0.0],
                   [0.0,   math.sin(theta),   math.cos(theta),     0.0],
                   [0.0,           0.0,              0.0,           1.0] ])
    return T
```

Usage: Rotated_vector = [x y z 1] * T_rotx(theta)

b) Rotation around the Y-axis

```
def T_roty(theta):
    """ Rotate points theta (radians)around the Y-axis.
    """
    T = np.matrix([[ math.cos(theta),   0.0,   math.sin(theta),     0.0],
                   [          0.0,       1.0,           0.0,         0.0],
                   [ -math.sin(theta),   0.0,   math.cos(theta),     0.0],
                   [          0.0,       0.0,           0.0,         1.0] ])
    return T
```

Usage: Rotated_vector = [x y z 1] * T_roty(theta)

c) Rotation around the Z-axis

```
def T_rotz(theta):
    """ Rotate points theta (radians)around the Z-axis.
    """
```

```
T = np.matrix([ [math.cos(theta),    -math.sin(theta),    0.0,    0.0],\
                [ math.sin(theta),     math.cos(theta),    0.0,    0.0],\
                [           0.0,                 0.0,      1.0,    0.0],\
                [           0.0,                 0.0,      0.0,    1.0] ])
    return T
```

Usage: Rotated_vector = [x y z 1]*T_rotz(theta)

Shape Size Amplification or Shrinking.

```
def T_scaling(sx, sy, sz):
    """ Expand points by sx in the X-direction,
            sy in the Y-direction and
            sz in the Z direction.
    """
    T  = np.matrix([ [ sx,    0.0,    0.0,    0.0],\
                     [0.0,     sy,    0.0,    0.0],\
                     [0.0,    0.0,     sz,    0.0],
                     [0.0,    0.0,    0.0,    1.0] ])
    return T
```

Usage example: Scaled_vector = [x y z 1] * T_scaling(150.0 , 200.0, 0.0)

Shape Translation (Shifting).

```
def T_translate(tx, ty, tz):
    """ Shift points tx in the X-direction,
            ty in the Y-direction and
            tz in the Z direction.
    The apparent direction of Z increasing seems to be negative!!!.
    """
    T = np.matrix([[1.0,    0.0,    0.0,    0.0],\
                   [0.0,    1.0,    0.0,    0.0],\
                   [0.0,    0.0,    1.0,    0.0],\
                   [ tx,     ty,     tz,    1.0] ])
    return T
```

Usage example: Scaled_vector = [x y z 1] * T_translate(300.0, 300.0, 0.0)

Matrix Transformation Module

For convenience we collect the matrix transformation functions together as a Python module as shown below. Each transformation returns a numpy format matrix. Multiplying this matrix by a 3D (x, y, z) vector will transform that vector in the required way. For example multiplying the position vector [2.0, 2.0, 2.0 , 1.0] by the scaling function **def T_scaling(sx, sy, sz)** where sx = 2, sy = 3, sz = 5 would transform the position vector to [4.0, 6.0, 10, 0, 1.0]

```
"""
Program name: matrix_transforms.py
Objective: Providing a 3D module that performs the required matrix operations and transformations.
Perspective transformation is included,

Keywords: 3d matrix, geometric transformations, perspective transform.
===========================================================================79
Next problem:

1. Comprehensive test modules for each function including failure cases.
==================================
"""
import math
import numpy as np
#%%%%%%%%%%%         3D LINEAR TRANSFORMATIONS        %%%%%%%%%%%%%%%%%%%%%
#%%%%%%        STANDARD TRANSFORMATION MATRICES FOR 3D GEOMETRIC SHAPES:
# Transformations: Translation, rotation, shear, scaling. See appendix on Matrix Transforms for other
transformations.

def T_reflect_xy():
    """ Reflection through the X-Y plane
    """
    T = np.matrix([[1.0, 0.0,  0.0, 0.0],
            [0.0, 1.0,  0.0, 0.0],
            [0.0, 0.0, -1.0, 0.0],
            [0.0, 0.0 , 0.0, 1.0] ])
    return T

def T_reflect_yz():
    """ Reflection through the Y-Z plane
    """
    T = np.matrix([[-1.0, 0.0,  0.0, 0.0],
            [ 0.0, 1.0,  0.0, 0.0],
            [ 0.0, 0.0,  1.0, 0.0],
            [ 0.0, 0.0,  0.0, 1.0] ])
    return T

def T_reflect_zx():
    """ Reflection through the Z-X plane
    """
    T = np.matrix([[1.0,  0.0,  0.0, 0.0],
            [0.0, -1.0,  0.0, 0.0],
            [0.0,  0.0,  1.0, 0.0],
            [0.0,  0.0 , 0.0, 1.0] ])
    return T

def T_translate(tx, ty, tz):
    """ Shift points tx in the X-direction,
            ty in the Y-direction and
            tz in the Z direction.
    The apparent direction of Z increasing seems to be negative!!!.

    """
    T = np.matrix([[1.0, 0.0, 0.0,  0.0],
            [0.0, 1.0, 0.0,  0.0],
            [0.0, 0.0, 1.0,  0.0],
```

```python
                    [tx,  ty , tz,  1.0] ])
    return T

def T_scaling(sx, sy, sz):
    """ Expand points sx in the X-direction,
                  sy in the Y-direction and
                  sz in the Z direction.
    """
    T = np.matrix([[ sx, 0.0, 0.0, 0.0],
                   [0.0,  sy, 0.0, 0.0],
                   [0.0, 0.0,  sz, 0.0],
                   [0.0, 0.0, 0.0, 1.0] ])
    return T

def T_rotx(theta):
    """ Rotate points theta (radians)around the X-axis.
    """
    T = np.matrix([[1.0,          0.0,                  0.0,     0.0],
                   [0.0,  math.cos(theta),  -math.sin(theta),   0.0],
                   [0.0,  math.sin(theta),   math.cos(theta),   0.0],
                   [0.0,          0.0,                  0.0,     1.0] ])
    return T

def T_roty(theta):
    """ Rotate points theta (radians)around the Y-axis.
    """
    T = np.matrix([[  math.cos(theta),  0.0,  math.sin(theta),  0.0],
                   [          0.0,       1.0,              0.0,  0.0],
                   [ -math.sin(theta),  0.0,  math.cos(theta),  0.0],
                   [          0.0,       0.0,              0.0,  1.0] ])
    return T

def T_rotz(theta):
    """ Rotate points theta (radians)around the Z-axis.
    """
    T = np.matrix([ [math.cos(theta),    -math.sin(theta),   0.0,  0.0],
                    [math.sin(theta),     math.cos(theta),   0.0,  0.0],
                    [        0.0,                    0.0,    1.0,  0.0],
                    [        0.0,                    0.0,    0.0,  1.0] ])
    return T


def T_shear(sh_x, sh_y, sh_z):
    """ Shear or skew points points by sh_x in the X-direction,
                        sh_y in the Y-direction,
                        sh_z in the Z-direction.
    """
    T = np.matrix([ [ 1.0,   sh_x,   sh_z,   0.0],
                    [sh_x,    1.0,   sh_y,   0.0],
                    [sh_z,   sh_y,    1.0,   0.0],
                    [ 0.0,    0.0,    0.0,   1.0] ])

    return T
```

Rotate the Shape about the X, Y and Z axes

In the example below we rotate the simple fish shape three times in sucession and then shift it by x = 300 and y = 300 so that it is in the center of the viewing area. This entire sequence is repeated 160 times and this results in the wire-cage type of drawings shown below.

```
"""
Program name: 3d_2d_shape_conversion_and_rotation_1.py
Objective: Rotate a shape about X, Y, Z or all
selected axes in any position..

Keywords: 3d projections, 2d shapes, transforms, arbitrary rotation..
===============================================================================79
Comments: The five vertices constituting the fish shape are gives a a list of
x,y coordinates. The function "twod_shape_2_homogeneous_matrix(twod_shape)"
converts them to an augmented 4d (homogeneous) list of vectors.
Each vector is the location of a vertex in 3d (homogeneous) space.

Tested on: Python 2.7.3, Python 3.2.3
Author:  Mike Ohlson de Fine
==================================
"""
from Tkinter import *
#from tkinter import *   # Use this instead of the above for python version 3.x
import math
import numpy
import matrix_transforms

root = Tk()
root.title('Rotate Fish Shape around X,Y and Z simultaneously')
cw = 600                          # canvas width.
ch = 600                          # canvas height.
canvas_1 = Canvas(root, width=cw, height=ch, background="#110011")
canvas_1.grid(row=0, column=1)

cycle_period= 30

rad_one_deg = math.pi/180.0
rad_angle = 0.0

# 2D VERSION - CO-PLANAR
tiny_fish = [-1.61,0.50,   0.75,-0.50,   1.61,0.13,   0.87,0.49,   -1.43,-0.22]
#=================================================================
# 2 ESSENTIAL GRAPHIC VECTOR TYPE CONVERSIONS
#=================================================
# For Display - Downconvert a 3D/4D matrix down to a 2D list.
def fourd_shape_2_twod_line(numpy_threed_matrix, kula, line_thickness):
    """ Convert a 3D homogeneous matrix (numpy form) to a list for 'create_line'.
    """
    bbb = numpy_threed_matrix.tolist()
    twod_line = []
    for i in range(0, len(bbb)):
        twod_line.append( bbb[i][0] )
        twod_line.append( bbb[i][1] )
    canvas_1.create_line( twod_line, width = line_thickness,  fill=kula )
```

```
    return twod_line

# Expand a 2D shape -> A 4d (homogeneous) matrix array
def twod_shape_2_homogeneous_matrix(twod_shape):
    """ Convert a 2D shape list into a homogeneous 4D matrix (numpy form).
    The z coordinate is zero. z = 0.
    """
    homogenous_4d_array =[]
    for i in range(0, len(twod_shape), 2):
        new_x = twod_shape[ i]
        new_y = twod_shape[ i + 1]
        new_z = 0.0
        new_w = 1
        new_vertex = [new_x, new_y, new_z, new_w]
        homogenous_4d_array.append(new_vertex)
    homogenous_4d_mat = numpy.matrix(homogenous_4d_array)
    return homogenous_4d_mat


#=====================================================================
# CONVERT 2D SHAPES TO 4D MATRICES (NUMPY FORM)
fish_2d24d_mat = twod_shape_2_homogeneous_matrix(tiny_fish)
# Scale the tiny fish up into a big fish
bigfish_mat = fish_2d24d_mat * matrix_transforms.T_scaling(150.0 , 200.0, 0.0)

# Dynamic rotation of fish_1 around axes within the shape
bigfish_view = bigfish_mat * matrix_transforms.T_translate( 300.0, 300.0, 0.0)  # Viewing convenience.
fourd_shape_2_twod_line(bigfish_view, 'yellow', 4)

for i in range (160):
    bigfish_mat = bigfish_mat * matrix_transforms.T_rotx(rad_angle) # Rotation about X axis.
    bigfish_mat = bigfish_mat * matrix_transforms.T_roty(rad_angle) # Rotation about Y axis.
    bigfish_mat = bigfish_mat * matrix_transforms.T_rotz(rad_angle) # Rotation about Z axis.
    bigfish_view = bigfish_mat * matrix_transforms.T_translate( 300.0, 300.0, 0.0) # Viewing convenience.
    fourd_shape_2_twod_line(bigfish_view, 'green', 1)
    rad_angle = rad_one_deg * 5.0

root.mainloop()
```

Rotation around the X-axis:

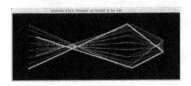

Rotation around the Y-axis:

Rotation around the Z-axis:

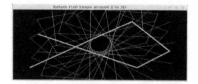

Combined rotation around the X, Y and Z axes:

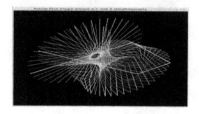

What have we accomplished so far?

- We have demonstrated how to convert 3D shapes into matrices. These matrices are in the form required by the Numpy module.
- Using Numpy versions of vertex lists (that, is matrix versions), we are able to matrix multiply our shapes with standard linear algebra matrices to rotate the shape around the X, Y and Z axes by any chosen amount.

The Next Step – Do the same with entire collections or sets of shapes.

Working with Shape Sets (Groups of Shapes)

The first task is to develop the Python code to deal with large sets of shapes. The shapes could be a three-dimensional human forms, an animal or mythical beast, a building or even complete villiage presented to our Python program as long lists of vertices.

For the sake of clarity we will use the set of four fish outlines shown below. We will handle them in our code as Python list of lists. A list of lists is another way of saying a two-index list, like

A_set = [a, b, c, d] where a = [e,f,g,h], b= [i,j,k,l,m,n,o] , c= [p,q, ...] and so on.

In the example we have

fish_set = [fish_1, fish_2, fish_3, fish_4]
where

fish_1 = [169.2,161.6 , 309.2,102.3 , 360.0,139.5 , 316.4,160.9 , 180.0,118.7]
fish_2 = [515.0,270.9 , 421.4,173.0 , 325.7,196.6 , 299.22,243.0 , 392.8,291.6 , 498.5,211.6]
fish_3 = [164.2,306.6 , 229.2,271.6 , 317.1,298.7 , 212.8,305.2 , 149.2,265.9]
fish_4 = [362.8,378.7 , 300.7,353.0 , 260.7,367.3 , 292.8,383.7 , 370.7,347.3 , 424.2,375.9 , 462.1,355.2 , 412.1,336.6 , 361.4,362.3]

A set of shapes to be processed as a unit:

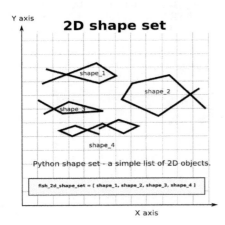

The way we handle complex sets of shapes is simply achieved by means of the following four lines of Python code:

```
fish_4d_set_mat = []
for set in range(len(fish_set)):
    temp = twod_shape_2_homogeneous_matrix(fish_1)
    fish_4d_set_mat . append(temp)
```

where the "twod_shape_2_homogeneous_matrix(fish_1) " function is the exact same one we used in the previous example for a single shape.

twod_shape_2_homogeneous_matrix(fish_1) is an abbreviated way of writing " **convert a 2D shape into a homogeneous Numpy matrix**". Python thus gives us a simple and powerful way of handling unlimited geometric complexity.

```
"""
Program name: 3d_shape_set_convert_2Dto4D_1.py
Objective: Convert a 2D planar shape into a list of 4D vertex vectors.

Keywords: 3d shape, 2d shapes, conversion function.
==================================================================================79
Comments: 2d shape vertices are converted to lists of 4d (homogeneous) matrix/vectors.
Each vector is the location of a vertex in 3d (homogeneous) space.

A 'shape' is a 2d planar line of arbtrary number of segments.
```

The final list corresponds to a shape object in 3 dimensions.
The shape object is a list of 4D vertices.

Tested on: Python 2.7.3, Python 3.2.3
Author: Mike Ohlson de Fine
=================================
"""

```python
import numpy

# 2D SHAPES - Four simple fish shapes in the x-y plane
fish_1 = [ 169.2,161.6 , 309.2,102.3 , 360.0,139.5 , 316.4,160.9 , 180.0,118.7 ]
fish_2 = [ 515.0,270.9 , 421.4,173.0 , 325.7,196.6 , 299.22,243.0 , 392.8,291.6 , 498.5,211.6 ]
fish_3 = [ 164.2,306.6 , 229.2,271.6 , 317.1,298.7 , 212.8,305.2 , 149.2,265.9 ]
fish_4 = [ 362.8,378.7 , 300.7,353.0 , 260.7,367.3 , 292.8,383.7 , 370.7,347.3 , 424.2,375.9 , 462.1,355.2 ,
412.1,336.6 , 361.4,362.3 ]

fish_set = [ fish_1, fish_2, fish_3, fish_4 ]  # Create the set.
#=====================================================================================
# CONVERSION OF A 2D LIST TO A MATRIX OF 4D VERTICES.
#=====================================================================================
def twod_shape_2_homogeneous_matrix(twod_shape):
    """ Convert a 2D shape list into a homogeneous 4D matrix (numpy form).
    The z coordinate is zero. ie. z = 0.
    """

    homogenous_4d_array = []
    for i in range(0, len(twod_shape), 2):
        new_x = twod_shape[i]
        new_y = twod_shape[i + 1]
        new_z = 0.0
        new_w = 1
        new_vertex = [new_x, new_y, new_z, new_w]
        homogenous_4d_array.append(new_vertex)

    homogenous_4d_mat = numpy.matrix(homogenous_4d_array)
    return homogenous_4d_mat


#=====================================================================================
# Convert 2D set SET to 4D matrices (NUMPY FORM).
#=====================================================================================
fish_4d_set_mat = []
for set in range(len(fish_set)):
    temp = twod_shape_2_homogeneous_matrix(fish_1)
    fish_4d_set_mat.append(temp)

print ('fish_4d_set_mat:')
print (fish_4d_set_mat)

''' RESULT
fish_4d_set_mat:
[matrix([[ 169.2,  161.6,   0. ,   1. ],
        [ 309.2,  102.3,   0. ,   1. ],
        [ 360. ,  139.5,   0. ,   1. ],
        [ 316.4,  160.9,   0. ,   1. ],
        [ 180. ,  118.7,   0. ,   1. ]]),
matrix([[ 169.2,  161.6,   0. ,   1. ],
        [ 309.2,  102.3,   0. ,   1. ],
        [ 360. ,  139.5,   0. ,   1. ],
```

```
        [ 316.4,  160.9,   0. ,   1. ],
        [ 180. ,  118.7,   0. ,   1. ]]),
matrix([[ 169.2,  161.6,   0. ,   1. ],
        [ 309.2,  102.3,   0. ,   1. ],
        [ 360. ,  139.5,   0. ,   1. ],
        [ 316.4,  160.9,   0. ,   1. ],
        [ 180. ,  118.7,   0. ,   1. ]]),
matrix([[ 169.2,  161.6,   0. ,   1. ],
        [ 309.2,  102.3,   0. ,   1. ],
        [ 360. ,  139.5,   0. ,   1. ],
        [ 316.4,  160.9,   0. ,   1. ],
        [ 180. ,  118.7,   0. ,   1. ]])]
'''
```

Rotate Complex Sets of Shapes about the X, Y and Z axes

As we did with a single shape, we can construct a program that easily uses the same code used for rotation of a single shape and apply it to complex sets of shapes.

No rotation:

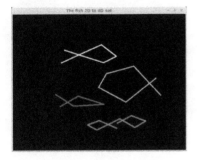

Rotation around the X axis:

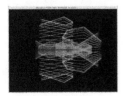

Rotation around the Y axis:

Rotation around the Z axis:

Combined rotation around the X, Y and Z axes:

3D Rotation around the X-axis

"""

Program name: 3d_shape_set_2Dto4D_rotation_1.py
Objective: Convert a 2D planar shape set into a list of 4D vertex vectors,
and then perform transform geometry (scaling, translation and rotation).

Keywords: 3d shape, 2d shapes, conversion of shape sets, transform sets.
===79
Comments: 2d shape vertices are converted to lists of 4d (homogeneous) matrix/vectors.
Each vector is the location of a vertex in 3d (homogeneous) space.

A 'shape' is a 2d planar line of arbtrary number of segments.
A 'set' is a collection of separate shapes.

The final list "fish_set" corresponds to a set of shape objects in 3 dimensions.
The shape object is a list of 4D vertices.

```
Tested on: Python 2.6, Python 2.7.3, Python 3.2.3
Author:  Mike Ohlson de Fine
==================================
"""

from Tkinter import *
#from tkinter import *    # Use this instead of the above for python version 3.x
import math
import numpy
import matrix_transforms

root = Tk()
root.title('Rotate Fish Set around X,Y and Z together')
cw = 600                        # canvas width.
ch = 550                        # canvas height.
canvas_1 = Canvas(root, width=cw, height=ch, background="#110011")
canvas_1.grid(row=0, column=1)


cycle_period= 30


rad_one_deg = math.pi/180.0
rad_angle = 0.0

# 2D SHAPE - A simple fish shape in the x-y plane
fish_1 = [ 169.2,161.6 , 309.2,102.3 , 360.0,139.5 , 316.4,160.9 , 180.0,118.7 ]
fish_2 = [ 515.0,270.9 , 421.4,173.0 , 325.7,196.6 , 299.22,243.0 , 392.8,291.6 , 498.5,211.6 ]
fish_3 = [ 164.2,306.6 , 229.2,271.6 , 317.1,298.7 , 212.8,305.2 , 149.2,265.9 ]
fish_4 = [ 362.8,378.7 , 300.7,353.0 , 260.7,367.3 , 292.8,383.7 , 370.7,347.3 , 424.2,375.9 , 462.1,355.2 ,
412.1,336.6 , 361.4,362.3 ]

fish_set = [ fish_1, fish_2, fish_3, fish_4 ]
kulas = [ 'yellow', 'orange', 'purple', 'magenta' ]
#=====================================================================================
# CONVERSION OF A 2D LIST TO A MATRIX OF 4D VERTICES.
#=====================================================================================
def twod_shape_2_homogeneous_matrix(twod_shape):
    """ Convert a 2D shape list into a homogeneous 4D matrix (numpy form).
        The z coordinate is zero. ie. z = 0.
    """
    homogenous_4d_array = []
    for i in range(len(0, twod_shape), 2):
        new_x = twod_shape[ i ]
        new_y = twod_shape[ i + 1]
        new_z = 0.0
        new_w = 1
        new_vertex = [new_x, new_y, new_z, new_w]
        homogenous_4d_array.append(new_vertex)

    homogenous_4d_mat = numpy.matrix(homogenous_4d_array)
    return homogenous_4d_mat

# For Display - Downconvert a 3D/4D matrix down to a 2D list.
def fourd_shape_2_twod_line(numpy_threed_matrix, kula, line_width):
    """ Convert a 3D homogeneous matrix (numpy form) to a list for 'create_line'.
    """
    bbb = numpy_threed_matrix.tolist()
    twod_line = []
```

```
    for i in range(0, len(bbb)):
        twod_line.append( bbb[i][0] )
        twod_line.append( bbb[i][1] )
    canvas_1.create_line( twod_line, width = line_width, fill=kula )
    return twod_line


#===============================================================================
# Convert 2D set SET to 4D matrices (NUMPY FORM).
fish_4d_set_mat = []
for set in range(len(fish_set)):
    temp = twod_shape_2_homogeneous_matrix(fish_set[set])
    fish_4d_set_mat.append(temp)

# Move origin to center-of-rotation(cor).
for set in range(len(fish_set)):
    fish_4d_set_mat[set] = fish_4d_set_mat[set] * matrix_transforms.T_translate(-300.0, -330.0, 0.0)

# Dynamic rotation of fish_1 around axes within the shape
for i in range (100):
    for set in range(len(fish_4d_set_mat)):
        fish_4d_set_mat[set] = fish_4d_set_mat[set] * matrix_transforms.T_rotx(rad_angle)   # X rotation.
        fish_4d_set_mat[set] = fish_4d_set_mat[set] * matrix_transforms.T_roty(rad_angle)   # Y rotation.
        fish_4d_set_mat[set] = fish_4d_set_mat[set] * matrix_transforms.T_rotz(rad_angle)   # Z rotation.
        view_fish_set = fish_4d_set_mat[set] * matrix_transforms.T_translate( 300.0, 280.0, 0.0)
        fourd_shape_2_twod_line(view_fish_set, kulas[set], 1)

    rad_angle = rad_one_deg * 10.0

root.mainloop()
```

Combining Matrix Operations

We have been using multiplication by special 4 x 4 square matrices to achieve geometric transformations of scaling, rotation and shifting. If we need to achieve four transformations in sequence we just do four multiplications in sequence, one after the next.

The order is important – we will get different results if we change the order in which we do the multiplications.

Now here is a small piece of magic that comes out of matrix algebra – any number of matrix multiplications of square matrices can be achieved by one single multiplication. What is this single magic matrix? It is just the matrix that comes from multiplplying the sequence of individual transformations together.

For example we could combine 3D rotation around the x-axis, the y-axis and the z-axis into a single multiplication. We will not do this as it makes the elements of our transformation matrices unnecessarily complex and, very importantly, difficult to debug.

An interesting and useful consequence of multiple matrix transformations:
A whole long sequence of matrix multiplications can all be combined into a single matrix. This matrix has an inverse that can be used to undo the whole sequence of trnsforms in a single short multiplication. In OpenGL, which we learn to use in the last few chapters in this book, the transform matrices and their inverses are used in a stack – a region of memory that saves a list of the last few matrix transforms. We make use of this later.

Organize the Geometry Transforms as a Python Module

Collect all the 3D Geometry Transformation Functions into a "matrix_transforms.py" module.
The 3D object geometry transforms have been collected together into a single module and can then be used simply by putting "**matrix_transforms.** " in front of the module being used.

The following functions are included in the matrix_transforms module.

T_reflect_xy():   """ Reflection through the X-Y plane """

T_reflect_yz():   """ Reflection through the Y-Z plane """

T_reflect_zx():   """ Reflection through the Z-X plane """

T_translate(tx, ty, tz):   """ Shift points in the X, Y and/or Z directions """

T_scaling(sx, sy, sz):   """ Expand points sx in the X, Y and/or Z directions """

T_rotx(theta):   """ Rotate points theta (radians)around the X-axis. """

T_roty(theta):   """ Rotate points theta (radians)around the Y-axis. """

T_rotz(theta):   """ Rotate points theta (radians)around the Z-axis. """

T_shear(sh_x, sh_y, sh_z):   """ Shear or skew points points by sh_x in the X, Y and/or Z directions """

T_Z_perspective(xyz_numpy_point, kz):   """ Single point perspective. Vanishing point on the z-axis """

T_Y_perspective(xyz_numpy_point, ky):   """ Single point perspective. Vanishing point on the y-axis """

T_X_perspective(xyz_numpy_point, kx):   """ Single point perspective. Vanishing point on the x-axis """

T_ortho_xy(): """ Orthogonal projection onto XY-plane """

T_ortho_xz(): """ Orthogonal projection onto XZ-plane """

T_ortho_zy(): """ Orthogonal projection onto ZY-plane """

5

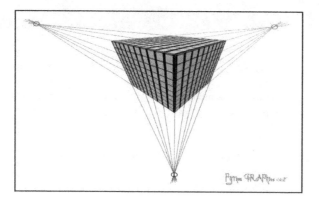

Perspective Transforms

"The only thing you sometimes have control over is perspective. You don't have control over your situation. But you have a choice about how you view it. "
Chris Pine.

"The divisions of Perspective are 3, as used in drawing; of these, the first includes the diminution in size of opaque objects; the second treats of the diminution and loss of outline in such opaque objects; the third, of the diminution and loss of colour at long distances." Leonardo da Vinci.

The topics covered in this chapter are:
- **The Brain Magic of Perspective Projections**
- **The Geometric Principle of Perspective Projection**
- **A Single Vanishing Point**
- **Two Vanishing Points**

- **Three Vanishing Points**
- **Looking Up**
- **Looking Down**

The Brain Magic of Perspective Projections

The human brain is good at making models of the real world inside our heads. A hungry hunter can throw a spear at a running boar and thereby save his family from starvation. All he has are "maps" in his brain that guide his spear throwing muscles. It's a miracle so profound that almost all human entertainment, especially sport, is constructed around it . We humans celebrate it endlessly in sport.

The key to a convincing looking representations of the real world on sheets of paper, canvas or computer screens, are the rules of perspective projection. In this chapter we explore the use of linear algebra matrices to achieve a meaningful representation of real world shapes, through the rules of drawing perspective.

Plane projections of a constellation of boxes.

Two-dimensional projections of rectangular objects. No perspective has been applied and so the actual shape cannot be known. The objects could be flat sheets, or boxes, or long beams.

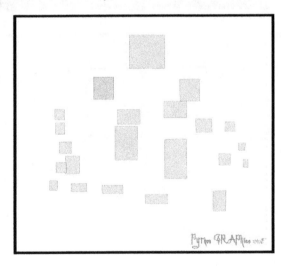

Orthograpgic projection allows relative size to be perceived.

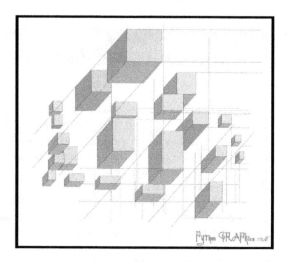

The Geometric Principle of Perspective Projection

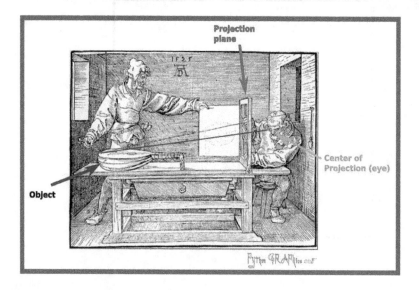

The fundamental rule of perspective drawing: The further away an object is from the observer, the smaller it appears. Parallel lines running away from the observer seem to converge at a single point, the vanishing point.

Case 1: A Single Vanishing Point

The most common artistic perspective has a single vanishing point.

Single vanishing point perspective.
The trigonometry of a single vanishing point perspective model. A group of objects inside a 3D world are projected as 2D images onto a flat translucent screen. The further away objects are from the screen, the smaller will be their images on the screen.

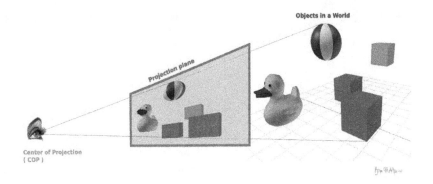

The conceptual arangement for the construction of of perspective projections.

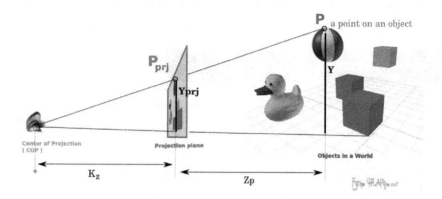

The geometric distances that relate the position of points on the 3D objects to the position of the images of those 3D objects on the projection screen.

The Perspective Equation

$$\frac{Yprj}{Kz} = \frac{Y}{Kz + Zp} \quad \text{(from similar triangles)}$$

can be re-arranged as:

$$Yprj = \frac{Y}{1 + \dfrac{Zp}{Kz}}$$

If we put $\; fz = 1 + \dfrac{Zp}{Kz}$

then $\boxed{Yprj = fz\,Y}$ this is the perspective equation!
It gives the height (y position)
of points on the projection plane.

fz is the "focal length" used in
camera lens terminology.

Geometric distances for deriving perspective relations:

Position of P in world coordinates is P = [x y z 1]

$$\begin{bmatrix} x & y & z & 1 \end{bmatrix} \times \begin{bmatrix} f_z & 0 & 0 & 0 \\ 0 & f_z & 0 & 0 \\ 0 & 0 & 1 & 0 \\ 0 & 0 & 0 & 1 \end{bmatrix} = \begin{bmatrix} X_{prj} & Y_{prj} & Z_{prj} & 1 \end{bmatrix}$$

Which is the same as:

$$X_{prj} = \frac{x}{1 + \dfrac{Zp}{Kx}}$$

$$Y_{prj} = \frac{y}{1 + \dfrac{Zp}{Kx}}$$

$$Z_{prj} = z$$

The Python function that will deliver a single point perspective view is the following:

```python
def T_Z_perspective(xyz_numpy_point, kz):
    """
    Using matrix multiplication, convert a 3D homogeneous matrix (numpy form) to an equivalent
    perspective matrix.
    z_component is the z-component of the point being transformed to perspective coordinates.
    kz is that distance to the projection plane.
    The returned matrix is the plane projection of the object, correctly scaled.
    """
    z_component = xyz_numpy_point.item(2)
    fz = 1/(z_component/kz + 1)

    Pz = np.matrix([ [fz,  0.0,  0.0,  0.0],\
                     [0.0,  fz,  0.0,  0.0],\
                     [0.0, 0.0,  1.0,  0.0],\
```

```
                        [0.0, 0.0,   0.0,    1.0] ])
        return Pz
```

Note that transformation has to be computed for every individual vertex belonging to the shape set being transformed into the perspective view. This means that every time the position vector of a point is multiplied by the transformation matrix, the matrix will have different values for the elements (entries) of the matrix. That is the value
z_component = xyz_numpy_point.item(n)
will be the unique value belonging to the specific vertex being transformed.

Single Vanishing Point Animation Example

Now we look at an example where we animate the rotations of a 3D object with a single vanishing point perspective.

The instructions that apply the perspective transform to each vertex belonging to our 3D object are:

```
#2: Apply perspective transforms in Z directions - single-vanishing point perspective.
    for h in range(len(object_vertices)):
        for i in range(len(object_vertices[h])):
            perspective_vertices[h][i] = perspective_vertices[h]
[i]*matrix_transforms.T_Z_perspective(perspective_vertices[h][i], f)
```

The T_Z_perspective(..., f) function is inside the **matrix_transforms.py** module.

The Planar Object
The code used to assemble the planar object is:

```
# Generate Planar Surface of Rectangular Strips.
def stripface(n, x0, y0, z0, w, h):
    """ Generate a planar set of n rectangular strips starting at x0, y0, z0
        width w in the x direction, and length h in the y direction.
    """
    x_new = x0
    xy_strip_set = []
    for i in range(n):
        xy= [ [ x_new,  y0,   z0, 1.0 ], [ x_new+w, y0,   z0, 1.0 ], [ x_new+w, y0+h, z0, 1.0 ], [ x_new,   y0+h, z0,
1.0 ] ]
        xy_mat = np.matrix(xy)
        xy_strip_set.append(xy_mat)
        x_new += 2*w
    return xy_strip_set
```

In the example that follows this one we will extend this function to create three such planar objects at right angles to each other. This illustrates the perspective projection effect clearly.

The complete program

```
"""
Program name: 3d_shape_groups_in_perspective_1.py
Objective: Create 3D perspective transform and display.


Keywords: 3d projections, perspective, transforms, display.
====================================================================================79
Comments: This program uses the matrix_transformation module as an import.
An array of planar strips is used to demonstrate the concept.

Tested on: Python 2.6, Python 2.7.3, Python 3.2.3
Author:  Mike Ohlson de Fine
=====================================
"""

from Tkinter import *
#from tkinter import *   # Use this instead of the above for python version 3.x
import math
import copy
import numpy as np
import matrix_transforms


root = Tk()
root.title('Move any old shapes in perspective')
cw = 800                        # canvas width.
ch = 800                        # canvas height.
canvas_1 = Canvas(root, width=cw, height=ch, background="#110011")
canvas_1.grid(row=0, column=1)
cycle_period= 30
#################################################################################
# Generate Planar Surface of Rectangular Strips.
def stripface(n, x0, y0, z0, w, h):
    """ Generate a planar set of n rectangular strips starting at x0, y0, z0
        width w in the x direction, and length h in the y direction.
    """

    x_new = x0
    xy_strip_set = []
    for i in range(n):
        xy= [ [ x_new,   y0,   z0, 1.0 ], [ x_new+w, y0,   z0, 1.0 ], [ x_new+w, y0+h, z0, 1.0 ], [ x_new,   y0+h, z0, 1.0 ] ]
        xy_mat = np.matrix(xy)
        xy_strip_set.append(xy_mat)
        x_new += 2*w
    return xy_strip_set
#===================================================================================
def display_matrix_object(numpy_threed_matrix,kula):
    """ Convert a 3D homogeneous matrix (numpy form) to a list for a tkinter 'create_polygon'.
    """

    bbb = numpy_threed_matrix.tolist()
    twod_line = []
    for i in range(0, len(bbb)):
        twod_line.append( bbb[i][0] )
        twod_line.append( bbb[i][1] )
    #canvas_1.create_line( twod_line, width = 1, tag = 'lines_1', fill= kula )
    canvas_1.create_polygon( twod_line, width = 1,  tag = 'lines_1', fill= kula )
```

```
    return twod_line

def scale_shift_3d_object(object_vertices, scale_y, scale_z, x_shift, y_shift):
    """ This places a 3D piece "object" at a convenient viewing position and at a
    a convenient size.
    """
    view_vertices = copy.deepcopy(object_vertices)
    for h in range(len(view_vertices)):
        for j in range(len(view_vertices[h])):
            view_vertices[h][j] = view_vertices[h][j] * matrix_transforms.T_scaling(scale_x, scale_y, scale_z)
            view_vertices[h][j] = view_vertices[h][j] * matrix_transforms.T_translate(x_shift, y_shift, 0.0)
    return view_vertices
#=================================================================================
# Initialization of variables and data.
rad_ninety_deg = 90 * math.pi/180.0
rad_one_deg = math.pi/180.0
rad_angle = 0.0

f = 8.0  # f is an analog of focal length for perspective projections.

# A General Planar Strip in x-y plane, width w, height h
x0 = 0.0
y0 = 0.0
z0 = 0.0
w = 0.1
h = 6.0

# Locate the shape-set (for temporary display purposes only) at x_shift, y_shift.
x_shift = 200.0
y_shift = 100.0
scale_x = 40.0
scale_y = 40.0
scale_z = 40.0
#^^^^^^^^^^^^^^^^^^^^^^^^^^^^^^^^^^^^^^^^^^^^^^^^^^^^^^^^^^^^^^^^^^^^^^^^^^^^^^^^^^^
# Create (instantiate) objects and position them.
assemblage_A = stripface(30, x0, y0, z0, w, h)  # Make an instance of the planar object.
for h in range(len(assemblage_A)):       # Disposition and setup - Shift to a new location.
    assemblage_A[h] = assemblage_A[h] * matrix_transforms.T_translate(2.2, 2.2, 0)
#^^^^^^^^^^^^^^^^^^^^^^^^^^^^^^^^^^^^^^^^^^^^^^^^^^^^^^^^^^^^^^^^^^^^^^^^^^^^^^^^^^^
# Dynamic (animated) rotation of the object).

def transform_display(object_vertices, rad_angle, kula):
    """ Transform and then Display.
    There are two very distinct and separate operations here:
    A) Rotate the object around the X, Y and Z axes. This alters the position of every vertex permanently.
    B) Translate and scale each vertex temporarily for viewing. These operations are performed on a separate
       copy of the rotated object. After each view the copy has no worth - it will be overwritten when the
       next view is created.
    """
    #1: Strips: Rotate Assemblage. Any other transforms may be applied to the vertices here. Their effect will be
permanent.
    #   For this example only rotation by a common angle is considered.
    for h in range(len(object_vertices)):
        object_vertices[h] = object_vertices[h] * matrix_transforms.T_rotx(rad_angle)   # Rotate around x.
        object_vertices[h] = object_vertices[h] * matrix_transforms.T_roty(rad_angle)   # Rotate around y.
        object_vertices[h] = object_vertices[h] * matrix_transforms.T_rotz(rad_angle)   # Rotate around z.
```

```
    perspective_vertices = copy.deepcopy(object_vertices)   # Preserve the original and view an independent
copy.

    #2: Apply perspective transforms in Z directions - single-vanishing point perspective.
    for h in range(len(object_vertices)):
        for i in range(len(object_vertices[h])):
            perspective_vertices[h][i] = perspective_vertices[h]
[i]*matrix_transforms.T_Z_perspective(perspective_vertices[h][i], f)

    #3: Position and size the strip-grid for convenient viewing.
    view_perspective_vertices = []
    for h in range(len(perspective_vertices)):
        one_component = scale_shift_3d_object(perspective_vertices[h], scale_y, scale_z, x_shift, y_shift)
        view_perspective_vertices.append(one_component)

    # 4: Display perspective projections.
    for h in range(len(object_vertices)):
        display_matrix_object(view_perspective_vertices[h], kula)

for i in range (200):
    transform_display(assemblage_A, rad_angle, "#880000")
    rad_angle = rad_one_deg * 1.0
    canvas_1.update()                  # This refreshes the drawing on the canvas.
    canvas_1.after(cycle_period)   # This makes execution pause for 30 milliseconds, nominally.
    canvas_1.delete('lines_1')

root.mainloop()
```

Three Planar Objects

We now modify the above example by extending the stripfaces(..) function to create three planes made of strips. The planes are mutually perpendicular to each other, as follows:

```
def stripface(n, x0, y0, z0, w, h):
    """ Generate a planar set of n rectangular strips starting at x0, y0, z0
        width w in the x direction, and length h in the y direction.
    """
    # Rectangular strips in the x-y plane.
    x_new = x0
    xy_strip_set = []
    for i in range(n):
        xy= [ [ x_new,  y0,  z0, 1.0 ], [ x_new+w, y0,  z0, 1.0 ], [ x_new+w, y0+h, z0, 1.0 ], [ x_new,  y0+h, z0,
1.0 ] ]
        xy_mat = np.matrix(xy)
        xy_strip_set.append(xy_mat)
        x_new += 2*w
    # Rectangular strips in the x-z plane.
    x_new = x0
    xz_strip_set = []
    for i in range(n):
        xz= [ [ x_new,  y0,  z0, 1.0 ], [ x_new+w, y0,  z0, 1.0 ], [ x_new+w, y0, z0+h, 1.0 ], [ x_new,  y0, z0+h,
1.0 ] ]
        xz_mat = np.matrix(xz)
        xz_strip_set.append(xz_mat)
        x_new += 2*w
```

```
# Rectangular strips in the z-y plane.
y_new = y0
yz_strip_set = []
for i in range(n):
    yz= [ [ x0,  y_new,  z0, 1.0 ], [ x0, y_new+w,  z0, 1.0 ], [ x0, y_new+w, z0+h, 1.0 ], [ x0,  y_new, z0+h,
1.0 ] ]
    yz_mat = np.matrix(yz)
    yz_strip_set.append(yz_mat)
    y_new += 2*w

return xy_strip_set, xz_strip_set, yz_strip_set
```

Then the instructions to create and position the three instances are:

```
# Create (instantiate) objects and position them.
xyz_strip_sets = stripface(30, x0, y0, z0, w, h)
assemblage_A = xyz_strip_sets[0]
assemblage_B = xyz_strip_sets[1]
assemblage_C = xyz_strip_sets[2]

for h in range(len(assemblage_A)):      # Disposition and setup - Shift to a new location.
        assemblage_A[h] = assemblage_A[h] * matrix_transforms.T_translate(2.2, 2.2, 0)
        assemblage_B[h] = assemblage_B[h] * matrix_transforms.T_translate(2.2, 2.2, 0)
        assemblage_C[h] = assemblage_C[h] * matrix_transforms.T_translate(2.2, 2.2, 0)
```

The final execution loop is:

```
# Main execution.
for i in range (200):
    transform_display(assemblage_A, rad_angle, "#880000")
    transform_display(assemblage_B, rad_angle, "#008800")
    transform_display(assemblage_C, rad_angle, "#000088")
    rad_angle = rad_one_deg * 1.0
    canvas_1.update()              # This refreshes the drawing on the canvas.
    canvas_1.after(cycle_period)   # This makes execution pause for 200 milliseconds.
    canvas_1.delete('lines_1')

root.mainloop()
```

Slow Execution and Graphics Bottlenecks

When the above example is run the execution and display are extremely slow. The vast number of floating mathematical operations compounded by slow graphics display methods that are associated with the use of Tkinter, demonstrate that the methods we have used so far are inadequate for producing the fast image production that would be needed to produce a video game.

The advantage of the use of Python with Tinker is the elegant simplicity of constructing 2D and 3D objects as well as the value of making the matrix functions that perform the transforms. There is no clearer way to do it. But now that we have obviously reached the limit of what we can achieve with these methods, we need to know which new direction we need to move in to solve the graphics speed problem.

The Need for Speed

The solution to making 3D animated graphics fast is two-fold:
1. Use the OpenGL graphics functions instead of Tkinter.
2. Use fast hardware to speed up computation and graphics rendering.

We embark on this road in Chapter 8. OpenGL functions are not only very effective at rendering images fast but they painlessly solve the problem of sorting out which parts of any object should be invisible when there are many objects, some which should obscure others, in the field of view. OpenGL also deals with color shading, lighting, transparency and fog.

We need methods of creating complicated 3D objects when we work with OpenGL and in the next two chapters we explore two very useful open source packages that are ideal for our needs.

Case 2: Two Vanishing Points

We figured out the equation that will change the x and y positions of any point on an object when we apply a perspective transformation that creates a single vanishing point somewhere along the z-axis. The location along the axis is controlled by the focal length f.

A similar line of reasoning might allow us to apply the same ideas to arrive at equally simple matrices that apply two and three vanishing point perspective distortions along the x and y axes. Unfortunately it is not that simple and deducing the matrices for more than one point perspective distortion is beyond the scope of this book.

In the diagrams below we illustrate the desired outcome of effective two and three vanishing point perspective but we do not explore methods of achieving them with our matrix transforms. When we start using OpenGL we do not have to worry about this because OpenGL has solved the problem with a simple-to-use function.

Two vanishing point perspective:

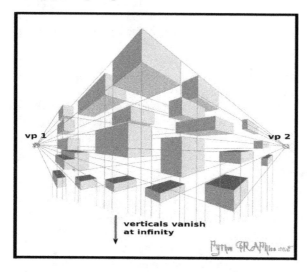

Case 3: Three Vanishing Points

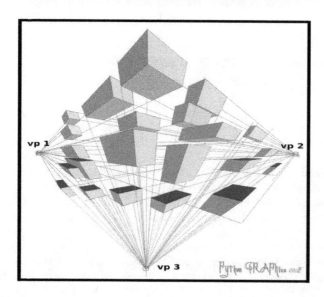

Vanishing Point Position to Control Viewer Altitude

High viewer altitude. This perspective is achieved by positioning the vanishing point below the object being viewed.

Low viewer altitude. This perspective is achieved by positioning the vanishing point above the object being viewed.

6

Using SVG and Inkscape for Python Drawings

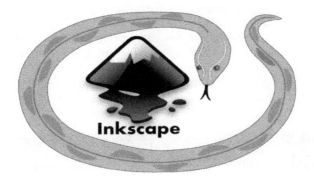

"How do you expect the children to eat a whale? asked Sanuk. "The same way they eat seal and small fish" said Maguyuk, "One bite at a time."

In this chapter we will cover:
- **How do we get Inkscape**
- **Adjust Inkscape to Export the Best SVG Format**
- **Inspect an Inkscape exported File**
- **Convert SVG 'M' Line into Python Lists**
- **A Composite Image from Layers**

In this chapter we follow the Inuit hunter's advice above by breaking up a complex and pain-in-the-head problem into small bite-sized chunks that are mentally easy to chew. When we draw cartoons, game characters, objects and landscapes we want to use the most convenient tools. When you want to cut a piece of wood with a saw you do not buy a sheet of steel and make a saw blade first. Nor do you buy a mallet and chisel (which *will* cut wood albeit wastefully). What we seek now are the most suitable, easy to use and readily available tools to produce drawings that can be used in bare-metal Python programs.

A good example is the drawing program *Inkscape* which conforms to the SVG standard. The universal language for web graphics is SVG (Scaled Vector Graphics). SVG is a vector graphics standard for web applications that is part of the World Wide Web Consortium's collection of standards. One of the best drafting programs around is Inkscape, a free and open source package that natively outputs its files in SVG format. So using Python we want be able to draw shapes in Inkscape (or anything else that outputs SVG files) and have a simple Python program to convert these drawings into a form that Python can use directly. In this chapter we do this.

How do we get Inkscape?

Simply type in https://inkscape.org/en/ into your web browser. This will take you to the Inkscape site.

Click on the "DOWNLOAD" button and then follow the instructions appropriate to your particular operating system: MS Windows, Mac OS 10, Linux Ubuntu, Linux Suse or compile Inkscape from the source packages. The help/tutorial document is excellent. In this book we assume that you will work your way through the tutorials and examples up to the point where you can produce shapes made of segments of straight lines.

Adjust Inkscape to Export the Best SVG Format

Inkscape can export it's SVG files in a variety of formats. The default format is wrong for us. It is most unsuitable because it makes the task of identifying and extracting the x and y coordinates from the exported files very complicated. Inkscape, by default, produces svg code for lines that are unnecessarily complicated because it mixes M, m, L, l, Z and z annotation within lines which makes the conversion routines for producing Python lists a complicated headache. So the most important part of the process is to change the default settings of Inkscape to ones what will make our job simple.

1. Open Inkscape and select (click on) the *file* menu at the top tool bar.

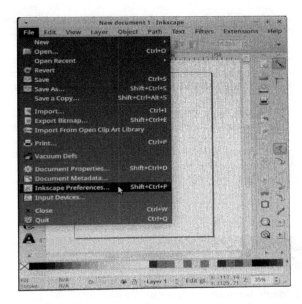

2. Select **Inkscape Preferenc**es near the bottom of the menu.
3. Scroll down the menu that pops up and select **SVG output**.
4. On the small panel that appears click inside the small box next to **Force repeat commands**.
   Un-check '*Allow relative coordinates*'. This is the critical step.

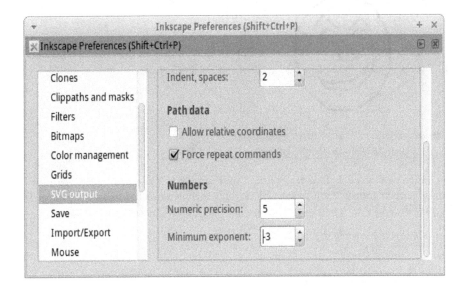

The settings for Indent, spaces and numeric precision may be changed to the settings shown here but that is not important - it is just a preference that is not critical to the usable format of the output files.

The key task in this chapter is to build up to a python program that can take a drawing in the form of an SVG file made in Inkscape and convert it into a list of coordinate values that can be drawn directly onto a Python canvas. This is a first step in producing animations of complex drawings.

In this chapter we do hardly any drawing code. What we do now is focus on text processing as a means of converting files produced by the Inkscape vector drawing package into the much simpler form used by Python (Tkinter). It is a pretty useful exercise because it covers the more general problem of converting one file type into another. The SVG (Scaled Vector Graphics) format is used to produce much of the graphics on cell phones and tablets. There is no reason you cannot convert cartoons and games prototyped in Python into Javascript versions that can work on smartphones and tablets.

"There are no rules, only tools." ~ *Glenn Vilppu (renowned animator, artist, teacher).*

Inspect an Inkscape Exported File

Using Inkscape the following rough drawing of a face was drawn.

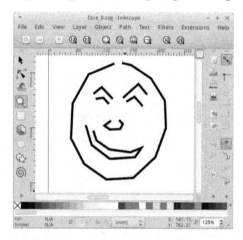

This image was saved as face_0.svg and if we examine this file in a text editor like gedit or context we see the following SVG file, which is a mix of html and SVG code. The only lines of interest to us are the lines in blue text. The rest we can ignore.

```
<?xml version="1.0" encoding="UTF-8" standalone="no"?>
<!-- Created with Inkscape (http://www.inkscape.org/) -->

<svg
   xmlns:dc="http://purl.org/dc/elements/1.1/"
   xmlns:cc="http://creativecommons.org/ns#"
   xmlns:rdf="http://www.w3.org/1999/02/22-rdf-syntax-ns#"
```

```
xmlns:svg="http://www.w3.org/2000/svg"
xmlns="http://www.w3.org/2000/svg"
version="1.1"
width="744.09448"
height="1052.3622"
id="svg3998">
<defs
 id="defs4000" />
<metadata
 id="metadata4003">
 <rdf:RDF>
  <cc:Work
    rdf:about="">
   <dc:format>image/svg+xml</dc:format>
   <dc:type
     rdf:resource="http://purl.org/dc/dcmitype/StillImage" />
   <dc:title></dc:title>
  </cc:Work>
 </rdf:RDF>
</metadata>
<g
 id="layer1">
<path
   d="M 64.285714,85.219325 L 97.142857,56.647896 L 160,89.505039"
   id="path2985"
   style="fill:none;stroke:#000000;stroke-width:4;stroke-linecap:butt;stroke-linejoin:miter;stroke-
miterlimit:4;stroke-opacity:1;stroke-dasharray:none" />
  <path
   d="M 205.71429,92.362182 L 268.57143,59.505039 L 292.85714,93.790754"
   id="path2987"
   style="fill:none;stroke:#000000;stroke-width:4;stroke-linecap:butt;stroke-linejoin:miter;stroke-
miterlimit:4;stroke-opacity:1;stroke-dasharray:none" />
  <path
   d="M 147.34013,154.07171 L 167.14286,163.79075 L 183.19184,155.05198"
   id="path2989"
   style="fill:none;stroke:#000000;stroke-width:2;stroke-linecap:butt;stroke-linejoin:miter;stroke-
miterlimit:4;stroke-opacity:1;stroke-dasharray:none" />
  <path
   d="M 110,180.93361 L 167.14286,212.36218 L 264.28571,162.36218"
   id="path2991"
   style="fill:none;stroke:#000000;stroke-width:10;stroke-linecap:butt;stroke-linejoin:miter;stroke-
miterlimit:4;stroke-opacity:1;stroke-dasharray:none" />
  <path
   d="M 120,105.21933 L 140.71428,110.56158"
   id="path3780"
   style="fill:none;stroke:#000000;stroke-width:3;stroke-linecap:butt;stroke-linejoin:miter;stroke-
miterlimit:4;stroke-opacity:1;stroke-dasharray:none" />
  <path
   d="M 220.71428,113.79075 L 241.42857,108.79075"
   id="path3782"
   style="fill:none;stroke:#000000;stroke-width:3;stroke-linecap:butt;stroke-linejoin:miter;stroke-
miterlimit:4;stroke-opacity:1;stroke-dasharray:none" />
 </g>
</svg>
```

The lines in this file that contain the essential drawing shapes are:

```
d="M 64.285714,85.219325 L 97.142857,56.647896 L 160,89.505039"
d="M 205.71429,92.362182 L 268.57143,59.505039 L 292.85714,93.790754"
d="M 147.34013,154.07171 L 167.14286,163.79075 L 183.19184,155.05198"
d="M 110,180.93361 L 167.14286,212.36218 L 264.28571,162.36218"
d="M 110,180.93361 L 167.14286,212.36218 L 264.28571,162.36218"
d="M 120,105.21933 L 140.71428,110.56158"
d="M 220.71428,113.79075 L 241.42857,108.79075"
```

These are lists of xy position coordinates of points which are joined by lines of the form
d="M x1,y1 L x2,y2   L x3,y3   etc."

The M specifies that the values are to interpreted as absolute positions, in pixels, on a
canvas. We therefore need to make Python code that will do the following:
- Scan through the Inkscape.svg file and pick out sub-strings of text lines that
  start with "M" or less ambiguously **'d="M'** ,
- Convert each 'L' into a comma, (,)
- Convert the string characters into Python lists of the form [*x1,y1 x2,y2 x3,y3*].

Convert SVG "M" Lines into Python Lists

The Python code we use to discover the string of characters ' d="M ' is the following:

```
id_start = ' d="M '        # Id signature for a valid vertex list in the inkscape.svg Data source.

line_set = []
file_lines = 0
''' Note: to open a file and process its contents, and make sure to close it, you can simply do:
    with open("x.txt") as f:
'''
with open(obj_file_name) as ff:
    counter = 0                 # Slice position counter.
    for line in ff:             # For each line ( line is the string contents of the line) .
       line_length = len(line)  # Total length of line. Needed for number of slices.
       file_lines += 1          # Keep a count of the number of lines.
       ''' Whenever id_start is discovered line.find(id_start) will be true.
       This method returns index (string slice location) if found and -1 otherwise.
       '''
       if line.find(id_start) != -1:  # id_start string discovered. This denotes an SVG line of vertices.
          slice_loc = line.find(id_start) # The next character will be what we have been seeking - a float.
          line_string = line
          floats_list = extract_floats(line)  # This function is in the program below.
          line_set.append(floats_list)
```

The final Program is

```
"""
Program name: inkscape2python_1.py
```

Objective: Transform an inkscape.svg drawing file into a usable Python vertex lists.
Specifically: Identify 2D vertices in all lines saved in a SVG file from an
Inkscape drawing.
Each .svg line like: d="M 82.833,90.697 L 97.985,78.575 L 118.19,99.788"
is converted to a Python list like:
[82.833,90.697 , 97.985,78.575 , 118.19,99.788]

Keywords: inkscape, conversion, drawing, vertices, lines,
===79
Comments: Method:Identify 2D vertices in all lines saved in a SVG file from an
Inkscape drawing.
Each .svg line like: d="M 82.833,90.697 L 97.985,78.575 L 118.19,99.788"
is converted to a Python list like:
[82.833,90.697 , 97.985,78.575 , 118.19,99.788]

Input data used is an SVG file exported from Inkscape.

Tested on: Python 2.6, Python 2.7.3, Python 3.2.3
Author: Mike Ohlson de Fine
"""

```python
obj_file_name = "/home/mikeodf/constr/face_0.svg" # Inkscape output file.


def extract_floats(line):
    """ Objective: Extract a complete floating point number, including sign.
        Assumption: An appropriate line of characters ( the "line" argument)
        for parsing has been found.
        Now we work through it character by character looking for minus signs, decimal points
        and digits. These are added to a string xx which will be converted to a float.
        A non-digit will signal the completion of the float.
    """
    slice_loc = 0            # Slice position counter.
    line_length = len(line)  # Total length of line.
    sign = ''                # The sign (negative or positive) of the number.
    jadigit = 0              # Digit 'present' toggle flag.
    xx = ''                  # xx will become the CURRENT floating point number.
    float_seq = 0            # The number of floats obtained. When == 3 add 1.0 for augmentation.
    float_list = []

    # Pad the line with a space. Necessary to avoid loop index errors.
    line = line + ' '
    for chr in line:

        # Overriding condition. Only proceed if we are working inside the line length.
        if slice_loc <= line_length-1:

            # Is the character a non-digit?
            if line[slice_loc].isdigit() == False:

                # Is the character a minus sign?
                if line[slice_loc] == '-':
                    sign = '-'
                    xx = sign
                slice_loc = slice_loc + 1

            # Is the character a digit?
            if line[slice_loc].isdigit():
                jadigit = 1
```

```python
      xx = xx + line[slice_loc]    # Add the new digit to xx
      slice_loc = slice_loc + 1


    # Is the character a decimal point?
    if  line[slice_loc] == '.':
      jadigit = 1
      xx = xx + line[slice_loc]       # Add this digit to xx
      slice_loc = slice_loc + 1


    # The previous character was a digit but the current one is not,
    # therefore the current floating point number is now complete.
    if  line[slice_loc].isdigit() == False and jadigit == 1:  # Terminate float.
      jadigit = 0                                  # Clear 'working up float' flag.
      float_seq = float_seq + 1
      sign = "                                     # Clear the sign flag.
      float_list.append(float(xx))                 # Add the latest float to the list .
      slice_loc = slice_loc + 1
      xx = "

  return float_list


id_start = ' d="M '        # Id signature for a valid vertex list in the inkscape.svg  - Data source.

line_set = []
file_lines = 0
''' note to open a file and process its contents, and make sure to close it, you can simply do:
    with open("x.txt") as f:
  '''
with open(obj_file_name) as ff:
    counter = 0                                    # Slice position counter.
    for line in ff:                                # For each line ( line is the string contents of the line)
      line_length = len(line)                      # Total length of line. Needed for number of slices.
      file_lines += 1                              # Keep a count of the number of lines.
      #Whenever id_start is discovered line.find(id_start) will be true.
      # This method returns index (string slice location) if found and -1 otherwise.

      if line.find(id_start) != -1:         # id_start string discovered. This denotes an SVG line of vertices.
        slice_loc = line.find(id_start)     # The next character will be what we have been seeking -  a float.
        line_string = line
        floats_list = extract_floats(line)
        line_set.append(floats_list)


# ============================
# CONVERTED SHAPE  TESTING
# ============================
#from Tkinter import *
from tkinter import *   # Use this instead of the above for python version 3.x
root = Tk()
root.title('Inkscape shapes converted to Python list.')
cw = 350                          # canvas width.
ch = 300                          # canvas height.
canvas_1 = Canvas(root, width=cw, height=ch, background="#eeeeee")
canvas_1.grid(row=0, column=1)

for i in range(len(line_set)):
    canvas_1.create_line( line_set[i], width = 3,  fill= 'blue' )
```

root.mainloop()

And the result, on a Python-Tkinter canvas is:

A Composite Image from Layers

Now we look at how to produce a complex image extracted from a photograph using code almost identical to that used above

The original photograph:

Layers of detail, light and shade were obtained from the image by tracing over the jpg image in Inkscape. When we have traced the lines we must save each particular layer of detail as a separate SVG file as shown below.

98

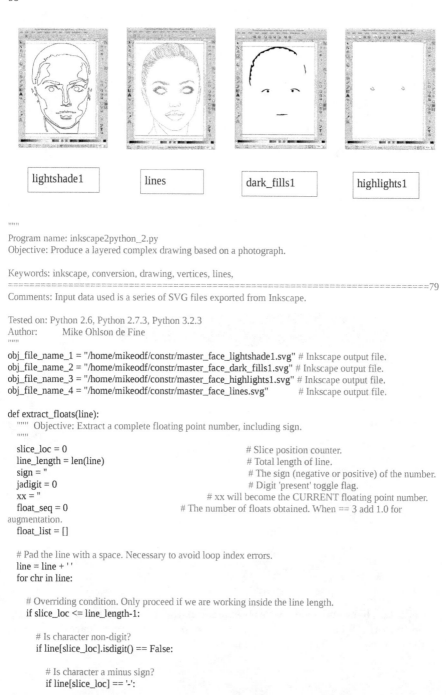

| lightshade1 | lines | dark_fills1 | highlights1 |

```
"""
Program name: inkscape2python_2.py
Objective: Produce a layered complex drawing based on a photograph.

Keywords: inkscape, conversion, drawing, vertices, lines,
===================================================================================79
Comments: Input data used is a series of SVG files exported from Inkscape.

Tested on: Python 2.6, Python 2.7.3, Python 3.2.3
Author:        Mike Ohlson de Fine
"""
obj_file_name_1 = "/home/mikeodf/constr/master_face_lightshade1.svg" # Inkscape output file.
obj_file_name_2 = "/home/mikeodf/constr/master_face_dark_fills1.svg" # Inkscape output file.
obj_file_name_3 = "/home/mikeodf/constr/master_face_highlights1.svg" # Inkscape output file.
obj_file_name_4 = "/home/mikeodf/constr/master_face_lines.svg"       # Inkscape output file.

def extract_floats(line):
    """ Objective: Extract a complete floating point number, including sign.
    """
    slice_loc = 0                                   # Slice position counter.
    line_length = len(line)                         # Total length of line.
    sign = ''                                       # The sign (negative or positive) of the number.
    jadigit = 0                                     # Digit 'present' toggle flag.
    xx = ''                         # xx will become the CURRENT floating point number.
    float_seq = 0               # The number of floats obtained. When == 3 add 1.0 for
augmentation.
    float_list = []

    # Pad the line with a space. Necessary to avoid loop index errors.
    line = line + ' '
    for chr in line:

        # Overriding condition. Only proceed if we are working inside the line length.
        if slice_loc <= line_length-1:

            # Is character non-digit?
            if line[slice_loc].isdigit() == False:

                # Is character a minus sign?
                if line[slice_loc] == '-':
```

```
            sign = '-'
            xx = sign
          slice_loc = slice_loc + 1

        # Is character a digit?
        if line[slice_loc].isdigit():
          jadigit = 1
          xx = xx + line[slice_loc]      # Add the new digit to xx .
          slice_loc = slice_loc + 1

        # Is character a decimal point?
        if line[slice_loc] == '.':
          jadigit = 1
          xx = xx + line[slice_loc]      # Add this digit to xx .
          slice_loc = slice_loc + 1

        # The previous character was a digit but the current one is not ,
        # therefore the current floating point number is now complete.
        if line[slice_loc].isdigit() == False and jadigit == 1:          # Terminate float.
          jadigit = 0                                                    # Clear 'working up float' flag.
          float_seq = float_seq + 1
          sign = ''                                                      # Clear the sign flag.
          float_list.append(float(xx))                                   # Add the latest float to the list .
          slice_loc = slice_loc + 1
          xx = ''

    return float_list


def get_xy_strings(obj_file_name):
    """ Identify lines containing x-y coordinates and extract the floating point pairs.
        The argument is the name and directory locations of the SVG file to be parsed.
    """
    id_start = ' d="M '      # Id signature for a valid vertex list in the inkscape.svg Data source.
    line_set = []
    file_lines = 0

    with open(obj_file_name) as ff:
        counter = 0                    # Slice position counter.
        for line in ff:                # For each line ( line is the string contents of the line) .
          line_length = len(line)      # Total length of line. Needed for number of slices.
          file_lines += 1              # Keep a count of the number of lines.

          if line.find(id_start) != -1:              # id_start string discovered. This denotes an SVG line of vertices.
            slice_loc = line.find(id_start)           # The next character will be what we have been seeking - a float.
            line_string = line
            floats_list = extract_floats(line)
            line_set.append(floats_list)
    return line_set

# Extract from each of four files.
line_set_1 = get_xy_strings(obj_file_name_1)
line_set_2 = get_xy_strings(obj_file_name_2)
line_set_3 = get_xy_strings(obj_file_name_3)
line_set_4 = get_xy_strings(obj_file_name_4)

    # ===============================
```

```
#  CONVERTED SHAPE  TESTING
# ============================
from Tkinter import *
#from tkinter import *   # Use this instead of the above for python version 3.x
root = Tk()
root.title('Inkscape shapes converted to Python list.')
cw = 800                           # canvas width.
ch = 1200                          # canvas height.
canvas_1 = Canvas(root, width=cw, height=ch, background="#eeeeee")
canvas_1.grid(row=0, column=1)

for i in range(len(line_set_1)):                 # Light shadows.
    canvas_1.create_polygon( line_set_1[i], width = 1,  fill= '#cccccc' )

for i in range(len(line_set_2)):                 # Dark shadows.
    canvas_1.create_polygon( line_set_2[i], width = 1,  fill= '#444444' )

for i in range(len(line_set_3)):                 # Highlights.
    canvas_1.create_polygon( line_set_3[i], width = 1,  fill= '#ffffff' )

for i in range(len(line_set_4)):                 # Lines
    canvas_1.create_line( line_set_4[i], width = 1,  fill= '#444444' )

root.mainloop()
```

And the resulting Tkinter image is:

7

Blender as a Python Tool

"The most potent muse of all is our own inner child." Stephen Nachmanovitch

"A rock pile ceases to be a rock pile the moment a single man contemplates it, bearing within him the image of a cathedral." — Antoine de Saint-Exupéry

Topics covered in this chapter are:
- **Blender Skill**
- **From Blender Object to Python Object**
- **Exporting the Blender Object**
- **Extract Vertices**
- **Extract Faces**
- **Extracting the Complete Shape from Blender**
- **The Proof is in the Animation**
- **Cautions and Warnings**

Now we want to create sophisticated 3D objects like people, animals, castles and cathedrals. We want to have these objects in the form of Python lists of vertices. Then we can use the Python matrix transforms to make them do interesting things. In the next chapter we start learning how to use OpenGL and this opens up many more possibilities. OpenGL and a subset of it called OpenES, is a basic tool that is needed to produce graphic applications on mobile devices like cellphones and tablets. Blender is the tool that can help us achieve this. Of course Blender is a potent 3D animation tool in it's own right but that is not what this book is about.

We have been assembling methods and tools for controlling and manipulating three-dimensional objects. Obtaining the geometric data to create 3D objects is tricky. One practical method of doing this could be to make cardboard models of objects and then take their measurements and get the x, y and z measurements of key points on their surface. For complicated shapes this is difficult. Is there a simpler way? The answer is a qualified yes, by using Blender as a kind of sketching tool. Blender is sophisticated and somewhat difficult to use for a beginner. There is a steep and sometimes frustrating learning curve. But there is a lot of help on the internet. There are also a lot of ready made Blender objects which we can download and use without restriction. The website "http://www.blendswap.com/" has more than twelve thousand 3D objects. To have the privelege to download any we have to contribute at least one object then we can sign up as member and access everything.

In this chapter we concentrate on methods of converting existing 3D models produced in Blender into Python lists that can be controlled and transformed using the matrix operations we have developed in this book so far. We start off with simple objects like triangles and progress to more complicated ones. One of the big advantages of Blender is that we can produce 3D objects from flat images like drawings and photos.

History of Blender: Blender started its life as a commerical product, which was not very sucessful and was withdrawn. A small group of people asked the company what they would sell the code for. 100,000 euros was the answer. The group asked for donations so the source code could be purchased and set free under the GPL.

The original man behind the company that created it, Ton Roosendaal, is still very much masterminding its continuing development. It was his determination that kept it alive, and has seen it thrive. It was a far sighted, generously human thing Ton did. We all benefit.

Blender has been selected as a tool for constructing 3D objects because:
- It is free and Open Source.
- It is very, very powerful (It can do so MUCH).
- We can get help, advice and instruction videos how to use it all over the internet, especially YouTube.
- It will export objects in a form we can use with Python

The disadvantage of Blender is that because it is so powerful it is difficult to learn in the beginning. But the effort is rewarding.

From Blender Object to Python Object

In this section we shall use a simple shape, a triangle, created with Blender and develop the tools needed to convert it to a Python shape.

We use very similar techniques to those used in the previous chapter to develop the Python techniques for converting Inkscape drawings into shapes that can be used to create Python lists of vertices.
The differences with the previous program, *inkscape2python_1.py* are:

- The source data comes from a Blender created object.
- The Blender data must be exported from Blender as a Wavefront file. These will have .obj extensions.
- Vertices are useless if we do not specify the surfaces that they define. In other words we need a list of faces that specify which vertices are used to construct each face. (In Chapter 10 we are introduced to OpenGL vertex arrays that simplifies things and speeds up image animation).
- The three dimensional [x, y, z] vertices need to be converted to the augmented form [x, y, z, 1.0] to make them transformable by the standard 3D transform matrices introduced in chapter 4.

The conversion from 3d to the augmented form is achieved using the simple function

```python
def augment_vertices(vertex_list):
    """ Just augment the vertex position vector by inserting 1.0 at the end.
    """

    for i in range(len(vertex_list)):
        vertex_list[i].append(1.0)
    return vertex_list
```

Exporting the Blender Object

When we are ready to export a wavefront.obj file from Blender we must select the export format as shown in the screenshot below.

For our first example we will use the simple triangle object shown below as our blender 3D object.

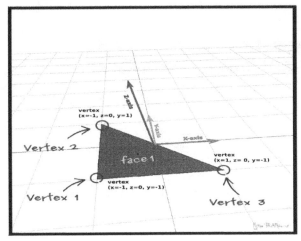

The "triangle.obj" text file exported by Blender is:

```
# Blender v2.62 (sub 0) OBJ File: 'triangle_pyramid.blend'
# www.blender.org
mtllib triangle.mtl
o Plane
v 1.000000 0.000000 1.000000
v -1.000000 0.000000 1.000000
v -1.000000 0.000000 -1.000000
usemtl Material.001
s 1
f 1 2 3
```

In this file the first line contains the title. The third line is an accompanying file that contains information on how to color and texture the object. We will ignore this.
The line "o Plane" states that what follows are the vertices defining a plane. The three vertices are:

```
v 1.000000 0.000000 1.000000
v -1.000000 0.000000 1.000000
v -1.000000 0.000000 -1.000000
```

It is important to know that the vertices are numbered in sequence. Later, in chapter 10, we see that sequence can determine whether a surface is in light or shadow. The numbers are used later to define the various faces (surfaces) making up our object. For example vertex number 2 is the second one (= v -1.000000 0.000000 1.000000).
"s 1" states that what follows is the surface made up by joining vertices 1, 2, 3 and 1.

With this information we now develop Python code that will extract the vertices as Python position vectors of 3D coordinates expressed as augmented 3D vectors. We also need code that will define the faces so that they can be drawn as 3D objects in Python.

Task 1: Extract Vertices

What we need to do is:
1. Scan through the triangle.obj file line by line,
2. For each line starting with "v" pull out the floating point numbers ('floats').
3. Place the floats into a Python list.
4. Augment each vertex with 1.0 to make it fully transformable. Recall that in order to allow matrix multiplication to be able to shift a vertex it needs to be in the augmented form [x, y, z, 1.0]

```
"""
```

Program name: blender_vertices_extraction_1.py
Objective: Transfer a blender.obj 3D object file into single Python vertex list.

Keywords: blender, geometry, vertices, list
===79
Comments: Wavefront.obj files exported form Blender. Blender 3D objects are the source objects.

Tested on: Python 2.6, Python 2.7.3, Python 3.2.3
Author: Mike Ohlson de Fine
"""""
# File containing 3D objects exported from Blender.
obj_file_name = "/home/mikeodf/constr/blender_objects/triangle.obj" # Data source.

def extract_floats(line):
    """" Objective: identify 3D vertices in a line of Wavefront .obj file.
    Each .obj line on the form "v x1 y1 z1 " is converted to a Python list like
    "[xa, y1, z1]" where x1, y1 and z1 are floating point numbers.
    Assumption: An appropriate line of characters for parsing has been found.
    Then we work through it character by character looking for minus signs, decimal points
    and digits. These are added to a string xx which will be converted to a float.
    A non-digit will signal the completion of the floating point number.
    """""
    slice_loc = 0   # Slice position counter.
    line_length = len(line)   # Total length of line.
    sign = "   # The sign (negative or positive) of the number.
    yesdigit = 0   # 'Digit present' toggle flag.
    xx = "   # xx will become the CURRENT floating point number.
    float_seq = 0   # The number of floats obtained.
    float_list = []

    # Pad the line with a space. Necessary to avoid loop index errors.
    line = line + ' '
    for chr in line:

        # Overriding condition. Only proceed if we are working inside the line length.
        if slice_loc <= line_length-1:

            # Is character non-digit?
            if line[slice_loc].isdigit() == False:

                # Is character a minus sign?
                if line[slice_loc] == '-':
                    sign = '-'
                    xx = sign
                slice_loc = slice_loc + 1

            # Is character a digit?
            if line[slice_loc].isdigit():
                yesdigit = 1
                xx = xx + line[slice_loc]   # Add the new digit to xx.
                slice_loc = slice_loc + 1

            # Is character a decimal point?
            if line[slice_loc] == '.':
                yesdigit = 1
                xx = xx + line[slice_loc]   # Add this decimal point to xx.
                slice_loc = slice_loc + 1

```python
            # The previous character was a digit but the current one is not
            # Therefore the current floating point number is now complete.
            if line[slice_loc].isdigit() == False and yesdigit == 1:   # Terminate float.
                yesdigit = 0                                           # Clear 'working up float' flag.
                float_seq = float_seq + 1
                sign = ''                                              # Clear the sign flag.
                float_list.append(float(xx))                          # Add the latest float to the list.
                slice_loc = slice_loc + 1
                xx = ''

    return float_list

def augment_vertices(vertex_list):
    """ Just augment the vertex position vector by inserting 1.0 at the end.
    """
    for i in range(len(vertex_list)):
        vertex_list[i].append(1.0)
    return vertex_list

# Find vertices and transform into augmented vertex vectors.
vertex_list = []
with open(obj_file_name) as ff:
    counter = 0                                # Slice position counter.
    for line in ff:                            # For each line in ff:
        line_length = len(line)                # Total length of line.
        if line.find('v') != -1:               # Is there a 'v' anywhere in the line? This denotes a vertex.
            slice_loc = line.find('v')         # If yes, return lowest index in string where 'v' occurs.
            if slice_loc == 0:                  # If the first character is 'v' then:
                digit_list = extract_floats(line)
                vertex_list.append(digit_list)

    augmented_vertex_list = augment_vertices(vertex_list)

print ( 'vertex_list: ', vertex_list)
```

The result of this execution is:
vertex_list: [[1.0, 0.0, 1.0, 1.0], [-1.0, 0.0, 1.0, 1.0], [-1.0, 0.0, -1.0, 1.0]]

Task 2: Extract Faces

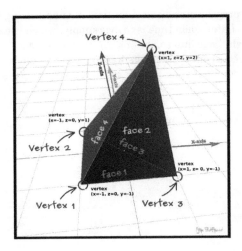

In this next example we will use the Blender object shown above. It is a truly 3D object that has four separate faces.

The exported Waveform file is:

```
# Blender v2.62 (sub 0) OBJ File: 'triangle_pyramid.blend'
# www.blender.org
mtllib triangle_pyramid.mtl
o Plane
v 2.146835 0.130339 3.153294
v 0.146835 0.130339 3.153293
v 0.146835 0.130339 1.153293
v 2.146835 2.130339 0.153294
usemtl Material.001
s 1
f 1 2 3
f 1 3 4
f 2 4 3
f 1 4 2
```

Each face is described by three integers. For example the first face is f 1 2 3 where "1" refers to the first vertex v 2.146835 0.130339 3.153294 , "2" refers to the second vertex v 0.146835 0.130339 3.153293 and "3" refers to the third vertex and so on.

So now we need a function designed to extract the face numbers which are integers. We have taken the easy, logical decision to use our previous function *extract_floats()* and modify it to handle integers by just adding the line:

$vertex\_index = int(xx) - 1$

The *extract_integers(line)* can be made shorter and more compact but there is a

110

substantial advantage in programmer distraction-time in simply using something tried, tested and bug free. Later when time is in oversupply, which it hardly ever is, we could buff and polish the code into something pretty and compact.

The minus one is there because all Python lists have zero as the index of the first element in any list of objects. So Python indices are always one less the wavefront indices.

We put this all together in the following program.

```
"""
Program name: blender_faces_extraction_1.py
Objective: Extract faces from a .obj file and convert them to Python face lists.

Keywords: blender, geometry, vertices, faces
==============================================================================79
Comments:  Data used in this program:
1. Wavefront.obj files exported form Blender. Blender 3D objects are the source objects.

Tested on: Python 2.6, Python 2.7.3, Python 3.2.3
Author:       Mike Ohlson de Fine
"""
# File containing 3D objects exported from Blender.
obj_file_name = "/home/mikeodf/constr/triangle_pyramid.obj"          # Data source.

def extract_integers(line):
    """ Objective: identify 3D object faces in a line of Wavefront .obj file.
        Each .obj line of the form "f a1  b1 c1 d1" is converted to a Python list like
        "[ a1,  b1, c1, d1 ]" where a1,  b1, c1 and d1 are integers.
        These integers are indexes of the array of vertices.
        Each face of the object (triangular or four sided) is defined as a list
        "faces[n][ vertex_list[a1],  vertex_list[b1], vertex_list[c1], vertex_list[d1] ]"

        Assumption: An appropriate line of characters for parsing has been found.
        Now we work through it character by character looking for minus signs, decimal points
        and digits. These are added to a string xx which will be converted to an integer.
        A non-digit will signal the completion of the line.
    """
    slice_loc = 0                              # Slice position counter.
    line_length = len(line)                    # Total length of line.
    sign = ''                                  # The sign (negative or positive) of the number.
    jadigit = 0                                # Digit 'present' toggle flag.
    xx = ''                                    # xx will become the CURRENT floating point number.
    float_seq = 0                              # The number of floats obtained.
    digit_list = []

    # Pad the line with a space. Necessary to avoid loop index errors.
    line = line + ' '
    for chr in line:

        # Overriding condition. Only proceed if we are working inside the line length.
        if slice_loc <= line_length-1:

            # Is character non-digit?
            if line[slice_loc].isdigit() == False:
```

```
        # Is character a minus sign?
        if line[slice_loc] == '-':
            sign = '-'
            xx = sign
        slice_loc = slice_loc + 1

    # Is character a digit?
    if line[slice_loc].isdigit():
        jadigit = 1
        xx = xx + line[slice_loc]      # Add the new digit to xx
        slice_loc = slice_loc + 1

    # Is character a decimal point?
    if line[slice_loc] == '.':
        jadigit = 1
        xx = xx + line[slice_loc]      # Add this digit to xx
        slice_loc = slice_loc + 1

    # The previous character was a digit but the current one is not
    # Therefore the current integer number is now complete.
    if line[slice_loc].isdigit() == False and jadigit == 1:   # Terminate float.
        jadigit = 0   # Clear 'working up float' flag.
        float_seq = float_seq + 1
        sign = ''   # Clear the sign flag.
        vertex_index = int(xx)-1
        digit_list.append(vertex_index)               # Add the latest integer to the list
        slice_loc = slice_loc + 1
        xx = ''

return digit_list

faces_integers = []
# 2. Find Wavefront faces and form into lists.
with open(obj_file_name) as ff:
    counter = 0                        # Slice position counter.
    for line in ff:                    # For each line in ff:
        line_length = len(line)        # Total length of line.
        if line.find('f') != -1:       # Is there a 'f' anywhere in the line? This denotes a face.
            slice_loc = line.find('f') # If yes, return lowest index in string where 'v' occurs.
            if slice_loc == 0:         # If the first character is 'v' then:
                integers_list = extract_integers(line)

            faces_integers.append(integers_list)

print ( 'faces_list: ', faces_integers)
```

The correct result is:
faces_list: [[0, 1, 2], [0, 2, 3], [1, 3, 2], [0, 3, 1]]

Extracting the Complete Shape from Blender: Vertices and Faces

The Blender object we use now is a brilliant mask created by a man known as

112

"Kongorilla" (Stephen Kongsle) on the internet site
http://www.thingiverse.com/thing:32189/#files. It is elegant in it simplicity of
form, using a small number of polygons.

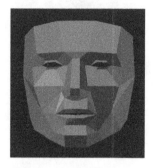

Putting everything together to extract the vertices and create lists of faces that Python
can display we have:

```
"""
Program name: blender_vertices_faces_1.py
Objective: Transform a blender.obj 3D object file into usable Python vertex and face lists
as well as OpenGL object triangles.

Keywords: blender, geometry, vertices, faces
=========================================================================79
Comments: Data used in this program:
Wavefront.obj files exported form Blender. Blender 3D objects are the source objects.

Tested on: Python 2.7.3, Python 3.2.3
Author:       Mike Ohlson de Fine
"""

import numpy
import copy

# File containing 3D objects exported from Blender.
obj_file_name = "/home/mikeodf/constr/LowPolyMaskFace_Kongorilla.obj"   # Wavefront data source.

def extract_floats(line):
    """ Objective: identify 3D vertices in a line of Wavefront .obj file.
        Each .obj line of the form "v x1  y1 z1 " is converted to a Python list like
        "[ xa, y1, z1 ]" where x1, y1 and z1 are floating point numbers (position coordinates).
        Assumption: An appropriate line of characters for parsing has been found.
        Now we work through it character by character looking for minus signs, decimal points
        and digits. These are added to a string xx which will be converted to a float.
        A non-digit will signal the completion of the float.
    """
    slice_loc = 0              # Slice position counter.
    line_length = len(line)    # Total length of line.
    sign = ''       # The sign (negative or positive) of the number.
    jadigit = 0     # Digit 'present' toggle flag.
    xx = ''         # xx will become the CURRENT floating point number.
    float_seq = 0   # The number of floats obtained. When == 3 add 1.0 for augmentation.
```

```
float_list = []

# Pad the line with a space. Necessary to avoid loop index errors.
line = line + ' '
for chr in line:

    # Overriding condition. Only proceed if we are working inside the line length.
    if slice_loc <= line_length-1:

        # Is character non-digit?
        if line[slice_loc].isdigit() == False:

            # Is character a minus sign?
            if line[slice_loc] == '-':
                sign = '-'
                xx = sign
            slice_loc = slice_loc + 1

        # Is character a digit?
        if line[slice_loc].isdigit():
            jadigit = 1
            xx = xx + line[slice_loc]     # Add the new digit to xx
            slice_loc = slice_loc + 1

        # Is character a decimal point?
        if line[slice_loc] == '.':
            jadigit = 1
            xx = xx + line[slice_loc]        # Add this digit to xx
            slice_loc = slice_loc + 1

        # The previous character was a digit but the current one is not
        # Therefore the current floating point number is now complete.
        if line[slice_loc].isdigit() == False and jadigit == 1:   # Terminate float.
            jadigit = 0   # Clear 'working up float' flag.
            float_seq = float_seq + 1
            sign = ''    # Clear the sign flag.
            float_list.append(float(xx))  # Add the latest float to the list .
            slice_loc = slice_loc + 1
            xx = ''

return float_list

def extract_integers(line):
    """ Objective: identify 3D object faces in a line of Wavefront .obj file.
    Each .obj line on the form "f a1  b1 c1 d1" is converted to a Python list like
    "[ a1,  b1, c1, d1 ]" where a1,  b1, c1 and d1 are integers.
    These integers are indexes of the array of vertices.
    Each face of the object (triangular or four sided) is defined as a list
    "faces[n][ vertex_list[a1],  vertex_list[b1], vertex_list[c1], vertex_list[d1] ]"

    Assumption: An appropriate line of characters for parsing has been found.
    Now we work through it character by character looking for minus signs, decimal points
    and digits. These are added to a string xx which will be converted to an integer.
    A non-digit will signal the completion of the line.
    """
    slice_loc = 0              # Slice position counter.
    line_length = len(line)    # Total length of line.
```

```python
sign = ''                    # The sign (negative or positive) of the number.
jadigit = 0                  # Digit 'present' toggle flag.
xx = ''          # xx will become the CURRENT floating point number.
float_seq = 0    # The number of floats obtained. When == 3 add 1.0 for augmentation.
digit_list = []

# Pad the line with a space. Necessary to avoid loop index errors.
line = line + ' '
for chr in line:

    # Overriding condition. Only proceed if we are working inside the line length.
    if slice_loc <= line_length-1:

        # Is character non-digit?
        if line[slice_loc].isdigit() == False:

            # Is character a minus sign?
            if line[slice_loc] == '-':
                sign = '-'
                xx = sign
            slice_loc = slice_loc + 1

        # Is character a digit?
        if line[slice_loc].isdigit():
            jadigit = 1
            xx = xx + line[slice_loc]    # Add the new digit to xx
            slice_loc = slice_loc + 1

        # Is character a decimal point?
        if line[slice_loc] == '.':
            jadigit = 1
            xx = xx + line[slice_loc]       # Add this digit to xx
            slice_loc = slice_loc + 1

        # The previous character was a digit but the current one is not
        # Therefore the current integer number is now complete.
        if line[slice_loc].isdigit() == False and jadigit == 1:  # Terminate float.
            jadigit = 0                         # Clear 'working up float' flag.
            float_seq = float_seq + 1
            sign = ''                           # Clear the sign flag.
            vertex_index = int(xx)-1
            digit_list.append(vertex_index)  # Add the latest integer to the list
            slice_loc = slice_loc + 1
            xx = ''

    return digit_list

# 1. Find all vertices and collect into a list of vertices.
#=================================================================
vertex_list = []
with open(obj_file_name) as ff:
    counter = 0                          # Slice position counter.
    for line in ff:                      # For each line in ff:
        line_length = len(line)          # Total length of line.
        if line.find('v') != -1:         # Is there a 'v' anywhere in the line? ie. a vertex.
            slice_loc = line.find('v')   # If yes, return lowest index in string where 'v' occurs.
            if slice_loc == 0:           # If the first character is 'v' then:
```

```
        digit_list =  extract_floats(line)
        vertex_list.append(digit_list)

# 1B Make an additional list of augmented (4D) vertices.
augmented_vertex_list = copy.deepcopy(vertex_list)
for i in range(len(vertex_list)):
  augmented_vertex_list[i].append(1.0)

# 2. Find Wavefront faces and form into lists.
#================================================
face_indices = []
with open(obj_file_name) as ff:
    counter = 0                            # Slice position counter.
    for line in ff:                        # For each line in ff:
      line_length = len(line)              # Total length of line.
      if line.find('f') != -1:             # Is there a 'f' anywhere in the line? ie. a face.
        slice_loc = line.find('f')         # If yes, return lowest index in string where 'f' occurs.
        if slice_loc == 0:                 # If the first character is 'f' then:
          integers_list =  extract_integers(line)
          face_indices.append(integers_list)

# 3. Make faces lists - OpenGL amenable.
#=============================================
""" That is a three dimensional Python list array: It is a list of triangular faces.
  Each face consists of three vertices representing the corners of a triangle.
"""
faces_gl = copy.deepcopy(face_indices)
for i in range(len(face_indices)):
  for j in range(len(face_indices[i])):
    faces_gl[i][j] = vertex_list[face_indices[i][j]]

# 4. Make faces lists - Tkinter compatible. For verification by display
faces_tk = copy.deepcopy(faces_gl)
for i in range(len(faces_gl)):
  for j in range(len(faces_gl[i])): #
    faces_tk[i][j] = augmented_vertex_list[face_indices[i][j]]
```

The Proof is in the Animation

We must prove that the shape we extract from a blender 3D object is correct. The most effective way to do this is to cause Python to create a drawing that we can see from all angles to make sure it is a true representation of the original Blender object.

We can do this with the following code which we should just add onto the end of the previous program.

```
#===============================================
#  SHAPE TRANSFORM TESTING BY DRAWING
# =================================================
''' The code below is just for quick visual confirmation that the data is good.
```

```
'''
from Tkinter import *
#from tkinter import *     # Use this instead of the above for python version 3.x
import math
import matrix_transforms
root = Tk()
root.title("Show the current 3D triangles model.")
cw = 600                    # canvas width.
ch = 600                    # canvas height.
canvas_1 = Canvas(root, width=cw, height=ch, background="#110011")
canvas_1.grid(row=0, column=1)


# For Display - Downconvert a 3D/4D matrix down to a 2D list.
def fourd_shape_2_twod_line(numpy_threed_matrix,kula,l_width):
    """ Convert a 3D homogeneous matrix (numpy form) to a list for 'create_line'.
    """

    bbb = numpy_threed_matrix.tolist()
    twod_line = []
    for i in range(0, len(bbb)):
        twod_line.append( bbb[i][0] )
        twod_line.append( bbb[i][1] )
    canvas_1.create_line( twod_line, width = l_width,  tag = 'lines_1', fill= kula )
    #canvas_1.create_polygon( twod_line, width = l_width,  tag = 'lines_1', fill= kula )
    return twod_line

# Dynamic rotation.
def show_shape(vertex_set):
    """ Demonstrate the 3D animated transformations of shapes composed of vertices and edges.
    """

    cycle_period= 100
    rad_one_deg = math.pi/180.0
    rad_angle = 0.0

    for i in range(len(faces_tk)):
        for j in range(len(faces_tk[i])):
            faces_tk[i][j] = faces_tk[i][j] * matrix_transforms.T_scaling(50 , 50, 50)

    # Animation by rotation around 3 axes.
    for i in range (500):

        # Faces.
        for i in range(len(faces_tk)):
            faces_tk[i] = faces_tk[i] * matrix_transforms.T_roty(-rad_angle)
            faces_tk[i] = faces_tk[i] * matrix_transforms.T_rotx(rad_angle*0.2)
            faces_tk[i] = faces_tk[i] * matrix_transforms.T_rotz(rad_angle*1.3)
            view_faces =faces_tk[i] * matrix_transforms.T_translate( 300.0,  300.0, 0.0)
            fourd_shape_2_twod_line(view_faces , '#ffff00', 1)

        rad_angle = rad_one_deg * 1.0
        canvas_1.update()                # This refreshes the drawing on the canvas.
        canvas_1.after(cycle_period)   # This makes execution pause for 100 milliseconds.
        canvas_1.delete('lines_1')

show_shape(vertex_list)
root.mainloop()
```

117

The result of this execution is given here.

Cautions and Warnings

Warning #1: Lines are not Polygons

The faces as extracted from the Wavefront.obj files consist of a list of vertices to form closed polygons. We have used the canvas_1.create_line(twod_line, width = l_width, tag = 'lines_1', fill= kula) Tkinter function to display our lines. To display a polygon using the create_line function we need to add an extra vertex to the line as follows: take a copy of the first vertex and just add it to the end. This is only necessary for faces on the edge of our object. We could avoid this problem by using canvas_1.create_polygon(twod_line, width = l_width, tag = 'lines_1', fill= kula) function instead of create_line but this gives rise to new problem. The new problem is that we do not have a simple or convenient method of dynamically adjusting the order of polygon drawing to ensure that the faces closest to the viewer always get drawn last. This procedure is known as the "Painters Algorithm". It is a tricky and computation-expensive activity.

OpenGL solves this problem by keeping track of the distance from the viewer of every single pixel in a piece of special memory called the **depth buffer.** Only the pixel closest to the viewer is sent to the screen display. In chapters 9 and 10 OpenGL deals with this problem painlessly.

Warning #2: Blender objects look upside-down to Python.

You will notice that any object extracted from a Blender .obj file is upside-down when displayed in Python. This is because Belnder and Python use opposite direction conventions for the Y-direction when they create vertices. Whenever this is a problem we must just reverse the arithmetic sign of the y-coordinates in Python.

Conclusion

Now we have a method of creating almost any 3D shape for Python using Blender.

However this comes at a cost. The price we have to pay is to put aside a lot of time and mental energy to sufficiently master Blender. My estimate is that anyone determined to achieve some competence using Blender will need to devote around thirty hours to working with it. About a third of that time will probably be spent watching Youtube videos and writing notes to yourself. The biggest barrier is learning where to find the correct menu items on Blender. There seem to be hundreds of selections that have to be made. Once we have started to get a bit familiar with the interface there are only about thirty selections and buttons we need to know how to use.
It is well worth the effort.

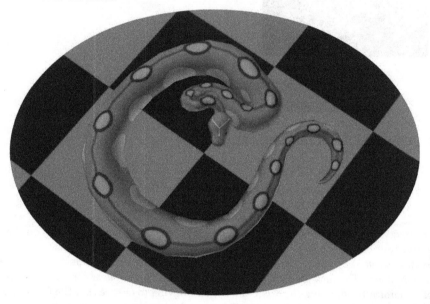

8

OpenGL: Basic Drawing

"The first writing of the human being was drawing, not writing." Marjane Satrapi

" I prefer drawing to talking. Drawing is faster, and leaves less room for lies. " Le Corbusier

Topics covered in this chapter:
- **What is OpenGL**
- **Why is OpenGL so complicated**
- **OpenGL and Frame Buffers**
- **OpenGL Primitives**
- **A Short OpenGL Program**
- **All the OpenGL Primitives Demonstrated**
- **Now we Discover GLUT**
- **All the GLUT Wireshapes**
- **Independently Rotating Cubes**
- **Labour Saving using Python (x,y) Coordinate Lists**

In this chapter we take an introductory look at using OpenGL with Python. OpenGL is a very, very sophisticated 2D and 3D grapics library designed to use the full potential of specialized graphics hardware (GPUs). If we do not have a GPU installed on our computer OpenGL still works, only not as quickly. The hardware is changing fast with new designs appearing every few months. The OpenGL standard is evolving at a similar pace in order to take advantage of improving hardware capabilities. So OpenGL is complicated and difficult to learn. Because GPU's are rapidly evolving, OpenGL is also changing and this makes it confusing to learn because when we google questions about OpenGL it is difficult to tell how relevant the advice is. The answers will vary depending on the version being discussed.

However basic concepts do not change and good software application interfaces like OpenGL remain backwards compatible. This means that older programs we may have written will still run on later versions of OpenGL. Modern cutting-edge graphics programming changes the functioning of Graphics hardware through *shading language* instructions. We will not deal with this new stuff in this book because it adds too much complexity to a subject that is already difficult.

We keep things relatively simple in this chapter by just using a subset of OpenGL that can be used to perform similar functions to Tkinter. This will allow us to start using OpenGL without needing to know much about modern graphics hardware and the sophisticated shader languages. We are going to work through some basic tasks using OpenGL that use techniques that are similar to the ones we have used so far in this book with Python. OpenGL handles tricky issues like hidden surface removal, surface textures and lighting very well and this makes it extremely useful.

We will explore how to draw basic lines and shapes as well as perform the basic matrix transformations to re-size, translate and rotate 3D graphic objects. A method of converting 3D objects produced in Blender into OpenGL objects is also developed.

What is OpenGL?

OpenGL is a low-level graphics library. OpenGL stands for Open Graphics Language. OpenGL is how your program instructions on the CPU talks to the hardware on your GPU – two separate and distinct computer hardware engines. OpenGL's main job is to help a programmer create code that creates points, lines, and polygons, and then convert those objects into pixels on a screen. The conversion process of objects into pixels is called the "pipeline" of the OpenGL renderer.

OpenGl is a collection of functions that provide a software interface to graphics hardware. It's strengths are:

- It is works across the major operating systems of Linux, Apple OS, Microsoft and Android.
- It is designed to work effectively with all Graphic Processing Units (GPUs) to make high resolution graphics work fast.

- It is Open Source, free, widely available, widely used and well supported.

History of OpenGL:

OpenGL started off as IrisGL (Integrated **R**aster **I**maging **S**ystem **G**raphics **L**ibrary), a proprietary graphics API Developed by Silicon Graphics Inc. (SGI), the computer graphics market leader at the time. IrisGL was used as the starting point of an open standard for computer graphics that would save time porting applications by avoiding direct hardware access. After SGI cleaned up IrisGL and opened up the standard in 1992 to other companies, OpenGL was born. The standard was maintained and and updated by the the the OpenGL Architectural Review Board (OpenGL ARB). In 2006, the ARB and the Khronos Board of Directors voted to transfer control of the OpenGL API standard to the Khronos Group. The Khronos group included AMD, Intel, Nvidia, Apple, Google, Motorola, Oracle, Samsung, Sony, Mozilla, Creative Labs and many, many others. In 2014 Microsoft quietly joined the Khronos group. See "http://www.theregister.co.uk/2014/08/11/hell_freezes_over_microsoft_joins_kh ronos/"

and "http://www.phoronix.com/scan.php?page=news_item&px=MTc2MDE".

Why is OplenGL so complicated?

The highly simplified explanation is the following.

OpenGL is a language designed to give the programmer control of graphics hardware. A GPU is a highly specialized, fast computer in it own right. Its chief property is that it is designed to fire colored pixels at a computer screen in parallel. It has similarities to a vast array of light cannons, each one aimed at a separate individual screen pixel. Every cannon is fired simultaneously.

In fact there are three independent sets of cannons, one for each of the primary colors of red, green and blue. In the GPU there are three memory values (red, green, blue) in a special memory matrix (RAM) called the frame buffer. This frame buffer stores the complete image in separate red, green and blue storage frames and this stored image is 'fired' at the screen about 60 times per second. Frames rates are increasing for interesting reasons. For example virtual reality technology attempts to reduce a sensation of nausea by using 90 frames per second. See http://arstechnica.com/gaming/2015/06/steamvr-the-room-scale-vr-world-that-feels-like-an-imax-in-your-house/

Upstream of the framebuffer are several specialized buffers that that contain information about the distance of pieces of objects from the screen (the depth buffer), the transparency of objects (alpha buffer), the reflectivity (material buffer) etc. There are OpenGL instructions to control all these hardware buffers. The idea behind all this is that teams of programmers and artists can produce stunningly appealing video games. In this book we will do our best to avoid as much of this complexity as possible. Instead we will focus on using the Python Graphics know-how that we have acquired so far.

In this chapter we will be using the Python module "OpenGL" as the graphics module used by Python via the instruction **from OpenGL.GL import *** . In previous chapters we used Tkinter as our software "graphics engine".

So although we are forced to include these instructions in our programs we will not go into them much. Comments on their function will be short.

OpenGL and Frame Buffers

The basic requirement of the hardware is that it should contain a graphics frame buffer. A framebuffer or frame store is a section of RAM memory that stores a complete pixel-for-pixel replica of the computer screen. So the complete picture intended for the screen can be sent out with a single 'refresh' command. Every pixel needs to have red, green and blue values stored as well as other information like optical surface properties, lighting and relative geometric position.

OpenGL's main purpose is to write color values (the process called *rendering*) into a framebuffer. OpenGL also reads values stored in the framebuffer.

For our purposes as new programmers OpenGL is a set of commands that specify geometric objects in two or three dimensions.

OpenGL Primitives

OpenGL defines primitives. Each primitive is a point, a line segment, a polygon, a rectangle or a pixel. Primitives in turn are specified as a group of vertices. A vertex defines a point, an endpoint of an edge, or a corner of a polygon where two edges meet. Data such as positional coordinates, colors, normals, and texture coordinates are associated with each vertex. Normals are discussed in chapter 10.

So the basic shapes listed below are called primitives. The OpenGL format to define a shape is

```
glBegin(GL_primitive)
glColor3f(red, green, blue)
glVertex3f( x0, y0, z0)
glVertex3f(x1, y1, z1)
glVertex3f(x2, y2, z2)
...
glVertex3f(xn, yn, zn)
glEnd()
```

where a GL-primitive can be one of the following:

GL_POINTS – individual pixels.
GL_LINES - pairs of vertices interpreted as individual line segments
GL_LINE_STRIP – a series of connected line segments
GL_LINE_LOOP - same as above, with a segment added between last and first vertices
GL_TRIANGLES - triples of vertices interpreted as triangles
GL_TRIANGLE_STRIP – a linked strip of triangles
GL_TRIANGLE_FAN – a linked fan of triangles
GL_QUADS - quadruples of vertices interpreted as four-sided polygons
GL_QUAD_STRIP – a linked strip of quadrilaterals
GL_POLYGON - boundary of a simple, convex polygon

Here is a relatively short OpenGL-Python program for drawing a straight line. It is typical OpenGL code which is characterized by several instructions whose specific purpose is difficult to figure out. These are instructions that make adjustments to the GPU graphics *pipeline*. At this stage we will just accept that they are needed and that it is not vital that we understand their complete purpose at this stage.

```
"""
Program name: opengl_one_line_1.py
Objective: Using openGL draw a single line which is specified by means of
variables passed to a vertex 'glBegin/glEnd' set.
```

124

Keywords: OpenGL, line, linewidth
==79
Comments: glLineWidth(float width);
Sets the width in pixels for rendered lines; width must be greater than 0.0 and by default is 1.0.

Tested on: Python 2.7.3, Python 3.2.3
Author: Mike Ohlson de Fine
===================================
"""

```python
from OpenGL.GL import *
from OpenGL.GLUT import *
from OpenGL.GLU import *
window = 0

x0 =  1.0    # Line start
y0 =  1.0
x1 = -1.0    # Line finish
y1 =  1.0

def InitGL(Width, Height):
    """ Initialize and setup the Graphics Software/Hardware pipeline.
    """
    glClearColor(0.0, 0.0, 0.0, 0.0)
    glMatrixMode(GL_PROJECTION)
    glLoadIdentity()
    gluPerspective(45.0, float(Width)/float(Height), 0.1, 100.0)
    glMatrixMode(GL_MODELVIEW)

def any_line(x0,y0,x1,y1, kula):
    """ Specification of the line vertices.
    """
    glBegin(GL_LINES)
    glVertex3f(x0, y0,-1.0)
    glVertex3f(x1, y1,-1.0)
    glEnd()

def DrawGLScene():
    """ Specification of the line position, width and color.
    """
    glClear(GL_COLOR_BUFFER_BIT | GL_DEPTH_BUFFER_BIT)
    glLoadIdentity()
    glTranslatef(0.0,0.0,-6.0)
    glLineWidth(10.0)
    any_line(x0,y0,x1,y1, glColor3f(1.0,1.0,0.0) ) # Our line to be drawn.
    glutSwapBuffers()

def main():
    """ Main Program.
    """
    glutInit(sys.argv)
    glutInitWindowSize(300,80)           # Width,Height. The line gets scaled to the window.
    glutInitWindowPosition(10,30)        # Controls where the window starts - top-left corner of screen.
    window = glutCreateWindow(b'OpenGL-Python Line')
    glutDisplayFunc(DrawGLScene)  # Drawing.
    InitGL(5, 5)                         # Starting position of window on computer screen (top-left corner).
    glutMainLoop()
```

main()

Execution control is governed by the contents of the **main()** function.
In addition there will always be two principal functions. The first is InitGL(Width, Height)
which prepares the hardware platform, including the GPU, for execution. The second
is DrawGLScene() which contains information like color and line width that may change
during execution. If transformation instructions like resizing, shifting and rotating of
drawn objects were needed they would be included in DrawGLScene().

Difficulties with OpenGL and Python 3.x - "Wrong PATH"

If we try to run the above Python program using Python version 3, without modifying
the system variable that tells python programs where to hunt for modules, then we
may get an error message like:
ImportError: No module named OpenGL . The problem is solved if we make
appropriate changes to the system variable PYTHONPATH. Unfortunately it varies
from operating system to operating system. In the example program given above the
line sys.path.append("/usr/local/lib/python2.7/dist-packages/PyOpenGL-3.1.0-
py2.7.egg/") works for a version of Ubuntu called CAELinux. There is a systematic
way of solving the problem given in the Appendix: **Solving the Broken Path
Problem.**

GPU State:

InitGL(Width, Height) is an external expression (from our programmer' perspective), of
a fundamental design principal of OpenGL which is that is has a well defined **state**.
The state of every OpenGL graphics application we might write holds the values of
variable that are used frequently by the application. There is a special area of
memory set aside for the state and it is small at 12 kiloBytes. It typically contains,
among other similar such quantities, the current color being used. If a red triangle
were being drawn there is no need to keep loading the the floating point numbers
for the shade of red into one of the GPU's computation registers. It can simply be
read fron the state area. When a triangle of a different color is being drawn, only
then does the state color needs to be changed.

The details describing the shape of our particular drawn object are contained in:

```
def any_line(x0,y0,x1,y1, kula):
    """ Specification of the line vertices.
    """
    glBegin(GL_LINES)
    glVertex3f(x0, y0,-1.0)
    glVertex3f(x1, y1,-1.0)
    glEnd()
```

The vertices specifying our line are given by the statements between glBegin(GL_LINES)
and glEnd() . For long complicated shapes there can be thousands of glVertex3f(...) specifiers.

126

All the OpenGL Primitives Demonstrated

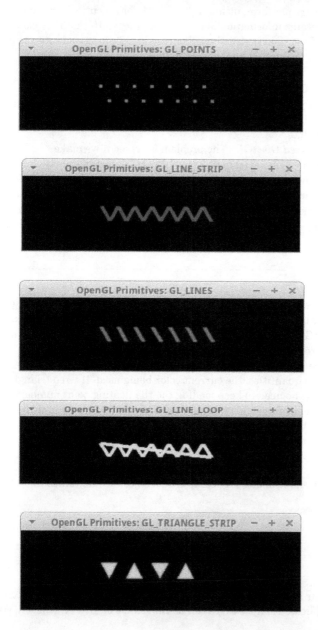

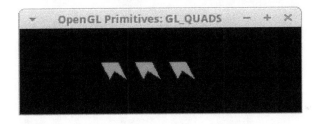

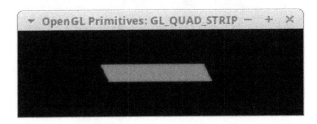

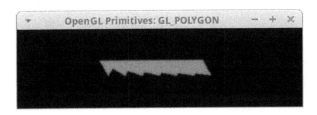

The program below demonstrates each of the primitives using a common set of vertices.

```
"""
Program name: opengl_primitives_1.py
Objective: Show each openGL primitive using a common set of points.

Keywords: OpenGL, line. strip, triangle, quad, polygon, points
=====================================================================================79
Comments: NOTE: For GL_QUADS, GL_QUAD_STRIP, and GL_POLYGON, all primitives must be both
planar and convex.
Otherwise, OpenGL behavior is undefined.
The GLU library supports polygon tessellation, which allows applications to render
filled primitives that are nonconvex or self-intersecting, or that contain holes.

Tested on:  Python 2.7.3, Python 3.2.3
Author:  Mike Ohlson de Fine
=================================
"""


from OpenGL.GL import *
from OpenGL.GLUT import *
from OpenGL.GLU import *
window = 0

# A Zig-zag stripe of points.
v1 = [-1.4 ,  0.5 , 0.0 ]
v2 = [-1.2 , -0.5 , 0.0 ]

v3 = [-1.0 ,  0.5 , 0.0 ]
v4 = [-0.8 , -0.5 , 0.0 ]

v5 = [-0.6 ,  0.5 , 0.0 ]
v6 =  [-0.4 , -0.5 , 0.0 ]

v7 = [-0.2 ,  0.5 , 0.0 ]
v8 = [ 0.0 , -0.5 , 0.0 ]

v9 = [0.2 ,  0.5  , 0.0 ]
v10 = [0.4 , -0.5  , 0.0 ]

v11 = [0.6 ,  0.5  , 0.0 ]
v12 = [0.8 , -0.5  , 0.0 ]

v13 = [1.0 ,  0.5  , 0.0 ]
v14 = [1.2 , -0.5  , 0.0 ]

def vertex_set():
    glVertex3f(v1[0], v1[1], v1[2])
    glVertex3f(v2[0], v2[1], v2[2])
    glVertex3f(v3[0], v3[1], v3[2])
    glVertex3f(v4[0], v4[1], v4[2])
    glVertex3f(v5[0], v5[1], v5[2])
    glVertex3f(v6[0], v6[1], v6[2])
    glVertex3f(v7[0], v7[1], v7[2])
    glVertex3f(v8[0], v8[1], v8[2])
    glVertex3f(v9[0], v9[1], v9[2])
```

```python
        glVertex3f(v10[0], v10[1], v10[2])
        glVertex3f(v11[0], v11[1], v11[2])
        glVertex3f(v12[0], v12[1], v12[2])
        glVertex3f(v13[0], v13[1], v13[2])
        glVertex3f(v14[0], v14[1], v14[2])


def unjoined_line():
    """ Joins PAIRS of unconnected segments. """
    glBegin(GL_LINES)
    glColor3f(1.0, 0.0, 0.0)  # Red
    vertex_set()
    glEnd()

def joined_line():
    """ Joins all points in sequence. """
    glBegin(GL_LINE_STRIP)
    glColor3f(0.2, 0.2, 1.0)  # Blue
    vertex_set()
    glEnd()

def line_loop():
    """ Joins all points in sequence, closing the loop. """
    glBegin(GL_LINE_LOOP)
    glColor3f(0.0, 1.0, 1.0)  # Turquoise
    vertex_set()
    glEnd()

def triangles():
    """ Makes triangles of groups of three. """
    glBegin(GL_TRIANGLES)
    glColor3f(0.0, 1.0, 0.0)  # Green
    vertex_set()
    glEnd()

def triangle_strip():
    """ First triangle using the first, second, and third vertices, and then another using the second,
        third, and fourth vertices, and so on. """
    glBegin(GL_TRIANGLE_STRIP)
    glColor3f(0.8, 1.0, 0.0)  # Orange
    vertex_set()
    glEnd()

def triangle_fan():
    """ First triangle using the first, second, and third vertices, and then another using the second,
        third, and fourth vertices, and so on. """
    glBegin(GL_TRIANGLE_FAN)
    glColor3f(1.0, 0.8, 0.0)  # Orange
    vertex_set()
    glEnd()

def quads():
    """ First quadrilateral using the first four vertices, and then another using the next four,
        and so on.
    """
    glBegin(GL_QUADS)
    glColor3f(1.0, 0.40, 0.0)  # Orange
```

130

```python
    vertex_set()
    glEnd()

def quads_strip():
    """ A linked strip of four-sided polygons. """
    glBegin(GL_QUAD_STRIP)
    glColor3f(1.0, 0.20, 0.0)  # Dark Orange
    vertex_set()
    glEnd()

def polygon():
    """ A linked strip of four-sided polygons. """
    glBegin(GL_POLYGON)
    glColor3f(1.0, 0.0, 1.0)  # Purple
    vertex_set()
    glEnd()

def points():
    """ Each vertex defines a point. """
    glPointSize( 4.0 )
    glBegin(GL_POINTS)
    glColor3f(1.0, 0.0, 1.0)  # Purple
    vertex_set()
    glEnd()

def InitGL(Width, Height):
    """ Initialize and setup the Graphics Software/Hardware pipeline.
    """
    glClearColor(0.0, 0.0, 0.0, 0.0)
    glMatrixMode(GL_PROJECTION)
    glLoadIdentity()
    gluPerspective(45.0, float(Width)/float(Height), 0.1, 100.0)
    glMatrixMode(GL_MODELVIEW)

def DrawGLScene():
    """ Test each primitive. For each primitive to be tested, un-comment the relevant line.
        Ensure all the others are commented out to keep the situation simple.
    """
    glClear(GL_COLOR_BUFFER_BIT | GL_DEPTH_BUFFER_BIT)
    glLoadIdentity()
    glTranslatef(0.0,0.0,-6.0)
    glLineWidth(10.0)
    # Test the primitives. Uncomment each line by itself to demonstrate it.
    # ========================================================
    unjoined_line()
    #joined_line()
    #line_loop()
    #triangles()
    #triangle_strip()
    #triangle_fan()
    #quads()
    #quads_strip()
    #polygon()
    #points()
    glutSwapBuffers()
```

```
def main():
    """ Main Program.
    """

    glutInit(sys.argv)
    glutInitWindowSize(350,100)    # W,H. Line gets scaled to the window.

    glutInitWindowPosition(10,30) # Controls where the window starts - top-left corner.
    window = glutCreateWindow(b'OpenGL Primitives: GL_POINTS')

    glutDisplayFunc(DrawGLScene)    # The actual 'draw now' command.
    InitGL(640, 480)
    glutMainLoop()

main()
```

Now we discover GLUT

GLUT (pronounced like the glut in gluttony) is the OpenGL Utility Toolkit.
GLUT is a separate library of utilities for OpenGL programs, which mainly perform
system-level Input and Output with the operating system. This includes display
window definition, window control, as well as monitoring of keyboard and mouse
input. Routines for drawing a number of geometric primitives in both solid and
wireframe mode are also provided. These include spheres, the Platonic solids and the
famous Utah teapot.
GLUT makes it easier to learn about and explore OpenGL programming. GLUT is
simple, easy, and small.

GLUT supports
- Multiple display windows for OpenGL rendering.
- Callback driven event processing (mouse and keyboard input).
- Sophisticated input devices.
- An 'idle' routine and timers.
- A simple, cascading pop-up menu facility.
- Utility routines to generate various solid and wire frame objects .
- Support for bitmap and stroke type fonts.
- Miscellaneous window management functions.

```
"""
Program name: opengl_wirecube_1.py
Objective: Simplified Example.

keywords: opengl, wirecube
===============================================================================79
Comments:

Tested on:  Python 2.7.3, Python 3.2.3
```

132

Author: Mike Ohlson de Fine
=====================================
"""

```python
from OpenGL.GL import *
from OpenGL.GLUT import *

def init():
    glClearColor(1.0, 1.0, 1.0, 0)
    glLoadIdentity()


def display_1():
    glClear(GL_COLOR_BUFFER_BIT | GL_DEPTH_BUFFER_BIT)
    glColor3f(1.0, 0.0, 0.0)
    glutWireCube(1.0)
    glFlush()

glutInit('')
glutInitWindowSize(300, 300)
glutCreateWindow(b'Wire Cube')
glutDisplayFunc(display_1)
init()
glutMainLoop()
```

All the GLUT Wireshapes

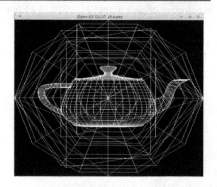

"""

Program name: glut_wireshapes_1.py
Objective: Draw all the GLUT predefined shapes.

keywords: opengl, cube, hexagon, teapot, cone, platonics, extrusion shapes.
==79
Comments:

Tested on: Python 2.6, Python 2.7.3, Python 3.2.3
Author: Mike Ohlson de Fine
=================================
"""

```python
from OpenGL.GL import *
from OpenGL.GLUT import *
```

```python
from OpenGL.GLU import *

# Rotation angle for the shapes.
rangle = 0.0
rot_axis = [1.0, 1.0, 0.0 ]


def InitGL(Width, Height):
    """ Initialize our OpenGL window. Sets all of the initial parameters.
    """
    glClearColor(0.0, 0.0, 0.0, 0.0)          # Set the background to black
    glMatrixMode(GL_PROJECTION)
    glLoadIdentity()
    gluPerspective(45.0, float(Width)/float(Height), 0.1, 100.0)  # Aspect ratio.
    glMatrixMode(GL_MODELVIEW)
#==========================================================================
# Variable position variables.
location_1 = [2.0, -3.0, -5.0]
location_2 = [-1.0, 0.0, -1.0]
location_3 = [4.0, 0.0, -4.0]
location_4 = [-2.0, 0.0, -2.0]

def DrawGLScene():
    """ The drawing function
    """
    global rangle  # Angular rotation
    global location_1, location_2, location_3, location_4
    glClear(GL_COLOR_BUFFER_BIT | GL_DEPTH_BUFFER_BIT);  # Clear The Screen And The Depth Buffer.
    rot_axis = [ 0.0, 1.0, 1.0 ]

    # Draw a cube, Icosahedron and torus
    glLoadIdentity();
    location_1[1] += 0.001
    location_1[2] -=0.05
    glTranslatef(location_1[0], location_1[1], location_1[2])
    glRotatef(rangle , rot_axis[0], rot_axis[1], rot_axis[2] )
    glutWireCube(2.5)
    glutWireIcosahedron()
    glutWireTorus(0.4, 4.4, 12, 8)

    # Draw octahedron and sphere.
    glLoadIdentity();
    location_2[0] += 0.01
    location_2[2] -= 0.03
    glTranslatef(location_2[0], location_2[1], location_2[2])
    glRotatef(rangle , rot_axis[0], rot_axis[1], rot_axis[2] )
    glutWireOctahedron()
    glutWireSphere(2.0, 4, 3)

    # Draw cone and dodecahedron
    glLoadIdentity();
    location_3[0] -= 0.001
    location_3[2] -= 0.01
    glTranslatef(location_3[0], location_3[1], location_3[2])
    glRotatef(rangle , rot_axis[0], rot_axis[1], rot_axis[2] )
    glutWireCone(2.5, 2.0, 6, 6)
    glutWireDodecahedron()
```

```
# Draw Teapot
glLoadIdentity();
location_4[0] += 0.05
location_4[2] -= 0.5
glTranslatef(location_4[0], location_4[1], location_4[2])
glRotatef(rangle , rot_axis[0], rot_axis[1], rot_axis[2] )
glutWireTeapot(1.5)

rangle += 0.5
glutSwapBuffers()

def main():
    """ Main Program.
    """

    glutInit(sys.argv) # initialization openGL window. Must be first GLUT function called.
    glutInitDisplayMode(GLUT_RGBA | GLUT_DOUBLE | GLUT_DEPTH)   # Display mode
    glutInitWindowSize(800, 800)
    glutInitWindowPosition(0, 0)
    window = glutCreateWindow(b"GLUT Wireshapes")
    glutDisplayFunc(DrawGLScene)
    glutIdleFunc(DrawGLScene)  # When we are doing nothing, redraw the scene. No animation without this.
    InitGL(800, 800)           # Call our custom initialization function.
    glutMainLoop()             # Start GLUT's Event Processing Engine

main()
```

Independently Rotating Cubes

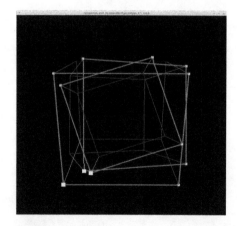

```
    """
```

Program name: opengl_perspective_rotations_1.py
Objective: Construct a general cube. Demonstrate independent rotation of multiple
instances of the cubes .

keywords: opengl, points, lines, variable cube, independent rotation

===79

```
Comments: A wire cube is defined interms of variables inside vertices.

Tested on: Python 2.6, Python 2.7.3, Python 3.2.3
Author:  Mike Ohlson de Fine
==================================
"""
from OpenGL.GL import *
from OpenGL.GLUT import *
from OpenGL.GLU import *
import sys

x0 = -1.0    # Line start .
y0 = -1.0
z0 = 1.0
rangle = 0.0

def InitGL(Width, Height):
    """ initial parameters. This is called right after the OpenGL window is created.
    """
    glClearColor(0.0, 0.0, 0.0, 0.0)  # Clear background to black .
    glMatrixMode(GL_PROJECTION)
    glLoadIdentity()                   # Reset projection matrix.
    gluPerspective(45.0, float(Width)/float(Height), 0.1, 100.0)
    glMatrixMode(GL_MODELVIEW)

def any_cube(x0,y0,z0, hite):
    """ Specification of the line and point positions and their color.
    """
    glColor3f(1.0,0.0,0.0)
    glLineWidth(8.0)
    glBegin(GL_LINE_STRIP)
    glVertex3f( x0     , y0     , z0)       # 1
    glVertex3f( x0     , y0+hite , z0)      # 2
    glVertex3f( x0+hite, y0+hite , z0)      # 3
    glVertex3f( x0+hite, y0     , z0)       # 4
    glVertex3f( x0     , y0     , z0)       # 1
    glEnd()

    glPointSize( 20.0)
    glColor3f(1.0, 1.0, 0.0)
    glBegin(GL_POINTS);         # Every vertex specified is a point.
    glVertex3f( x0     , y0     , z0) # 1
    glEnd()

    glPointSize( 12.0)
    glColor3f(0.0, 1.0, 0.0)
    glBegin(GL_POINTS);
    glVertex3f( x0     , y0+hite , z0)   # 2
    glVertex3f( x0+hite, y0+hite , z0)   # 3
    glVertex3f( x0+hite, y0     , z0)    # 4
    glEnd()

    glLineWidth(2.0)
    glColor3f(0.1,0.1, 1.0)
    glBegin(GL_LINE_STRIP)
    glVertex3f( x0     , y0     , z0-hite)     # 5
```

```python
    glVertex3f( x0      , y0+hite , z0-hite)   # 6
    glVertex3f( x0+hite  , y0+hite , z0-hite)  # 7
    glVertex3f( x0+hite  , y0    , z0-hite)  # 8
    glVertex3f( x0       , y0    , z0-hite)   # 5
    glEnd()

    glColor3f(1.0,0.0,0.0,0.5)
    glBegin(GL_LINES)
    glVertex3f( x0, y0+hite,    z0)     # 2
    glVertex3f( x0, y0+hite, z0-hite)   # 6
    glEnd()

    glBegin(GL_LINES)
    glVertex3f( x0+hite, y0+hite, z0  )   # 3
    glVertex3f( x0+hite, y0+hite, z0-hite)  # 7
    glEnd()

    glColor3f(0.5,0.0,1.0)
    glBegin(GL_LINES)
    glVertex3f( x0+hite, y0   , z0  )   # 4
    glVertex3f( x0+hite, y0   , z0-hite)  # 8
    glEnd()

    glColor3f(1.0,1.0,0.0)
    glBegin(GL_LINES)
    glVertex3f( x0, y0 , z0  )   # 1
    glVertex3f( x0, y0 , z0-hite)  # 5
    glEnd()

def DrawGLScene():
    """ Specification of the line and point positions and their color.
    """
    global rangle
    glClear(GL_COLOR_BUFFER_BIT | GL_DEPTH_BUFFER_BIT) # Clear screen and depth buffer.
    size    = [ 1.0, 1.0,  1.0 ]          # Change size if desired.
    location = [ 0.0,  0.0, -5.0 ]
    glLoadIdentity();
    glTranslatef(location[0], location[1], location[2]) # Shift to convenient position.
    glScale(size[0],size[1],size[2])         # Change size if desired.
    glRotatef(rangle*0.4, 1.0, 0.0, 0.0);  # Rotate cube around X.
    any_cube(-1.0,-1.0, 1.0, 2.0 )         # Largest cube.

    glLoadIdentity();
    glTranslatef(location[0], location[1], location[2]) # Shift to convenient position.
    glScale(size[0],size[1],size[2])         # Change size if desired.
    glRotatef(rangle*0.4, 0.0, 1.0, 0.0);  # Rotate cube around X.
    any_cube(-0.9,-0.9, 0.9, 1.8 )         # Intermediate size cube.

    glLoadIdentity();
    glTranslatef(location[0], location[1], location[2]) # Shift to convenient position.
    glScale(size[0],size[1],size[2])         # Change size if desired.
    glRotatef(rangle*0.4, 0.0, 0.0, 1.0);  # Rotate cube around X.
    any_cube(-0.8,-0.8, 0.8, 1.6 )         # Smallest cube.
    rangle += 1.0
    glutSwapBuffers()
#=============================================================
def main():
```

```
""" Specification of the line and point positions and their color.
"""
    glutInit(sys.argv)
    glutInitDisplayMode(GLUT_RGBA | GLUT_DOUBLE | GLUT_DEPTH)
    glutInitWindowSize(1000, 1000)
    glutInitWindowPosition(0, 0)
    window = glutCreateWindow(b"Perspective: 45.0, float(Width)/float(Height), 0.1, 100.0")
    glutDisplayFunc(DrawGLScene)
    glutIdleFunc(DrawGLScene)
    InitGL(1000, 1000)
    glutMainLoop()

main()
```

Labour Saving: Using Python (x, y) Coordinate Lists

```
"""
Program name: EVALpoints_rotations_gl_7.py
Objective: Draws a complex shape from a Python list of (x,y) coordinates using "eval".

keywords: eval, points, liness, rotate, draw
=============================================================================================79
Comments: Convert a Python list of (x,y) coordinates into a glVertex3f(x,y,z)
list of vertices. The OpenGL vertex statements are assembled for the Python
list as strings of the form "glVertex3f(x,y,z)" and transformed into OpenGL
statements using the eval() function.

Author:      Mike Ohlson de Fine
"""
from OpenGL.GL import *
from OpenGL.GLUT import *
from OpenGL.GLU import *
import shape_sun_face_1     # This the file that contains the complex Pyton list of (x, y) coordinates.

vts = shape_sun_face_1.sun_shape             # Short name for convenience.

rot_angle = 0.0                              # Rotation angle for the quadrilateral.

def InitGL(Width, Height):
    """ A general OpenGL initialization function that sets the initial parameters.
        It should be called immediately after our OpenGL window is created.
    """
    glClearColor(0.0, 0.0, 0.0, 0.0)                # This clears the background color to black .
    glMatrixMode(GL_PROJECTION)
    glLoadIdentity()                                # Reset the projection matrix.
    gluPerspective(45.0, float(Width)/float(Height), 0.1, 100.0)
    glMatrixMode(GL_MODELVIEW)


def yield_vertex(string_vertex, i, j):
    """ Assembles a "glVertex3f(x,y,z)" string then converts it to an OpenGL compatible
        glVertex3f(x,y,z) statement.
        Note that this function must not have an explicit 'return' statement.
```

```python
    """
    str_vt = 'glVertex3f('
    string_vert = str_vt + str(string_vertex[i][j]) +' , '+str(string_vertex[i][j+1]) +', -1.0 )'
    eval(string_vert)

def DrawCube():
    """ Assembles the correct vertex list for the " glBegin(GL_LINE_STRIP)"
        sequence of vertices.
    """
    glColor3f(1.0, 1.0, 0.0)
    glLineWidth(3.0)
    glBegin(GL_LINE_STRIP)              # Start line.
    for i in range(len(vts)):
        for j in range(0, len(vts[i]), 2):     # Synthesize vertices from Python list.
            yield_vertex(vts, i, j)
    glEnd()                            # End line.


def DrawGLScene():
    """" The main drawing function.
    """
    global rot_angle
    glClear(GL_COLOR_BUFFER_BIT | GL_DEPTH_BUFFER_BIT);  # Clear screen depth buffer .
    glLoadIdentity();
    glTranslatef( -13.0, -13.0, -18.0)
    glScale(0.06,  0.06,  0.06)
    #glRotatef(30.0, 0.0, 0.0, 1.0);         # Single rotation of the shape.
    glRotatef(rot_angle*0.6, 1.0, 1.0, 0.0);    # Continuous animated rotation.
    DrawCube()
    rot_angle += 1.0                       # Increment of angle for continuous rotation.
    glutSwapBuffers()

def main():
    """" Main event processing function.
    """
    global window
    glutInit(sys.argv)
    glutInitDisplayMode(GLUT_RGBA | GLUT_DOUBLE | GLUT_DEPTH)
    glutInitWindowSize(400, 400)
    glutInitWindowPosition(0, 0)
    window = glutCreateWindow("Python/OpengGL Rotate Complex Shapes")
    glutDisplayFunc(DrawGLScene)
    glutIdleFunc(DrawGLScene)               # When we are doing nothing, redraw the scene.
    InitGL(400, 400)                        # Initialize our window.
    glutMainLoop()                          # Start event processing engine

main()
```

9

Animation in 3D

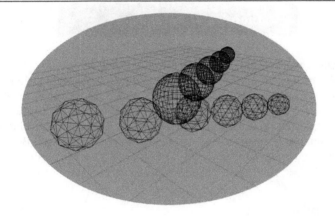

"Animation is not the art of drawings that move but the art of movements that are drawn" Norman McLaren.

"Animation can explain whatever the mind of man can conceive. This facility makes it the most versatile and explicit means of communication yet devised for quick mass appreciation." Walt Disney.

This chapter covers:
- **Principles of Animation**
- **Animation using Tkinter and Python**
- **Animation in 2D Using Tkinter**
- **Collision Detection**
- **Animation in 3D Using Tkinter**
- **OpenGL Animation and Timing Control**
- **Measurement of Graphic Rendering Times**
- **An Object Oriented Strategy for Animating Multiple Objects**

- **Three Choices for Animated Rendering in OpenGL**

The principles of animation are developed in Book 2 of this series. We are not going to repeat this development completely from scratch for 3D. Instead we will trim the code, demonstrations and explanations to shorter versions targeted to testing animation viability for 3D objects. OpenGL is the modern software specification for 3D graphics. It is relevant because it is designed to take advantage of continually improving Graphics Processing Unit (GPU) hardware.

OpenGL combined with Python provides a good approach to understanding how to create high quality animated 3D graphics. OpenGL is also suited to the development of graphics and animation on platforms like tablets and smart cellphones.

Principles of Animation

Animation is the art and science of making drawings appear to be alive. In essence all animation boils down to creating a sequence of drawings on some kind of surface and then controlling the rate at which they are displayed. We describe one such drawing as a movie frame. The frames are displayed one at a time for short, controlled periods of time. When the eye takes in the images and sends them to the brain, the human brain perceives the sequence as smooth, and to some degree, realistic motion. Because Python is such a well designed language it is unexpectedly easy to animate drawn objects.

Principles of motion

Animation is about creating the illusion of movement and life. Creating the illusion of movement from still pictures is linked strongly with the way the human brain processes sequences of images. If a series of images with a small amount of change or difference between any two images in sequence is presented in a regular time sequence then the human brain perceives continuous movement. This is the focus in this chapter. First we demonstate it with a Python–Tkinter program. After that we demonstrate it with some Python-OpenGL programs. Using Python with OpenGL offers more than one approach.

As we saw in chapter 7 there are convenient methods of converting 3D static objects created in Blender into lists of vertices that OpenGL can display as high quality 3D objects. Therefore the powerful alliance of Blender, Python and OpenGL gives us practically unlimited scope for creativity that takes advantage of cutting edge technology graphics as it is evolving.

There are 5 phases to creating an animation which creates the sensation of motion to a viewer.

1. Draw the object that is going to be animated.
2. Keep the image visible for a short period.
3. Erase the object from view.
4. Re-draw the object in slightly different position.
5. Repeat the cycle.

When using a computer to display the animation there are limitations imposed by the time it takes to compute the drawing using software commands plus the time needed to execute other parts of software.

Animation using Tkinter and Python

This how we go about drawing and animating in Python:
1. We use the Tkinter module and invoke it with
   from Tkinter import *

2. Then we draw the set of 3D shapes by first projecting them onto a 2D plane:
   fourd_shape_2_twod_line(view_faces , '#ff0000', 1)

3. *canvas_1.update()*   # This refreshes the drawing on the canvas.

4. *canvas_1.after(cycle_period)*   # Makes execution pause for 30 milliseconds.

5. *canvas_1.delete('lines_1')*   # Clear everything off the canvas.

The weakness of Tkinter is that it is not designed to take advantage of modern GPU technology. Producing highly detailed, fast 3D images using Tkinter is not possible. We must use OpenGL when we want fast 3D animated graphics.

Animation in 2D using Tkinter

In the example given below we simulate a bouncing rubber ball that is not perfectly elastic. This means that is loses some energy each time it bounces and eventually ends up rolling along the floor. The simulation includes a graphic trace that records the path or trajectory that was followed by the ball in its motion.

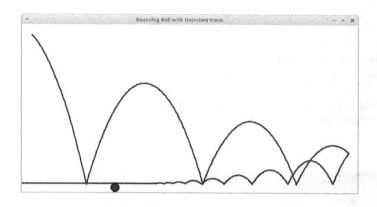

```
"""
Program name: elastic_gravity_ball_1 .py
Objective: A ball bouncing subject to gravity and energy loss with each impact.

Keywords: ball, bounce, gravity, time, movement, mutual impact
==================================================================================79
Comments: The "canvas_1.delete("ball_1")" method delets the drawn ball_1.
This tag (label) in the "canvas_1.create_oval( ball_1['posn_x'], ... tags="ball_1") instruction says that any drawn
object with the identified with the tag "ball_1" must be deleted.
The use of different tags for different objects allows selective deletion.
Here we delete the ball but leave the trajectory line untouched.

Tested on: Python 2.6, Python 2.7.3, Python 3.2.3
Author: Mike Ohlson de Fine.
"""
from Tkinter import *
#from tkinter import *   # for python version 3.x
import time
import math
root = Tk()
root.title("Bouncing Ball with trajectory trace.")


cw = 800                        # canvas width
ch = 400                        # canvas height

GRAVITY = 2.5
canvas_1 = Canvas(root, width=cw, height=ch, background="white")
canvas_1.grid(row=0, column=0)

cycle_period = 20                       # The time between new positions of the ball (milliseconds).
time_scaling = 0.05                     # This governs the size of the differential steps
                                        # when calculating changes in position.

# The parameters determining the dimensions of the ball and it's position.
# Separate but similarly behaved objects can be made.
ball_1 = {'posn_x':25.0,                # x position of box containing the ball (bottom).
          'posn_y':25.0,                # x position of box containing the ball (left edge).
          'velocity_x':45.0,            # amount of x-movement each cycle of the 'for' loop.
          'velocity_y':50.0,            # amount of y-movement each cycle of the 'for' loop.
```

```
            'ball_width':20.0,        # size of ball - width (x-dimension).
            'ball_height':20.0,       # size of ball - height (y-dimension).
            'color':"blue",           # color of the ball .
            'coef_restitution':0.80}   # proportion of elastic enrgy recovered each bounce .

def detectWallCollision(ball_1):
    """ Detect ball-to-wall collision. This that detects collisions with the walls of the container
        and then reverses the direction of movement if a collision is detected.
    """
    if ball_1['posn_x'] > cw - ball_1['ball_width']:        # Collision with right-hand container wall.
        ball_1['velocity_x'] = -ball_1['velocity_x'] * ball_1['coef_restitution']   # Reverse direction.
        ball_1['posn_x'] = cw - ball_1['ball_width']
    if ball_1['posn_x'] < 1:                                 # Collision with left-hand  wall.
        ball_1['velocity_x'] = -ball_1['velocity_x'] * ball_1['coef_restitution']
        ball_1['posn_x'] = 1
    if ball_1['posn_y'] < ball_1['ball_height'] :           # Collision with ceiling.
        ball_1['velocity_y'] = -ball_1['velocity_y'] * ball_1['coef_restitution']
        ball_1['posn_y'] = ball_1['ball_height']
    if ball_1['posn_y'] > ch - ball_1['ball_height'] :      # Floor collision.
        ball_1['velocity_y'] = - ball_1['velocity_y'] * ball_1['coef_restitution']
        ball_1['posn_y'] = ch - ball_1['ball_height']


def diffEquation(ball_1):
    """ Difference Equation for approximate ball physics.
    """
    x_old = ball_1['posn_x']
    y_old = ball_1['posn_y']
    ball_1['posn_x'] += ball_1['velocity_x'] * time_scaling
    ball_1['velocity_y'] = ball_1['velocity_y'] + GRAVITY  # A crude equation incorporating gravity.
    ball_1['posn_y'] += ball_1['velocity_y'] * time_scaling
    canvas_1.create_oval( ball_1['posn_x'], ball_1['posn_y'], ball_1['posn_x'] + ball_1['ball_width'] \
        ,ball_1 ['posn_y'] + ball_1['ball_height'], fill= ball_1['color'], tags="ball_1")
    canvas_1.create_line( x_old, y_old, ball_1['posn_x'], ball_1 ['posn_y'], width = 3, fill= ball_1['color'])
    detectWallCollision(ball_1)      # Has the ball collided with any container wall?


for i in range(1, 1000):           # End the program after 1000 position shifts.
    diffEquation(ball_1)           # Apply physics to the motion of the ball.
    canvas_1.update()              # Refreshes the drawing on the canvas.
    canvas_1.after(cycle_period)   # Makes execution pause for 20 milliseconds.
    canvas_1.delete("ball_1")      # Erases everything on the canvas .
root.mainloop()
```

How it Works

The key feature of all simulations is to predict the change in state of an object or system during a given period time. In the case of our bouncing ball the state of the object is completely specified by the position and velocity of the ball. Velocity is a vector and therefore must include direction. The size of the velocity vector is the speed of the ball and the direction of the ball is given by the direction of the vector. We actually do not need to explicitly figure out the vector. We only need the algebra to calculate the position of the ball at fixed times in sequence. If we make the time intervals sufficiently small then we end up with a sufficiently smooth and realistic simulation.

The way we accurately predict the progressive changes of state of the object is to have a bunch of equations that keep an account of the forces on the object and relate how one affects the other. In applied math and physics this is called the differential equation governing the motion. For our simulation the physics are contained in the function:

```
def diffEquation(ball_1):
    """ Difference Equation for approximate ball physics.
    """
    ...
    ball_1['posn_x'] +=  ball_1['velocity_x'] * time_scaling
    ball_1['velocity_y'] = ball_1['velocity_y'] + GRAVITY  # A crude equation incorporating gravity.
    ball_1['posn_y'] += ball_1['velocity_y'] * time_scaling
    ...
```

These three equations say in effect that horizontal velocity will remain unchanged from one time interval to the next but vertical velocity is increased by an additional amount due to the force of gravity.

Collision Detection

An essential feature of most games that simulate moving objects like balls is the need to detect collisions and when a collision has been detected, to adjust the state of motion of the moving object to simulate rebound or reversal of direction. So there are two features of collisions that we have to incorporate in our computer code. First is to decide when two objects are approaching so closely that they will definitely hit each other in the next time interval. Second is to use a set of physics equations that will change the state of the moving objects to the state the object would have immediately after a collision.

In our simple and approximate simulation of a bouncing ball we detect imminent collision as being when the ball is sufficiently close to the wall by applying the following tests for nearness:

```
if ball_1['posn_x'] > cw - ball_1['ball_width']:       # Collision with right-hand container wall.
...
    if  ball_1['posn_x'] < 1:                          # Collision with left-hand  wall.
        ...
    if  ball_1['posn_y'] <  ball_1['ball_height'] :    # Collision with ceiling.
        ...
    if  ball_1['posn_y'] > ch - ball_1['ball_height'] :  # Floor collision.
        ...
```

And then when a collision has been detected to reverse the velocity directions in the x and y directions.

What about balls bouncing off each other?

When there is more than one ball bouncing around we need a way to discover imminent impacts between any two balls. The most straightforward way of doing this is to to focus on each ball in turn and then predict the position of every other ball in turn to see if any one of them will enter the collision proximity of the ball which is being focussed on. This technique is demonstrated in book 2 of this series, "Python Graphics for Games 2: animation".

Now we move from two dimensional objects to three dimensions.

Animation in 3D Using Tkinter

Once we start trying to follow the motions of objects in three dimensions, the best way to cover the complexity of simulating the state of objects and their trajectories in 3D space is through the use of matrix transforms. Here we use the matrix transforms shown in chapter 4 of this book. The matrix functions have been collected together in a Python module called **matrix_transforms.py**. The contents are given in the appendix section *The Matrix Transform Module*.
Individual function are called using the syntax:
matrix_transforms.*matrix_transform*
where *matrix_transform* is one of the many matrix geometry transformation functions contained in the *matrix_transforms.py* module.

In the example here we have a five-triangle object called *faces* which we animate by rotating around the x, y and z-axes at different speeds.

The use of matrix transforms means that we need to perform the following tasks:
1. Define our original shape by expressing the vertices of the triangles as four variables as explained in chapter 4. For example the first triangle is:

   [[1.0, 0.0, 0.0, 1.0], [-1.0, 0.0, -0.0, 1.0], [0.0, -1.5, -0.0, 1.0], [1.0, 0.0, 0.0, 1.0]]

2. Convert the 4-component vertices into Numpy matrices so they may be multiplied by other matrices.
3. Exeute the required matrix transform by matrix manipulation.
4. Convert the result into a 2D projection.
5. Display the 2D projection.

The step of projecting the geometrically transformed vertices onto a 2D plane is done with the function:

```
# For Display - Downconvert a 3D/4D matrix down to a 2D list.
def fourd_shape_2_twod_line(numpy_threed_matrix, kula, l_width):
    """ Project a set of 3D vertices (homogeneous matrix - numpy form) onto a 2D plane.
```

Input arguments are a 3D shape, a color and a line width.
The x and y compnents are drawn as a segmented line or a polygon.
"""

The act of projection consists simply of extracting on the the x and y components of the matrix through:

```
for i in range(0, len(bbb)):
    twod_line.append( bbb[i][0] )
    twod_line.append( bbb[i][1] )
```

and displaying it on a tkinter canvas. In the program there are two options for display. Either as a polygon or as a line. For polyons we only need to give three vertices to complete a triangle but for a tkinter "line" we need four. The last vertex is repeat of the first.

An animation of rotating triangles in Tkinter

"""

Program name: tkinter_object_rotate_1.py
Objective: Animated display of a 3D object using tkinter.

Keywords: tkinter, animation, rotation geometry, vertices, faces
==79
Comments: For objects or shapes with less than 100 vertices tkinter rendering speed are acceptable but are not adequate for high numbers of vertices.

Tested on: Python 2.6, Python 2.7.3, Python 3.2.3
Author: Mike Ohlson de Fine
"""

```
import math
import time
import matrix_transforms
import numpy

faces = [
  [[ 1.0,  0.0,   0.0, 1.0], [ -1.0, 0.0,  -0.0, 1.0], [ 0.0, -1.5,  -0.0, 1.0], [ 1.0, 0.0,   0.0, 1.0]],
  [[ -1.0,  -0.0, -1.05, 1.0], [ 0.0, 0.5, -0.05, 1.0], [ 1.0, -0.0, -1.05, 1.0], [ -1.0, -0.0, -1.05, 1.0]],
  [[-1.05,  -0.0, -1.0, 1.0], [-1.05, 0.0,  1.0, 1.0], [-0.05, 0.5, -0.0, 1.0], [-1.05, -0.0, -1.0, 1.0]],
  [[ 1.05,  0.0,  1.0, 1.0], [ 1.05, 0.0, -1.0, 1.0], [ 0.05, 0.5, -0.0, 1.0], [ 1.05, 0.0,  1.0, 1.0]],
  [[ -1.0,  0.0,  1.05, 1.0], [ 0.0, 0.5,  0.05, 1.0], [ 1.0, 0.0,  1.05, 1.0], [ -1.0, 0.0,  1.05, 1.0]]]
```

''' Above are the vertices for four triangles. One triangle per line.
The fourth vertex in each line and is a duplicate of the first.

This allows the triangle to be completed as three line segments if the "canvas_1.create_line(...)" option is chosen. For polygons the fourth vertex in each line is redundant.
'''

```python
for i in range(len(faces)):
    ''' This converts the simple python vertex lists into proper numpy matrices that are
        in the correct form for matrix transforms - necessary for the fast geometry transformation
        used to achieve the animation.
    '''

    for j in range(len(faces[i])):
        faces[i][j]  = numpy.matrix(faces[i][j])    # Convert to Numpy matrices.


# ================================================================================
# SHAPE TRANSFORM TESTING
# ============================
from Tkinter import *
#from tkinter import *  # for python version 3.x
root = Tk()
root.title('Move tkinter objects in 3D')
cw = 400                          # canvas width.
ch = 400                          # canvas height.
canvas_1 = Canvas(root, width=cw, height=ch, background="#110055")
canvas_1.grid(row=0, column=1)


# For Display - Downconvert a 3D/4D matrix down to a 2D list.
def fourd_shape_2_twod_line(numpy_threed_matrix,  kula, l_width):
    """ Project a set of 3D vertices (homogeneous matrix - numpy form) onto a 2D plane.
        Input arguments are a 3D shape, a color and a line width.
        The x and y compnents are drawn as a segmented line or a polygon.
    """

    bbb = numpy_threed_matrix.tolist()
    twod_line = []
    for i in range(0, len(bbb)):
        twod_line.append( bbb[i][0] )
        twod_line.append( bbb[i][1] )
    #canvas_1.create_line( twod_line, width = l_width, tag = 'lines_1', fill= kula )
    canvas_1.create_polygon( twod_line, width = l_width,  tag = 'lines_1', fill= kula )
    return twod_line



# Dynamic rotation.
def show_shape():
    """ Demonstrate the 3D animated transformations of shapes composed of vertices.
    """

    cycle_period= 30
    rad_one_deg = math.pi/180.0
    rad_angle = 0.0

    for i in range(len(faces)):
        for j in range(len(faces[i])):
            faces[i][j] = faces[i][j] * matrix_transforms.T_scaling(100.1 , 100.1, 100.1)

    # Animation by rotation around 3 axes.
    for sequence in range (1000):
        for i in range(len(faces)):
            faces[i] = faces[i] * matrix_transforms.T_roty(-rad_angle)
            faces[i] = faces[i] * matrix_transforms.T_rotx(rad_angle*0.7)
            faces[i] = faces[i] * matrix_transforms.T_rotz(rad_angle*1.3)
```

```
        view_faces = faces[i] * matrix_transforms.T_translate( 200.0, 200.0, 0.0)
        fourd_shape_2_twod_line(view_faces , '#ff0044',  1)

    rad_angle = rad_one_deg * 1.0
    canvas_1.update()                  # This refreshes the drawing on the canvas.
    canvas_1.after(cycle_period)   # This makes execution pause for 200 milliseconds.
    canvas_1.delete('lines_1')

show_shape()
root.mainloop()
```

Now we leave Tkinter behind and concentrate on OpenGL as the method of presenting graphic images. If we have become comfortable using tkinter, it feels like a step backward start trying to do similar things using OpenGL. It is worth the effort.

OpenGL Animation and Timing Control

In this example we send two objects flying down the z-axis in opposite directions. We use the GLUT sphere and dodecahedron because it is convenient to use the shapes without the need to explicitly provide vertices.

The main feature of this example is the technique we use for animation speed control. It is the closest we can get to the technique we have been using when we use Tkinter's sequence of instructions:

```
    canvas_1.update()                  # Refreshes the drawing on the canvas.
    canvas_1.after(cycle_period)   # Makes execution pause for 20 milliseconds.
    canvas_1.delete("ball_1")        # Erases everything on the canvas .
```

For GLUT/OpenGL we use, in the main loop:

```
glutTimerFunc(1, Freshframe, 0) # The initial time delay need only be token.
```

Where the function being called is:

```
def Freshframe(a):
    """ Interrupt driven animation control.
        This function does 3 things:
            1. Sets a start/callback time for itself 20 millisec in the future.
            2. Increments/decrements the position variables of the objects.
            3. executes the opengl 'draw objects' function.
    """
    global rotation_angle, location_sphere, location_dodec
    rotation_angle += 0.5
    location_sphere[0] += 0.008
    location_sphere[2] += 0.03
    location_dodec[0] -= 0.001
    location_dodec[2] -= 0.01
    DrawGLScene()
```

glutTimerFunc(20,Freshframe, 0) # After 20 milliseconds "Freshframe" is called.

The last line **glutTimerFunc(20,Freshframe, 0)** is calling it's own function. Thus we have a loop that will never terminate, that does the following:

1. Increment the variables that control geometry of rotation and translation.
2. Draw the whole scene using the new values of the position variables.
3. Set an alarm clock to wake myself up (ie. "Freshframe") in 20 milliseconds.
4. Go to sleep.
5. When awoken by the alarm clock start at step 1. again.

If we do not want the execution to continue without a software controlled end then we would create a *counter* variable with initial value zero. Every time either "Freshframe" or "DrawGLScene" was executed we would increment the counter with **counter +=1**. when the counter reached some predetermined value we would execute some other code. We will leave that extra complexity out for now, in the interests of simplicity.

```
"""
Program name: glut_timer_animation_wireshapes_1.py
Objective: Demonstrate animation frame-rate control.

keywords: opengl, animation, sphere, dodecahedron, extrusion shapes.
==============================================================================79
Comments: "glutTimerFunc registers a timer callback to be triggered in a specified number of milliseconds."
GLUT attempts to deliver the timer callback as soon as possible after the expiration of the callback's time interval.
Parameters (msec, callback, data):
- msec Milliseconds till invocation.
- callback Client function for timer event.
- data Arbitrary data; passed to callback .

Tested on: Python 2.6, Python 2.7.3, Python 3.2.3
Author:  Mike Ohlson de Fine
==================================
"""

from OpenGL.GL import *
from OpenGL.GLUT import *
from OpenGL.GLU import *

# Rotation angle for the shapes.
rotation_angle = 0.0
```

```
rotation_axis = [1.0, 1.0, 0.0 ]
# Location of the shapes.
location_sphere = [-20.0, 0.0, -110.0]
location_dodec = [3.0, 0.0, -3.0]

# A general OpenGL initialization function.  Sets all of the initial parameters.
def InitGL(Width, Height):                    # Initialize our OpenGL window.
    glClearColor(0.0, 0.0, 0.0, 0.0)          # Set The Background To Black
    glMatrixMode(GL_PROJECTION)
    glLoadIdentity()                          # Reset The Projection Matrix.
    gluPerspective(45.0, float(Width)/float(Height), 0.1, 100.0)  # Calculate Aspect Ratio.
    glMatrixMode(GL_MODELVIEW)

# The main drawing function.
def DrawGLScene():
    """ The pure drawing function - no animation control here.
    """

    global rotation_angle  # Angular rotation
    global location_sphere, location_dodec
    glClear(GL_COLOR_BUFFER_BIT | GL_DEPTH_BUFFER_BIT);
    rot_axis = [ 0.0, 1.0, 1.0 ]

    # Draw sphere.
    glLoadIdentity();
    glColor3f(0.0, 0.0, 0.7)
    glTranslatef(location_sphere[0], location_sphere[1], location_sphere[2])
    glRotatef(rotation_angle , rotation_axis[0], rotation_axis[1], rotation_axis[2] )
    glutWireSphere(5.0, 8, 8) # (radius, slices, stacks)

    # Draw dodecahedron
    glLoadIdentity();
    glColor3f(1.0, 0.0, 0.7)
    glTranslatef(location_dodec[0], location_dodec[1], location_dodec[2])
    glRotatef(rotation_angle , rotation_axis[0], rotation_axis[1], rotation_axis[2] )
    glutWireDodecahedron()

    glutSwapBuffers()

def Freshframe(a):
    """ Interrupt driven animation control.
        This function does 3 things:
            1. Sets a start/callback time for itself 20 millisec in the future.
            2. Increments/decrements the position variables of the objects.
            3. executes the opengl 'draw objects' function.
    """

    global rotation_angle, location_sphere, location_dodec
    rotation_angle += 0.5
    location_sphere[0] += 0.008
    location_sphere[2] += 0.03
    location_dodec[0] -= 0.001
    location_dodec[2] -= 0.01
    DrawGLScene()
    glutTimerFunc(20,Freshframe,0)  # After 20 milliseconds "Freshframe" is called.

def main():
    glutInit(sys.argv)# initialization openGL window. Must be first GLUT function called.
    glutInitDisplayMode(GLUT_RGBA | GLUT_DOUBLE | GLUT_DEPTH)  # Display mode
```

```
glutInitWindowSize(800, 800)
window = glutCreateWindow(b"GLUT Animated Wireshapes")
glutTimerFunc(1, Freshframe, 0) # The initial time delay need only be token.
InitGL(800, 800)              # Call our custom initialization function.
glutMainLoop()                # Start GLUT's Event Processing Engine


main()
```

Measurement of Graphic Rendering Times

When we are designing animation programs it is necessary to know how long calculations take. Rendering images takes up different amounts of time depending on what platform it is run on. We may need to modify and simplify images that have to run on slower hardware like mobile phones and tablets.

The program below is almost identical to the previous one.
The main difference is in the code sequence:

```
frame_count += 1
  if frame_count >= 1000: # Get fps averaged over 1000 frames.
    frame_count = 0
    end_time = glutGet(GLUT_ELAPSED_TIME)
    time_interval = end_time - start_time
    start_time = end_time
    fps = time_interval/1000.0   # Frames per second.
    print 'fps: ', fps, ' time_interval (millisec): ' , time_interval
    # Typical answer: "fps" 16.632  time_interval: 16632"
```

at the end of *DrawGLScene()*.
The function *glutGet(GLUT_ELAPSED_TIME)* takes a reading of a clock that has been running since the first time *glutGet(GLUT_ELAPSED_TIME)* was executed. It measure time in milliseconds (thousandths of a second). Thus the difference between any two sequential readings of the time is the time interval we are interested in. In our code sequence we cause the variable *frame_count* to reach one thousand before we take the average and this gives a pretty accurate measurement of the frame rendering rate.

```
"""
Program name: glut_timerfunction_measured_animation_wireshapes_1.py
Objective: Measure graphics frame-rate for glutIdleFunc or the glutTimerFunc.

keywords: opengl, animation, framerate, time measure, sphere, dodecahedron.
==============================================================================79
Comments: The glutGet(GLUT_ELAPSED_TIME) gives the millisecond count since the very first time it was
called. Thus the difference between the last time and the time before that provide a measure of the intervening
time.

Tested on: Python 2.6, Python 2.7.3, Python 3.2.3
Author:  Mike Ohlson de Fine
===================================
"""

from OpenGL.GL import *
from OpenGL.GLUT import *
from OpenGL.GLU import *

# Rotation angle for the shapes.
rotation_angle = 0.0
rotation_axis = [1.0, 1.0, 0.0 ]
# Location of the shapes.
location_sphere = [-20.0, 0.0, -105.0]
location_dodec = [3.0, 0.0, -3.0]
frame_count = 0
start_time = 0


# A general OpenGL initialization function.  Sets all of the initial parameters.
def InitGL(Width, Height):                  # Initialize our OpenGL window.
    global start_time
    glLineWidth(20.0)
    glClearColor(0.2, 0.4, 0.0, 0.0)        # Set The Background To Green
    glMatrixMode(GL_PROJECTION)
    glLoadIdentity()                        # Reset The Projection Matrix.
    gluPerspective(45.0, float(Width)/float(Height), 0.1, 100.0)
    glMatrixMode(GL_MODELVIEW)
    start_time = glutGet(GLUT_ELAPSED_TIME)

# The main drawing function.
def DrawGLScene():
    """ The pure drawing function - no animation control here.
    """

    global rotation_angle, frame_count, start_time  # Angular rotation
    global location_sphere, location_dodec
    glClear(GL_COLOR_BUFFER_BIT | GL_DEPTH_BUFFER_BIT);
    rot_axis = [ 0.0, 1.0, 1.0 ]

    # Draw sphere.
    glLoadIdentity();
    glColor3f(0.8, 0.8, 0.0)
    glTranslatef(location_sphere[0], location_sphere[1], location_sphere[2])
    glRotatef(rotation_angle , rotation_axis[0], rotation_axis[1], rotation_axis[2] )
    glutWireSphere(10.0, 8, 8) # (radius, slices, stacks)
```

```
# Draw dodecahedron
glLoadIdentity();
glColor3f(0.4, 0.0, 0.8)
glTranslatef(location_dodec[0], location_dodec[1], location_dodec[2])
glRotatef(rotation_angle , rotation_axis[0], rotation_axis[1], rotation_axis[2] )
glutWireDodecahedron()

glutSwapBuffers()

# Advance the variables.
rotation_angle += 0.5
location_sphere[0] += 0.008
location_sphere[2] += 0.03
location_dodec[0] -= 0.001
location_dodec[2] -= 0.01
frame_count += 1
if frame_count >= 1000: # Get fps averaged over 1000 frames.
    frame_count = 0
    end_time = glutGet(GLUT_ELAPSED_TIME)
    time_interval = end_time - start_time
    start_time = end_time
    fps = time_interval/1000.0   # Frames per second.
    print 'fps: ', fps, ' time_interval (millisec): ' , time_interval
    # Typical answer: "fps" 16.632   time_interval: 16632"


def Freshframe(a):       # One argment is demanded by the system.
    """ Interrupt driven animation control.
        This function does 3 things:
            1. Sets a start/callback time for itself 20 millisec in the future.
            2. Increments/decrements the position variables of the objects.
            3. executes the opengl 'draw objects' function.
    """
    global rotation_angle, location_sphere, location_dodec
    rotation_angle += 0.5
    location_sphere[0] += 0.008
    location_sphere[2] += 0.03
    location_dodec[0] -= 0.001
    location_dodec[2] -= 0.01
    DrawGLScene()
    glutTimerFunc(1,Freshframe,0)  # After 20 milliseconds "Freshframe" is called.

def main():
    glutInit(sys.argv)                       # Must be first GLUT function called.
    glutInitDisplayMode(GLUT_RGBA | GLUT_DOUBLE | GLUT_DEPTH)   # Display mode
    glutInitWindowSize(600, 600)
    window = glutCreateWindow("GLUT Animated Wireshapes")
    #glutIdleFunc(DrawGLScene)
    glutTimerFunc(30, Freshframe, 0) # The initial time delay need only be small token.
    InitGL(600, 600)                         # Call our custom initialization function.
    glutMainLoop()                           # Start GLUT's Event Processing Engine

main()
```

Free Running Frame Rate

The program above there is the the line

#glutIdleFunc(DrawGLScene) which has been commented out by the "#" in front.
If we remove the "#" and make the instruction active but now comment out the line
below it thus:
glutIdleFunc(DrawGLScene)
 #glutTimerFunc(30, Freshframe, 0) # The initial time delay need only be small token.
Then the frame rendering runs as fast as possible while still giving priority to all the
other activities of the GPU-CPU system. The measure of average frame rate now will
provide a good estimate of the highest frame rate our system is capable of for the type
of images we are rendering. The more vertices and triangles to be rendered, the slower
the frame rate will be. When 25000 vertices are being rendered a medium performance
computer will deliver frame rates in the region of one frame per second.

An Object Oriented Strategy for Animating Multiple Objects

Because we are using Python it is natural to ask if we can maximise the amount of
variable processing to be done by Python. Can we write most of our code as if we were
intending to use Tkinter as the graphics display mechanism? The answer is qualified
yes as demonstrated by the program below.

We use the concept of re-usable, re-configurable instances of objects from object-
oriented progrmming but without the pain of defining classes. The strategy pursued
here was to be able to render a general kind of shape whose precise dimensions could
be uniquely specified by set of specific dimension variables and then use this to create
multiple, different instances of the shape and then animate them.

The essential key to achieving this is in the instruction
box = TriBox(origin[0], origin[1], origin[2], width, height, depth) # For each box
 in the function def display_n(...).

TriBox(...) specifies the relative position of eight triangles that make up a rectangular
tube. The dimensions and position of the tube are variables. A particular set of values
of these variables effectively define a unique object and we could make as many as we
choose. The location and orientation of each object are also definable. Using this kind
of idea one could construct an Minecraft-like construction environment.

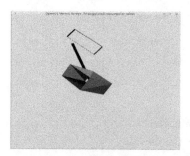

```
"""
Program name: opengl_boxy_triangles_1.py
Objective: Use variable parameters to define multiple objects.

keywords: opengl, glut, triangles, boxes, color control
=================================================================================79
Explanation: The idea is to be able pre-construct a shape like a box  and then be able to draw multiple instances
each with their own shape, position and rotation dynamics.
Variable parameters rather than constants are used to populate vertex arrays.
The names of the variables are used as OpenGL vertex arrays.
That is, that are referenced by their Python list names.
 This avoids the awkwardness and some of the speed performance penalty
associated with the "glBegin ... glEnd" style of 3D object definition.

Three different animation functions are available:
1. glutIdleFunc(all_displays)
2. glutDisplayFunc(all_displays)
3. glutTimerFunc(1,update,0) calling "update" which calls "all_displays()".


Tested on: Python 2.6, Python 2.7.3, Python 3.2.3
Author:        Mike Ohlson de Fine
"""
from OpenGL.GL import *
from OpenGL.GLUT import *
from OpenGL.GLU import *


#==============================================================================
# Individual object properties for each of three instances of the rectangular tube.
# there are the effective "state" parameters of the 3D objects controlled by Python.

rotate_angle_1 = 0.0
rotate_angle_2 = 0.0
rotate_angle_3 = 0.0

rotation_speed_1 = 0.2
rotation_speed_2 = 0.4
rotation_speed_3 = 0.3

rotation_axis_1 = [0.8, 0.3, 0.0]
rotation_axis_2 = [0.3, 0.8, 0.0]
rotation_axis_3 = [0.0, 0.5, 0.4]

shift_1 = [0,   0,    -20 ]
shift_2 = [0,   0,    -8 ]
shift_3 = [-2, 0.5,   -12 ]

origin_1 = [ -1, 1, 0 ]
origin_2 = [ 1, 1, 0 ]
origin_3 = [ 0, 0, 0 ]

w_1, w_2, w_3 = 0.2,  1.5, 2
h_1, h_2, h_3 = 0.2,  0.5, 1
d_1, d_2, d_3 = 5.0,  0.1, 2
```

```
kula = [ [ 0.0,  0.0,  0.4],
         [ 0.0,  0.0,  0.6],
         [ 0.0,  0.2,  0.3],
         [ 0.0,  0.3,  0.6],
         [ 0.0,  0.4,  0.0],
         [ 0.0,  0.6,  0.0],
         [ 0.3,  0.0,  0.0],
         [ 0.6,  0.2,  0.0]    ]
#========================================================================

def TriBox(org_x, org_y, org_z, width ,height ,depth ):
    ''' Draw a square tube (open ended box) from triangles.
       Arguments: origin (bottom left), given as tri1 and tri2.
               width(x-dirn.), height(y-dirn) and depth(z-dirn).
    '''

    tr1 = [org_x, org_y, org_z,  org_x+width, org_y+height, org_z-depth ]   # Parameters

    # vertex    1                    2                3
    #     -------------------------- | --------------------- | ---------------------------
    #        0     1     2        3     4     5      6     7     8

    vt1 = [  tr1[0], tr1[1], tr1[2],  tr1[3], tr1[1], tr1[5],  tr1[0], tr1[1], tr1[5] ]
    vt2 = [  tr1[0], tr1[1], tr1[2],  tr1[3], tr1[1], tr1[5],  tr1[3], tr1[1], tr1[2] ]
    vt3 = [  tr1[3], tr1[1], tr1[2],  tr1[3], tr1[4], tr1[5],  tr1[3], tr1[1], tr1[5] ]
    vt4 = [  tr1[3], tr1[1], tr1[2],  tr1[3], tr1[4], tr1[2],  tr1[3], tr1[4], tr1[5] ]

    vt5 = [  tr1[3], tr1[4], tr1[2],  tr1[0], tr1[4], tr1[5],  tr1[3], tr1[4], tr1[5] ]
    vt6 = [  tr1[3], tr1[4], tr1[2],  tr1[0], tr1[4], tr1[2],  tr1[0], tr1[4], tr1[5] ]
    vt7 = [  tr1[0], tr1[4], tr1[2],  tr1[0], tr1[1], tr1[5],  tr1[0], tr1[4], tr1[5] ]
    vt8 = [  tr1[0], tr1[4], tr1[2],  tr1[0], tr1[1], tr1[2],  tr1[0], tr1[1], tr1[5] ]

    return vt1, vt2, vt3, vt4, vt5, vt6, vt7, vt8

def InitGL(Width, Height):
    """" Initialize and setup the state of Graphics Software/Hardware pipeline.
    """"
    diffuse_lite_kula_white   = [1.0, 1.0, 1.0, 0.0]
    light0_position  = [  5.0, 1.0, 5.0, 0.0 ]
    glClearColor(0.8, 0.8, 1.0, 0.0)
    # ∧∧∧∧∧∧∧∧∧∧∧∧∧∧∧∧∧∧∧∧∧∧∧∧∧∧∧∧∧∧∧∧∧∧∧∧
    glEnable(GL_NORMALIZE)
    glEnable(GL_COLOR_MATERIAL)
    glEnable(GL_LIGHTING)
    glEnable(GL_LIGHT0)
    glLightfv(GL_LIGHT0, GL_POSITION, light0_position)
    glLightfv(GL_LIGHT0, GL_DIFFUSE,  diffuse_lite_kula_white)
    #∧∧∧∧∧∧∧∧∧∧∧∧∧∧∧∧∧∧∧∧∧∧∧∧∧∧∧∧∧∧∧∧∧∧∧∧∧∧∧∧∧
    glEnable(GL_DEPTH_TEST)
    glMatrixMode(GL_PROJECTION)
    glLoadIdentity()
    gluPerspective(45.0, float(Width)/float(Height), 0.1, 100.0)
    glMatrixMode(GL_MODELVIEW)

def all_displays():
    ''' This is the 'mothership' of the dynamic control of each instance of a shape ( box
       in this example). It controls the global values of the rotation angles.
       all_displays() calls display_n(...) passing individual properties to them
```

```
    as arguments.
    '''
    global rotate_angle_1, rotate_angle_2, rotate_angle_3

    glClear(GL_COLOR_BUFFER_BIT|GL_DEPTH_BUFFER_BIT) # Clear the colour and depth buffer
    glEnableClientState(GL_VERTEX_ARRAY);
    display_n(rotation_axis_1, kula, shift_1, rotate_angle_1, origin_1, w_1, h_1, d_1)
    display_n(rotation_axis_2, kula, shift_2, rotate_angle_2, origin_2, w_2, h_2, d_2)
    display_n(rotation_axis_3, kula, shift_3, rotate_angle_3, origin_3, w_3, h_3, d_3)

    glFlush() # Makes sure that we output the model to the graphics card
    glutSwapBuffers()
    glutPostRedisplay()

    rotate_angle_1 += rotation_speed_1
    rotate_angle_2 += rotation_speed_2
    rotate_angle_3 += rotation_speed_3

def display_n(rotation_axis, kula, shift, rotate_angle, origin, width, height, depth):
    """ Draw the object "box" which is an instance of TriBox(...).
    The shape and location of "box" are passed as variables to TriBox(...)
    and are draw as openGL vertex arrays.
    """
    glLoadIdentity()                          # Clear the modelview matrix stack
    glTranslatef(shift[0],shift[1],shift[2])       # Each object's seprate origin.
    glRotate(rotate_angle, rotation_axis[0],  rotation_axis[1],  rotation_axis[2])

    box = TriBox(origin[0], origin[1], origin[2],  width, height, depth) # For each box
    for i in range(0,len(box)):
        glColor3f(kula[i][0], kula[i][1],  kula[i][2])
        glVertexPointer(3, GL_FLOAT, 0, box[i])
        glDrawArrays(GL_TRIANGLES, 0, 3)

def update(a):
    """ Animation frame rate control.
    glutTimerFunc(frame-rate, update, 0). Frame-rate is in milliseconds.
    """
    all_displays()
    glutTimerFunc(2, update, 0)

def main():
    ''' Main Program.
    '''
    glutInit(sys.argv)
    glutInitWindowSize(600,600)    # Width, Height. Object gets scaled to the window.
    glutCreateWindow(b'OpenGL Vertex Arrays: Triangulated rectangular tubes')
    InitGL(600, 600)
    glutIdleFunc(all_displays)     # 1. Method 1 - During idle time redraw the frame.
    #glutDisplayFunc(all_displays)  # 2. Method 2
    #glutTimerFunc(1,update,0)       # 3. Method 3 - Control re-draw with timed interrups.
    glutMainLoop()

main()
```

Three Choices for Animated Rendering

At the end of the main() loop are the three lines:

```
glutIdleFunc(all_displays)      # 1. Method 1 - During idle time redraw the frame.
#glutDisplayFunc(all_displays)  # 2. Method 2
#glutTimerFunc(1,update,0)      # 3. Method 3 - Control re-draw with timed interrups.
```

These are different ways of achieving animated rendering of the objects.
The lst and third have already been demonstrated. The middle one
glutDisplayFunc(all_displays) also works. To experiment with each we can make sure the
one we wish to experiment with is active by removing the comment symbol "#" as the
first character, and ensure the other two are neutralized by being commented out with
the leading #.

Where to Next?

We leave the subject of animation now and move on to exploring methods of
constructing   objects.

10

OpenGL: Vertex Arrays and Normals

"According to String Theory, what appears to be empty space is actually a tumultuous ocean of strings vibrating at the precise frequencies that create the 4 dimensions you and I call height, width, depth and time." Roy H. Williams

" 3D graphics programming is a hell of a beast." Oliver Salzberg.

Topics we cover in this chapter:
- **OpenGL Complexity**
- **Vertex Array Instructions**
- **Model Assembly and Construction**
- **The Role of Normals**
- **The Calculation of Normal Vectors**
- **Normals Made Visible**
- **Centroid (Geometrics Center) of a Triangle**
- **Normal Arrow Vertices**

- **Intersection of Two Lines**

We will explore how to place objects together inside a scene like actors and props on a stage or a movie set. This is a model-making activity similar to that which model train hobbyists practice when they put together scenery around their model railways. We will then explore how to relate different models to each other in a common world.

The trick to understanding model construction in OpenGL is to understand how the matrix operations change geometry. We do not need to understand detail of the mathematical working of matrix algebra. We only need to understand how the sequence of instructions affect our model assembly. There are two geometry transformations that are key to object placement within a model: rotation and translation and we will use the construction of a model solar system to demonstrate this.

OpenGL Complexity and the Pursuit of Speed

OpenGL is not simple. There appear to be dozens of instructions whose exact purpose is not clear. There is an unavoidable overhead of incomprehensible instructions necessary in order to draw the most simple object. If we try to find information on the internet we get a flood of confusing and contradictory information. It can be frustrating because we can spend a lot of time figuring out how a certain method works only to discover some time later that it is *depricated*. Depricated means that its use is discouraged and may become obsolete in the future. This is because OpenGL is rapidly changing alongside the ongoing changes in graphics hardware. The hardware manufacturers are constantly striving for better performance – faster video frame rates, more detail in each frame, greater realism, quicker user response. To take advantage of the improving hardware performance the software has to evolve. The current trend is to place more control in the hands of the software programmer using *shading languages.*

In this book we do not experiment with shading languages. We are trying to simplify the learning process.
Our emphasis is on using OpenGL as a Python tool. As Python programmers we want to be able to produce high quality 3D graphics for art, game creation, scientific and business data vizualization.
We will be exploring vertex arrays in *immediate mode* rendering. We will not go into display lists or vertex buffer objects (vbo's) because it burdens us with a learning overload at a time when we are trying to keep things as simple as we can. Immediate mode is the method that assembles the primitive geometric shapes making up objects in the form of vertices and triangles and then transmit them across a data bus to the

graphics processor for immediate display. The main characterestics of immediate
mode are:

- Primitives like triangles are sent to the graphics card (aka. "pipeline") and
  displayed right away.
- The primitive data is erased/lost as soon as it has been rendered.
- Every new image is rebuilt from scratch. No advantage is taken of what has
  been arriving at the graphics pipeline previously.

The alternative to immediate mode is called *retained mode*. The strategy here is to
pass as much of the graphic work as possible to the graphics card. The main
characterestics of retained mode are:

- Primitives are stored in display lists, which is a type of compiled form. This
  means they are ready for execution as machine code - no translation required.
- These display lists are kept on the graphics card.
- Images are recreated by executing the display lists.

Vertex Array Instructions

Our first method of defining the vertices that are used to draw objects was in chapter
8 using the glBegin ... glEnd convention. This method is cumbersome and has been
superceded by vertex arrays which are much more efficient. Vertex arrays are perfect
with Python. If we take care to use triangles as the only type of graphics primitive, it
greatly simplifies how we construct models of 3D objects. Also when we want to do
OpenES graphic programming for smartphones, the traingles are the fundamental
building block.

The official web documents on vertex arrays are confusing, and they are not
accompanied by examples. Using them in Python makes them much easier to
understand and use.

The key instructions are:
1. glVertexPointer(3, GL_FLOAT, 0, Python list name for vertices)
2. glNormalPointer(GL_FLOAT, 0, Python list name for normals)
3. glDrawArrays(GL_TRIANGLES, 0, 9)

In the first one, glVertexPointer(...) the first argument is 3 because we will only be
handling triangles. The second arguments states that the entries in the list will be
floating point numbers. If you have integers mixed in your list, it will not cause
problems – they will be interpreted as floats. The third argument is the *stride,* which
is the number of memory locations to skip over to reach each vertex in sequence. We
do not have to vary anything here and should always have it as zero. The last
argument must be the name of a Python list of x,y and z vertices for the object to be
drawn.

In our example below this list is:

```
starry3tri = [ -1.0,  0.0,  0.5,    0.0, 1.1, 0.0,   1.0, 0.0, -0.5,  # 1st triangle
               -1.0,  0.0, -0.5,    0.0, 1.1, 0.0,   1.0, 0.0, 0.5,   # 2nd triangle
                0.0,  0.0, -1.0,    0.0, 0.0, 1.0,   0.0, 1.0, 0.0 ]  # 3rd triangle
```

The second key instruction, glNormalPointer(..) is an array of normal vectors that must match the vertex array. The first two arguments are the numerical type and the stride. The last argument should be the name of a Python array containing the normal vector at each vertex. Here is a bit of good news: if you do not want the bother of creating normal (using some equivalent of the vector cross product) then just use the same name as the Python vertex list in the glVertexPointer(...) instruction. It can give a better looking image sometimes.

In the third instruction, the first argument is the primitive type being use. We will always use triangles. The second argument is the integer start index in the array. We will always use 0. The last argument is the number of vertices to be used in drawing the object. In our example we use 9 vertices. If we used 3 instead of 9 then only one triangle would be drawn. If we used a different number for the start index then the vertices for the triangles would a different set of vertices for each triangle rendered.

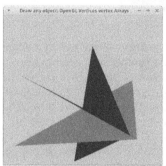 

Turning Vertex Arrays on and off

The use of vertex arrays is enabled in OpenGL with:

```
glEnableClientState(GL_VERTEX_ARRAY)
glEnableClientState(GL_NORMAL_ARRAY)
```

and it is turned off with:

```
glDisableClientState(GL_VERTEX_ARRAY)
glDisableClientState(GL_NORMAL_ARRAY)
```

The working program using vertex arrays to produce the animated images shown above is the following:

```
"""

Program name: opengl_starry3tri_vertex_arrays_1.py
Objective: A general purpose program for inspecting 3D objects supplied as
vertex arrays of triangles.
```

Keywords: OpenGL, triangle, objects, world model, normals, lighting.
==79
Comments: Demonstrate the futility of exporting unmodified Blender Wavefront.obj files. This illustrates the value of assembling 3D objects from of independent triangles.

Tested on: Python 2.7.3, Python 3.2.3
Author: Mike Ohlson de Fine
==================================
"""

```python
from OpenGL.GL import *
from OpenGL.GLUT import *
from OpenGL.GLU import *
import vector_2d3d_ops
import math

# The object to be displayed.
starry3tri = [
-1.0, 0.0, 0.5,    0.0, 1.1, 0.0,  1.0, 0.0, -0.5,  # 1st triangle
-1.0, 0.0, -0.5,   0.0, 1.1, 0.0,  1.0, 0.0, 0.5,   # 2nd triangle
 0.0, 0.0, -1.0,   0.0, 0.0, 1.0,  0.0, 1.0, 0.0  ] # 3rd triangle

# Display rotation axis.
rotate_y = 0.0
rotate_x = 0.0
#=======================================================
# The Objects in the world - given by their vertex and normal arrays.
starry3tri_vertices = len(starry3tri)/3
print 'starry3tri_vertices : ', starry3tri_ vertices
starry3tri_norm = vector_2d3d_ops.array_triangle_normals(starry3tri)
#===========================================================================

def InitGL(Width, Height):
    """ Initialize and setup the Graphics Software/Hardware pipeline.
    """
    glClearColor(0.8, 0.8, 0.0, 0.0)
    # /\/\/\/\/\/\/\/\/\/\/\/\/\/\/\/\/\/\/\/\/\/\/\/\/\/\/\
    diffuse_lite_kula_white  = [ 1.0, 1.0, 1.0, 0.0 ]
    light0_position       = [ -5.0, 1.0, 5.0, 0.0 ]
    # The 6 lines below create the lighting in the scene
    glEnable(GL_NORMALIZE)
    glEnable(GL_COLOR_MATERIAL)
    glEnable(GL_LIGHTING)
    glEnable(GL_LIGHT0)  # Create a light named "GL_LIGHT0"
    glLightfv(GL_LIGHT0, GL_POSITION, light0_position)
    glLightfv(GL_LIGHT0, GL_DIFFUSE,  diffuse_lite_kula_white)
    #/\/\/\/\/\/\/\/\/\/\/\/\/\/\/\/\/\/\/\/\/\/\/\/\/\/\/\
    glEnable(GL_DEPTH_TEST)
    glMatrixMode(GL_PROJECTION)
    glLoadIdentity()
    gluPerspective(45.0, float(Width)/float(Height), 0.1, 100.0)
    glMatrixMode(GL_MODELVIEW)

def DrawObject():
    """ All the objects to be drawn should be in this function.
        As far as possible there should be OpenGL instructions exclusively.
        Any calls to Python functions will slow rendering significantly.
        References to the names of vertex and normal arrays do not incur much of a penalty
```

```
"""
    global rotate_x, rotate_y
    glClear(GL_COLOR_BUFFER_BIT | GL_DEPTH_BUFFER_BIT)

    # Control of World Coordinates - the following 3 instructions.
    glLoadIdentity()
    glTranslatef(0.0,-0.6,-6.0)
    glRotatef(rotate_y, 0.0, 1.0, 0.0)
    glRotatef(rotate_x, 1.0, 0.0, 0.0)

    # Turn-on the vertex array processing
    glEnableClientState(GL_VERTEX_ARRAY)
    glEnableClientState(GL_NORMAL_ARRAY)

    # Display of 3D object: starry3tri
    glScale(2.0,  2.0,  2.0)
    glColor3f(0.6, 0.6, 1.0)                # Blue
    glVertexPointer(3, GL_FLOAT, 0, starry3tri)       #Arguments: (size, type, stride, pointer) .
    glNormalPointer(GL_FLOAT, 0, starry3tri_norm)  #Arguments: (type, stride, pointer).
    #glNormalPointer(GL_FLOAT, 0, starry3tri)   # Try this for blended shading.
    glDrawArrays(GL_TRIANGLES, 0, 3) # Arguments: (primitive type, starting index, number of vertices to
be rendered)

    # Turn-off the Vertex Array processing.
    glDisableClientState(GL_VERTEX_ARRAY)
    glDisableClientState(GL_NORMAL_ARRAY)

    rotate_y -= 0.05     # Rotation of the model world for display purposes.
    rotate_x += 0.005
    glutSwapBuffers()


def main():
    ''' Main Program.
    '''
    glutInit(sys.argv)
    glutInitWindowSize(400,400)    # Width,Height. The object gets scaled to the window.
    glutCreateWindow(b'Draw any object: OpenGL Vertices vertex Arrays')
    InitGL(400, 400)
    glutIdleFunc(DrawObject)         # Prepare the next frame during CPU idle time.
    glutMainLoop()

main()
```

Model Assembly and Construction

The Model-view idea of OpenGL is conceptually very similar to the idea of a model railway landscape layout shown above.

To understand OpenGL instructions we have to understand the design philosophy of how OpenGL places separate objects into a virtual world. A common term used for computer simulation/graphics for a virtual world is *model*. The idea is that the model is an assembly and arrangement of objects into a representation of part of a world, real or imagined. A model train layout within a small simulated landscape is one example.
We will create a small model called "dogs_world" using OpenGL vertex arrays.

We demonstrate the process of putting a model together using separate objects. We animate the model by continuously rotating it in order to see it from any position. We use the glModelView and glPerspective matrices to achieve this.

At the heart of OpenGL instructions are matrix operations. All control of objects, models and perspectives are achieved by matrix multiplication. There are four OpenGL matrices that are used and we are going to get acquainted with the first three. The fourth is dealt with in chapter 13 on lighting.
The four OpenGL matrices are:

The **model matrix** which specifies the position and orientation of an object in the modelspace. Each separate object has a matrix that places it into the correct position in model space. This matrix can combine a re-size operation, a rotation operation and a translation. Other slightly confusing names used for the model matrix are *world transform* or *object transform* or *global-space transform*. We will use **model matrix** because it embodies the idea that we shall be constructing a model, like a dolls house or a model train landscape.

The **view matrix** specifies where your "eye" or the camera capturing a view of the model is located in the scene. It must specify the direction and orientation of your line of sight. This may change from frame to frame, but it is always constant throughout the rendering for an individual frame.

The **projection matrix** essentially determines whether you are using a 3D or 2D view of the world – whether or not you have "perspective" in your view. In many applications, this is set up once and remains fixed for the entire application.

The **normal matrix** is used to calculate lighting. The lighting calculations performed by OpenGL use the normal vector to a surface (triangle) to determine how bright or dark to make pixels belonging to that surface and what other colors might be reflected off the particular pixel. In broad terms it is attached to a polygon (triangle) at right angles to the surface and it used in lighting calculations to determine how much light should bounce off the surface, to enter the eye or camera.

Surfaces Need Normals

In the programs that follow we always calculate and specify an array of normals that goes together with the vertices. Without a normal vector to match each vertex the GPU shading functions supply a uniform shade of color to each object. This is a bad idea as we can see in the two images below with the tree, the dog and the dog-house against a rising sun. The image with normals disabled is dark and uninteresting. The objects look flat and without depth. They show no gradations of light or shadow.

A normal vector to a plane surface such as a triangle is a vector at right angles to that surface. There are ways to handle curved surfaces but we will not deal with them for the sake of simplicity.
A unit normal is just a normal vector whose length has been adjusted to be one unit long. Mathematically we determine the normal as being the cross product of any two vectors in the plane of the object as long as the two vectors are not parallel. If we are only using triangles then any two edges will be in the plane of the triangle.

In the two images below the first image shows a normal vector calculated from the cross product of the triangle's edge AC (a vector) with the other edge AB. The product is written as AC x AB.
The second image shows the normal vector that results from the cross-product AB x AC

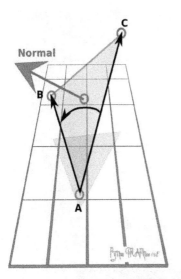 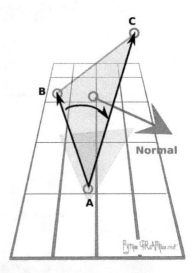

The Calculation of Normal Vectors

We are using triangles exclusively because, of all the possible plane polygons, they have the most robust properties. The most important property of triangles for us is that the vertices (points) of every triangle are always co-planar. No matter where we place the vertices in 3D space they will always be together on a perfectly flat plane. This makes calculation of the normal to the triangle a straight-forward bit of algebra. The method we use is to calculate the vector cross-product of any two vectors that lie along the edges of the triangle in question.

In the diagram above we will use the vectors AB and AC. What we see in the above diagrams is that the resulting normal vector will point in one direction for the product AB x AC and the opposite direction for the product AC x AB. This determines whether a triangle surface is reflecting light from it's surface or whether it is shadow.

```
def unit_normals(p,q,r):
    """ Compute the vector cross product from three vertices of a triangle.
        Three points are given by their position vectors p, q, and r.
        The result returned: The position vector of the unit normal
        to the plane containing the three points given.
    """
    vx1 = p[0] - r[0]  # x1 - x3.
    vy1 = p[1] - r[1]  # y1 - y3.
    vz1 = p[2] - r[2]  # z1 - z3.
```

```
vx2 = q[0] - r[0]  # x2 - x3.
vy2 = q[1] - r[1]  # y2 - y3.
vz2 = q[2] - r[2]  # z2 - z3.

vnx = vy1*vz2 - vz1*vy2
vny = vz1*vx2 - vx1*vz2
vnz = vx1*vy2 - vy1*vx2

len_vn = math.sqrt(vnx*vnx + vny*vny + vnz*vnz)
vnx = vnx/len_vn
vny = vny/len_vn
vnz = vnz/len_vn

return vnx, vny, vnz
```

A model assembled from 3D objects with normals enabled,
glEnable(GL_NORMAL)

The same model assembled from 3D objects without normals disabled.

Normals Made Visible

If normals are so important to the quality of our 3D images then we need a means of inspecting them in order to identify lighting flaws and understand our creative process.

How can we verify whether we have calculated our normals correctly?

One way is to see if our 3D objects look correct based on past experience. If we have not yet gained sufficient experience then we have a problem. The best way is to somehow *make* our normals visible. We want the normals to appear on the object as vector arrows or something similar. The arrow should be placed in the geometric center of the triangle and point in the direction of the normal. It's length can be one unit or any other visually convenient length. We have used long tapered folded triangles that clearly point in the same direction as the normal.

The structure of the Normal 'arrow' is produced by the three functions

tri_centroid(p,q,r), intersect(p1,p2, q1, q2) and
centroid_normals(vertex_array, dxy).

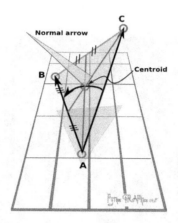

We construct the visible normal as follows:
1. Calculate the cross product of two vectors in the plane of the triangle.
2. Calculate the centroid of the triangle as the intersection of two lines joining a
   vertex of the triangle to the bisection point of the opposite side.
3. Draw the two slender triangles that comprise the normal arrow starting at the
   centroid and finishing a unit length (or other suitable proportion of this) away
   in the same direction as the normal.

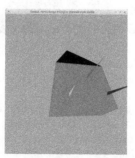

**Normal arrows in place on the triangles drawn from the vertex array
octet4tri.**

In the two diagrams on the right the top arrow is not visible because it's direction is
downward because the normal direction has been reversed by swapping the sequence
of two of the vertices defining that top triangle.

The following program was used to produce the drawings above.

```
"""
Program name: opengl_3D_visible_normals_1.py
Objective: Construct normals at the centroid of each face.

Keywords: OpenGL, triangle, normals, lighting.
============================================================================79
Comments: Each triangle face has its normal drawn on it pointing in the
positive direction.

Tested on: Python 2.6, Python 2.7.3, Python 3.2.3
Author:  Mike Ohlson de Fine
=====================================
"""

from OpenGL.GL import *
from OpenGL.GLUT import *
from OpenGL.GLU import *
import vector_2d3d_ops

rotation_y = 0.0
'''
octet4tri = [
-0.0, 0.7, 0.7,   -0.0, 1.0, 0.0,   -0.7, 0.7, 0.0,  # 1st triangle
-0.7, 0.0, 0.7,   -0.0, 0.7, 0.7,   -0.7, 0.7, 0.0,  # 2nd triangle
-0.0, 0.7, 0.7,   -0.7, 0.0, 0.7,   -0.0, 0.0, 1.0,  # 3rd triangle
-1.0, 0.0, 0.0,   -0.7, 0.0, 0.7,   -0.7, 0.7, 0.0 ] # 4th triangle
'''

octet4tri = [
-0.0, 0.7, 0.7,   -0.7, 0.7, 0.0,   -0.0, 1.0, 0.0,   # 1st triangle - sequence change. Reverses normal.
-0.7, 0.0, 0.7,   -0.0, 0.7, 0.7,   -0.7, 0.7, 0.0,   # 2nd triangle
-0.0, 0.7, 0.7,   -0.7, 0.0, 0.7,   -0.0, 0.0, 1.0,   # 3rd triangle
-1.0, 0.0, 0.0,   -0.7, 0.0, 0.7,   -0.7, 0.7, 0.0 ] # 4th triangle

#==============================================================
octet4tri_vertices = len(octet4tri)/3
print ( 'octet4tri_vertices: ', octet4tri_vertices)
octet4tri_norm = vector_2d3d_ops.array_triangle_normals(octet4tri)

octet4tri_arrows = vector_2d3d_ops.centroid_normals(octet4tri, 0.05)
octet4tri_arrows_vertices = len(octet4tri_arrows)/3
print ( 'octet4tri_arrows_vertices: ', octet4tri_arrows_vertices )
octet4tri_arrows_norm = vector_2d3d_ops.array_triangle_normals(octet4tri_arrows)
#==============================================================
def InitGL(Width, Height):
    """ Initialize and setup the Graphics Software/Hardware pipeline.
    """

    # Note - the value of the fourth parameter is immaterial for diffuse light.
    diffuse_lite_kula_white  = [1.0, 1.0, 1.0, 0.0]
    light0_position  = [ 5.0, 1.0, 5.0, 0.0 ]
    glClearColor(0.6, 0.6, 1.0, 0.0)
    # /\/\/\/\/\/\/\/\/\/\/\/\/\/\/\/\/\/\/\/\/\/\/\/\
    glEnable(GL_NORMALIZE)
    glEnable(GL_COLOR_MATERIAL)
    glEnable(GL_LIGHTING)
    glEnable(GL_LIGHT0)
```

```
glLightfv(GL_LIGHT0, GL_POSITION, light0_position)
glLightfv(GL_LIGHT0, GL_DIFFUSE,  diffuse_lite_kula_white)
#∧∧∧∧∧∧∧∧∧∧∧∧∧∧∧∧∧∧∧∧∧∧∧∧∧∧∧∧∧∧∧∧∧∧∧∧∧∧∧
glEnable(GL_DEPTH_TEST)
glMatrixMode(GL_PROJECTION)
glLoadIdentity()
gluPerspective(45.0, float(Width)/float(Height), 0.1, 100.0)
glMatrixMode(GL_MODELVIEW)

def Octocapsule():
    """ A four triangle open surface with normal arrows.
    """
    global rotation_y
    glClear(GL_COLOR_BUFFER_BIT | GL_DEPTH_BUFFER_BIT)

    # Enable vertex arrays
    glEnableClientState(GL_VERTEX_ARRAY)
    glEnableClientState(GL_NORMAL_ARRAY)

    # 1 first octant of Vertex arrays
    glLoadIdentity()
    glTranslatef(0.0,  -0.4,  -3.0)
    glRotatef(rotation_y, 0.0, 1.0, 0.0)
    glScale(1.0,  1.0,  1.0)
    glColor3f(1.0, 0.0, 0.0)            # Red
    glVertexPointer(3, GL_FLOAT, 0, octet4tri)    # (size, type, stride, pointer)
    glNormalPointer(GL_FLOAT, 0, octet4tri_norm)   # (type, stride, pointer).
    glDrawArrays(GL_TRIANGLES, 0, 12) # (primitive type, starting index, number of vertices to be rendered)

    # Yellow visible normal arrows/spikes.
    glColor3f(1.0, 1.0, 0.0)
    glVertexPointer(3, GL_FLOAT, 0, octet4tri_arrows)     # (size, type, stride, pointer)
    glNormalPointer(GL_FLOAT, 0, octet4tri_arrows_norm)   # (type, stride, pointer).
    glDrawArrays(GL_TRIANGLES, 0, 24) # (primitive type, starting index, number of vertices to be rendered)

    # Disable vertex arrays.
    glDisableClientState(GL_VERTEX_ARRAY)
    glDisableClientState(GL_NORMAL_ARRAY)

    rotation_y += 0.02  # Slow rotation around the y-axis.
    glutSwapBuffers()


def main():
    ''' Main Program.
    '''
    glutInit(sys.argv)
    glutInitWindowSize(600,600)    # Width, Height. Line gets scaled to the window.
    glutCreateWindow(b'OpenGL Vertex Arrays Triangles: Normals made visible')
    InitGL(600, 600)
    glutIdleFunc(Octocapsule)      # During idle time redraw the frame.
    glutMainLoop()

main()
```

Normals on an object composed of many triangles: The arrows all point inward because the normals are 'negative'. They can be altered to be positive either by exchanging the sequence of any two vertices defining each triangle or by altering the sequence of vectors in the cross- product function used to calculate the normals.

The functions needed to locate the centroid and assemble the vertices for the arrows are

- A function to find the position of the geometric center of the triangle under consideration,
- A function that calculates the point of intersection of two line segments given by their end points (vertices),
- A function that provides the vertex array that is used to draw the normal vector arrow whose base is at the centroid of the triangle and which points in the direction of the normal.

These functions are **tri_centroid(p,q,r)**, **intersect(p1,p2, q1, q2)** and **centroid_normals(vertex_array, dxy)**, and are given below.

They are incorporated into the **vector_2d3d_ops.py** module.

Centroids (geometric center of a triangle)

```
def tri_centroid(p,q,r):
    """ Locate the centroid of a triangle.
    The intersection of the lines joining a vertex
    with the mid-point of the opposite side is computed.
    Arguments: three vertices of a triangle.
    """
    # Mid-points of p-q and p-r.
    # Distances point-to-point.
    vx1 = r[0] - p[0]  # x1 - x3.
    vy1 = r[1] - p[1]  # y1 - y3.
    vz1 = r[2] - p[2]  # z1 - z3.

    vx2 = q[0] - p[0]  # x2 - x1.
    vy2 = q[1] - p[1]  # y2 - y1.
    vz2 = q[2] - p[2]  # z2 - z1.
```

```
        # Mid-points of p-q (position vector).
        pqx_mp = p[0] + vx2/2.0
        pqy_mp = p[1] + vy2/2.0
        pqz_mp = p[2] + vz2/2.0
        pq_mp = [pqx_mp, pqy_mp, pqz_mp ]

        # Mid-points of p-r (position vector).
        prx_mp = p[0] + vx1/2.0
        pry_mp = p[1] + vy1/2.0
        prz_mp = p[2] + vz1/2.0

        pr_mp = [prx_mp, pry_mp, prz_mp ]

        # Intersection.
        xi, yi, zi = intersect(r,pq_mp, q, pr_mp)
        return xi, yi, zi
```

Arrow of the Normal Vector

```
def centroid_normals(vertex_array, dxy):
    """ Calculate the vertex normal for each face, repeat it three times to furnish a Normal for each
        vertex of the triangle in the vertex array. The output is the target glNormaArray.
    """
    norm_arrows = []
    for i in range (0, len(vertex_array), 9): # Number of triangles
        # Each sequence of 9 floats from vertex_array supplies three vertices v1, v2, v3
        a1 = vertex_array[i]       # first vertex.
        a2 = vertex_array[i+1]
        a3 = vertex_array[i+2]
        v1 = [ a1,a2,a3]

        b1 = vertex_array[i+3]     # second vertex.
        b2 = vertex_array[i+4]
        b3 = vertex_array[i+5]
        v2 = [ b1,b2,b3]

        c1 = vertex_array[i+6]     # third vertex.
        c2 = vertex_array[i+7]
        c3 = vertex_array[i+8]
        v3 = [ c1,c2,c3]

        vnor = half_unit_normals(v1, v2, v3)
        vcen = tri_centroid(v1, v2, v3)
        vsum = [vnor[0]+vcen[0], vnor[1]+vcen[1], vnor[2]+vcen[2] ]
        # Now we produce twl triangles that point in the direction of the normal.
        # each must be added to an array of normal spikes - which are visible normals.

        tris = [ vcen[0], vcen[1], vcen[2],   vcen[0]+dxy, vcen[1], vcen[2],   vsum[0], vsum[1], vsum[2],
            vcen[0], vcen[1], vcen[2],   vcen[0], vcen[1]+dxy, vcen[2],   vsum[0], vsum[1], vsum[2 ] ]
        norm_arrows.append(tris)
    norm_arrows = list(itertools.chain(*norm_arrows))    # Ensure the array has been flattened.
```

```
return norm_arrows
```

Intersection of Two Lines

```python
def intersect(p1,p2, q1, q2):
    """ Intersection of 2 lines in 3D cartesian space. The lines should be coplanar.
    Inputs are the position vectors of two points on each line.
    There should be a test to confirm the the the two lines are co-planar,
    prior to any solution being computed. For the time being
    we will assume the lines are coplanar.
    """

    px1 = p1[0]
    py1 = p1[1]
    pz1 = p1[2]

    px2 = p2[0]
    py2 = p2[1]
    pz2 = p2[2]

    qx1 = q1[0]
    qy1 = q1[1]
    qz1 = q1[2]

    qx2 = q2[0]
    qy2 = q2[1]
    qz2 = q2[2]

    # Slopes
    # Q1: Are any divisors zero? ie. are lines paralell?
    if (px2 - px1) == 0:
        divsr_mp_xy = 0.000000001
    else: divsr_mp_xy = (px2 - px1)

    if (pz2 - pz1) == 0:
        divsr_mp_zy = 0.000000001

    else: divsr_mp_zy = (pz2 - pz1)

    if (qx2 - qx1) == 0:
        divsr_mq_xy = 0.000000001
    else: divsr_mq_xy = (qx2 - qx1)

    if (qz2 - qz1) == 0:
        divsr_mq_zy = 0.000000001
    else: divsr_mq_zy = (qz2 - qz1)

    mp_xy = (py2 - py1)/divsr_mp_xy
    mp_zy = (py2 - py1)/divsr_mp_zy

    mq_xy = (qy2 - qy1)/divsr_mq_xy
    mq_zy = (qy2 - qy1)/divsr_mq_zy
```

```
# Intercepts - constants.
cp_xy = py1 -mp_xy*px1
cp_zy = py1 -mp_zy*pz1

cq_xy = qy1 -mq_xy*qx1
cq_zy = qy1 -mq_zy*qz1

# Intersection in the x-y plane (ie. Projection onto the x-y plane.).
if (mp_xy - mq_xy) == 0:
    divsr_m = 0.000000001
else: divsr_m = (mp_xy - mq_xy)

xi = (cq_xy - cp_xy)/divsr_m

yi = xi*mp_xy +cp_xy

if (mp_zy - mq_zy) == 0:
    divsr_m = 0.000000001
else: divsr_m = (mp_zy - mq_zy)
zi = (cq_zy - cp_zy)/divsr_m

return xi, yi, zi
```

11

OpenGL: Model Construction and Assembly

*"Each of us is carving a stone, erecting a column, or cutting a piece of stained glass in the construction of something much bigger than ourselves. "*Adrienne Clarkson

Topics we cover in this chapter:
- **Construction of a Model**
- **Relating Multiple Reference Coordinates**
- **Constructing Symmetrical Objects from Small Chunks**
- **An Articulated Hand as a Model**
- **The Smartness of Push and Pop**
- **Deprecation**

We will explore how to place objects together inside a scene like actors and props on a stage or a movie set. This is a model making activity similar to what model train hobbyists do when they put together scenery around their model railways. We will then explore how to relate different models to each other in a common world.

The trick to understanding model construction in OpenGL is to understand how the matrix operations change geometry. We do not need to understand any detail of the mathematical working of matrix algebra. We only need to understand how the sequence of instructions affect our model assembly. There are two geometry transformations that are key to object placement within a model: rotation and translation. We will construct a small model of a dog and it's immediate environment. After this we will construction of a model solar system with a planet and a moon to demonstrate how moving geometries can be coordinated.

Construction of a Model

We are going to assemble some 3D objects and position them inside a model landscape that we construct and then we will view them from different vantage points.
Each of the objects is specified by it's own individual coordinates that are unique to its own personal or local reference axes. To construct the model landscape we have to scale, rotate and translate each object.

The objects will be:
- a rectangular piece of 'grass'
- a dog
- a dog house or kennel (walls only)
- the roof of the kennel
- a tree
- a tree trunk
- a backdrop showing a sunrise.

These objects will be placed relative to each other as a model and then we will display the complete model and rotate it as a single unit.
The separate objects were created using Blender and exported as wavefront.obj files. The Wavefront files were converted to vertex arrays.

The vertex arrays corresponding to each object are given here:

floor3 = [-0.88, 2.478, 1.07, 0.99, 2.51, 1.07, 1.0, 0.16, 1.07, 0.93, 0.16, 1.07, -0.96, 0.16, 1.07, -0.97, 2.47, 1.07]

backwall3 = [-0.36, -0.07, -0.97, -0.76, -0.06, -0.72, -0.19, 0.08, 0.56, -0.95, 0.04, 0.11, -0.27, 0.10, 0.73, -0.82, -0.04, -0.58, -0.28, 0.12, 0.87, -0.95, 0.03, 0.18, -0.88, 0.07, 0.78, 0.5, -0.05, -0.78, 0.29, -0.05, -0.94, 0.02, 0.09, 0.59, 0.12, 0.09, 0.62, 0.78, -0.06, -0.60, 0.62, -0.05, -0.76, 0.22, 0.11, 0.86, 0.79, 0.10, 0.86, 0.91, 0.02, -0.13, 0.91, 0.01, -0.24, 0.82, -0.03, -0.56, 0.18, 0.09, 0.70, 0.19, -0.06, -0.94, -0.28, -0.06, -0.95, -0.08, 0.09, 0.58]

dog3 = [0.23, 0.05, -0.0, 0.47, 0.10, -0.0, 0.43, -0.20, -0.11, 0.25, 0.04, 0.03, 0.50, 0.09, 0.02, 0.38, -0.25, 0.11, 0.33, -0.23, 0.0, 0.40, 0.13, 0.01, 0.81, -0.11, -0.0, 0.4, 0.13, 0.01, 0.85, 0.06, -0.0, 0.81, -0.11, -0.0, 0.11, -1.05, 0.15, 0.07, -0.34, 0.01, 0.21, -0.34, 0.01, 0.078, -0.34, -0.04, 0.21, -0.34, -0.04, 0.27, -1.05, -0.20, -0.56, -0.09, -0.0, 0.29, -0.37, -0.0, -0.55, -0.42, -0.0, -0.76, -0.33, -0.07, -0.54, -0.12, -0.03, -0.61, -1.04, -0.10, 0.29, -0.37, -0.0, -0.56, -0.09, -0.0, 0.40, 0.13, 0.01, -0.76, -0.33, 0.06, -0.54, -0.12, 0.02, -0.61, -1.04, 0.09, -0.54, -0.09, 0.01, -0.6, -0.22, 0.0, -0.89, 0.26, 0.02]

kennelwalls3 = [-0.62, -0.99, -0.62, 0.62, -0.99, -0.62, -0.62, 0.24, -0.62, -0.62, 0.23, 0.61, 0.62, -0.99, 0.61, 0.62, 0.24, 0.61, 0.62, -0.99, -0.6, 0.62, 0.24, -0.62, -0.62, 0.24, -0.62, -0.62, 0.23, 0.61, -0.62, -0.99, 0.61, 0.62, -0.99, 0.61, 0.62, 0.24, -0.62, 0.62, -0.99, -0.62, 0.62, -0.99, 0.61, 0.62, -0.99, 0.61, 0.62, 0.24, 0.61, 0.62, 0.24, -0.62]

kennelroof3 = [0.93, 0.99, -0.01, -0.93, 0.99, -0.01, 0.93, -0.06, -0.94, -0.93, 0.99, -0.01, -0.93, -0.06, -0.94, 0.93, -0.06, -0.94, -0.93, -0.06, 0.91, 0.93, 0.99, -0.01, 0.93, -0.06, 0.91, -0.93, -0.06, 0.91, 0.93, 0.99, -0.01, -0.93, 0.99, -0.01]

treetop3 = [0.49, -0.0, 0.29, 0.0, 1.59, 0.01, 0.48, -0.0, -0.26, 0.0, 1.59, 0.0, 0.0, -0.0, -0.54, 0.48, -0.0, -0.26, 0.0, 1.59, 0.015817, 0.0, -0.0, -0.54, -0.48, 0.0, -0.26, 0.0, 0.0, 0.57, 0.0, 1.59, 0.01, 0.49, 0.0, 0.29, -0.47, 0.0, 0.29, 0.0, 1.59, 0.01, -0.48, 0.0, -0.26, 0.0, 1.59, 0.01, -0.47, 0.0, 0.29, 0.0, 0.0, 0.57]

The Python program to assemble and display the model 'dogsworld' is given below.
Note that the two functions used for calculating the normal vertex arrays are held in
the module **vector_2d3d_ops.py**

```
"""
Program name: opengl_dogsworld_vertex_arrays_1.py
Objective: Assemble and move a miniature world made of several objects.

Keywords: OpenGL, triangle, objects, world model, normals, lighting.
=================================================================================79
Comments:

Tested on: Python 2.6, Python 2.7.3, Python 3.2.3
```

Author: Mike Ohlson de Fine
=====================================
"""

```python
from OpenGL.GL import *
from OpenGL.GLUT import *
from OpenGL.GLU import *
import vector_2d3d_ops
#===========================================================
# Lighting parameters. - the value of the fourth parameter is immaterial for diffuse light.
diffuse_lite_kula_white  = [1.0, 1.0, 1.0, 0.0]
light0_position  = [ 5.0, 1.0, 5.0, 0.0 ]
#===========================================================
# Model (world) rotation variables.
rotate_angle_y = 0.0
rotate_angle_x = 0.0
#===========================================================
# Objects in the world. Determine how many triangles and create normals.
dog3_faces = len(dog3)/3
print 'len dog3:', dog3_faces
dog3_norm = vector_2d3d_ops.array_triangle_normals(dog3)

kennelroof3_faces = len(kennelroof3)/3
print 'len kennelroof3:', kennelroof3_faces
kennelroof3_norm = vector_2d3d_ops.array_triangle_normals(kennelroof3)

kennelwalls3_faces = len(kennelwalls3)/3
print 'len kennelwalls3:', kennelwalls3_faces
kennelwalls3_norm = vector_2d3d_ops.array_triangle_normals(kennelwalls3)

treetop3_faces = len(treetop3)/3
print 'len treetop3:' ,treetop3_faces
treetop3_norm = vector_2d3d_ops.array_triangle_normals(treetop3)

backwall3_faces = len(backwall3)/3
print 'len backwall3:' ,backwall3_faces
backwall3_norm = vector_2d3d_ops.array_triangle_normals(backwall3)

floor3_faces = len(floor3)/3
print 'len floor3:' ,floor3_faces
floor3_norm = vector_2d3d_ops.array_triangle_normals(floor3)
#===========================================================
def InitGL(Width, Height):
    """ Initialize and setup the Graphics Software/Hardware pipeline.
    """

    glClearColor(0.0, 0.0, 0.0, 0.0)
    # /\/\/\/\/\/\/\/\/\/\/\/\/\/\/\/\/\/\/\/\/\/\/\/\/\/
    # The 6 lines below create the lighting (from a single light "LIGHT0") in the model scene.
    glEnable(GL_NORMALIZE)
    glEnable(GL_COLOR_MATERIAL)
    glEnable(GL_LIGHTING)

    glEnable(GL_LIGHT0)
    glLightfv(GL_LIGHT0, GL_POSITION, light0_position)
    glLightfv(GL_LIGHT0, GL_DIFFUSE,  diffuse_lite_kula_white)
    #/\/\/\/\/\/\/\/\/\/\/\/\/\/\/\/\/\/\/\/\/\/\/\/\/\/
    glEnable(GL_DEPTH_TEST)
    glMatrixMode(GL_PROJECTION)
```

```python
glLoadIdentity()
gluPerspective(45.0, float(Width)/float(Height), 0.1, 100.0)
glMatrixMode(GL_MODELVIEW)

def DrawDogsWorld():
    """ Dog's World is composed of a floor with a sunrise mural backdrop.
        Within it a dog, his house and a fir tree. The whole world rotates   as a unit - as if it were on the surface of
a planet.
    """
    global rotate_angle_x, rotate_angle_y
    glClear(GL_COLOR_BUFFER_BIT | GL_DEPTH_BUFFER_BIT)

    # Control of the Model Coordinates (Dog's World Coordinates)
    # - the following 5 instructions:
    glLoadIdentity()
    glTranslatef(0.5,0.4,-6.0)
    glRotatef(90.0, 1.0, 0.0, 0.0)
    glRotatef(rotate_angle_y,  0.0, 0.0, 1.0)
    glRotatef(rotate_angle_x,  1.0, 0.0, 0.0)

    # Turn-on the vertex array processing
    glEnableClientState(GL_VERTEX_ARRAY)
    glEnableClientState(GL_NORMAL_ARRAY)

    # 1 - Sunrise_rays
    glColor3f(1.0, 1.0, 0.1)            # Yellow
    glVertexPointer(3, GL_FLOAT, 0, backwall3)
    glNormalPointer(GL_FLOAT, 0, backwall3_norm)
    glDrawArrays(GL_TRIANGLES, 0, 24)

    # 2 - Grass_floor
    glColor3f(0.4, 0.6, 0.1)            # Green
    glVertexPointer(3, GL_FLOAT, 0, floor3)
    #glNormalPointer(GL_FLOAT, 0, floor3_norm)
    glNormalPointer(GL_FLOAT, 0, floor3)
    glDrawArrays(GL_TRIANGLES, 0, 6)

    # 3 - Dog
    glRotatef(-90.0, 1.0, 0.0, 0.0)
    glTranslatef(0.5, -0.4, 1.8)
    glScale(0.6,  0.6,  0.6)
    glColor3f(0.8, 0.1, 0.1)            # Brown
    glVertexPointer(3, GL_FLOAT, 0, dog3)
    glNormalPointer(GL_FLOAT, 0, dog3)
    #glNormalPointer(GL_FLOAT, 0, dog3_norm)
    glDrawArrays(GL_TRIANGLES, 0, 33)

    # 4 - Kennel roof
    glTranslatef(0.0, -0.1, -1.6)
    glScale(1.0,  1.0,  1.0)
    glColor3f(0.5, 0.5, 1.0)            # Blue
    glVertexPointer(3, GL_FLOAT, 0, kennelroof3)
    glNormalPointer(GL_FLOAT, 0, kennelroof3)
    #glNormalPointer(GL_FLOAT, 0, kennelroof3_norm)
    glDrawArrays(GL_TRIANGLES, 0, 12)

    # 5 - kennel walls
```

182

```python
glColor3f(0.8, 0.8, 0.8)                # White
glVertexPointer(3, GL_FLOAT, 0, kennelwalls3)
glNormalPointer(GL_FLOAT, 0, kennelwalls3)
#glNormalPointer(GL_FLOAT, 0, kennelwalls3_norm)
glDrawArrays(GL_TRIANGLES, 0, 18)

# 6 - Treetop (foliage)
glTranslatef(-2.1, 0.5, 1.0)
glScale(2.0,  2.0,  2.0)
glColor3f(0.0, 1.0, 0.1)                # Green
glVertexPointer(3, GL_FLOAT, 0, treetop3)
glNormalPointer(GL_FLOAT, 0, treetop3)
#glNormalPointer(GL_FLOAT, 0, treetop3_norm)
glDrawArrays(GL_TRIANGLES, 0, 18)

# 7 - Tree-trunk (similar shape to foliage)
glColor3f(0.9, 0.3, 0.3)                # Brown
glTranslatef(0.0, -0.75, 0.0)
glScale(0.2,  1.0,  0.2)
glVertexPointer(3, GL_FLOAT, 0, treetop3)
glNormalPointer(GL_FLOAT, 0, treetop3)
#glNormalPointer(GL_FLOAT, 0, treetop3_norm)
glDrawArrays(GL_TRIANGLES, 0, 18)

# Turn-off the Vertex Array processing.
glDisableClientState(GL_VERTEX_ARRAY)
glDisableClientState(GL_NORMAL_ARRAY)

rotate_angle_y += 0.05    # Rotation of the model world.
rotate_angle_x += 0.001
glutSwapBuffers()


def main():
    ''' Main Program.
    '''
    glutInit(sys.argv)
    glutInitWindowSize(1000,1000)    # W,H. Line gets scaled to the window.
    glutCreateWindow('Draw DogsWorld using OpenGL Vertex Arrays. Normals enabled')
    InitGL(1000, 1000)
    glutIdleFunc(DrawDogsWorld)      # When we are doing nothing, redraw the scene.
    glutMainLoop()

main()
```

The assembled model. **Normals enabled.**

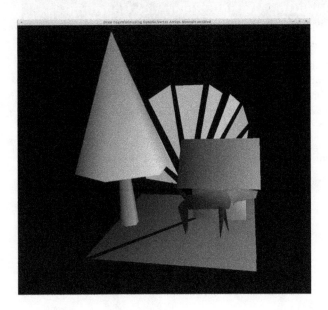

The assembled model. **Normals disabled.**
Without any normals. The colors lack shading that gives visual depth to the images.

Relating Multiple Reference Coordinates

Now we construct a small solar system that consists of:
- a central star, rotating about it's own central axis,
- a planet orbiting the star and spinning around its own local central axis,
- a moon that orbits the planet, spinning around it's own center,
- a spacecraft orbiting the moon.

A Planetary System: There are five bodies. Each spins around it's own axis.

Two craft orbit a moon. The moon orbits a planet and the planet orbits a star.

```
"""
Program name: opengl_planetary_system_1.py
Objective: Construct a simplified solar system with moon and spacecraft.

Keywords: OpenGL, triangle, normals, lighting, sun, planets, orbits.
=================================================================================79
Comments: Control of multiple orbiting bodies, spinning independently.

Tested on: Python 2.7.3, Python 3.2.3
Author:  Mike Ohlson de Fine
==================================
"""

from OpenGL.GL import *
from OpenGL.GLUT import *
from OpenGL.GLU import *
import vector_2d3d_ops
import itertools
import math
import copy
```

cube_triangles_1 = [1.0, 1.0, -1.0, 1.0, 1.0, 1.0, -1.0, 1.0, 1.0, -1.0, 1.0, -1.0, 1.0, 1.0, -1., -1.0, 1.0, 1.0, -1.0, -1.0,
1.0, -1.0, 1.0, -1.0, -1.0, 1.0, 1.0, -1.0, -1.0, -1.0, 1.0, -1.0, 1.0, -1.0, -1.0, 1.0, -1.0, 1.0, 1.0, -1.0, 1.0, -1.0, -1.0, 1.0, 1.0, -1.0,
-1.0, -1.0, -1.0, -1.0, -1.0, 1.0, -1.0, -1.0, 1.0, -1.0, 1.0, 1.0, -1.0, 1.0, -1.0, -1.0, 1.0, -1.0, 1.0, 1.0, -1.0, 1.0, 1.0, 1.,
1.0, 1.0, 1.0, -1.0, 1.0, -1.0, -1.0, -1.0, 1.0, -1.0, -1.0, 1.0, 1.0, -1.0, 1.0, 1.0, -1.0, -1.0, 1.0, -1.0, -1.0, -1.0, -1.0,
1.0, -1.0, -1.0, 1.0, 1.0, -1.0, 1.0, 1.0, 1.0, 1., 1.0, 1.0, 1.0, -1.0, 1.0, 1.0, -1.0, -1.0]

rotation_orbit = 0.0
rotation_spin = 0.0
#===
# Note - the value of the fourth parameter is immaterial for diffuse light.
diffuse_lite_kula_white = [1.0, 1.0, 1.0, 0.0]
light0_position   = [5.0, 1.0, 5.0, 0.0]
yellow_k   = [1.0 ,1.0, 0.0]
blue_k   = [0.0 ,0.0, 1.0]
moon_blue_k = [0.4 ,0.4, 1.0]
red_k   = [1.0 ,0.4, 0.4]
green_k   = [0.4, 1.0, 0.4]

def unit_normals(p,q,r):
    """ Compute the vector cross-product of vectors drawn between three points.
    Three points are given by their position vectors p, q, and r.
    Compute the vector cross product from three vertices of a triangle.
    The result returned: The position vector of the unit normal
    to the plane containing the three points given.
    """

    vx1 = p[0] - r[0] # x1 - x3.
    vy1 = p[1] - r[1] # y1 - y3.
    vz1 = p[2] - r[2] # z1 - z3.

    vx2 = q[0] - r[0] # x2 - x3.
    vy2 = q[1] - r[1] # y2 - y3.
    vz2 = q[2] - r[2] # z2 - z3.

    vnx = vy1*vz2 - vz1*vy2
    vny = vz1*vx2 - vx1*vz2
    vnz = vx1*vy2 - vy1*vx2

    len_vn = math.sqrt(vnx*vnx + vny*vny + vnz*vnz)
    if len_vn == 0:
        vnx = 0
        vny = 0
        vnz = 0
    else:
        vnx = vnx/len_vn
        vny = vny/len_vn
        vnz = vnz/len_vn
    return vnx, vny, vnz

def array_triangle_normals(vertex_array):
    """ Calculate the vertex normal for each face, repeat it three times to furnish a Normal for each
    vertex of the triangle in the vertex array. The output is the target glNormaArray.
    """

    norm_array = []
    for i in range (0, len(vertex_array), 9): # Number of triangles
        # Each sequence of 9 floats from vertex_array supplies three vertices v1, v2, v3
        a1 = vertex_array[i]   # first vertex.
        a2 = vertex_array[i+1]

```
        a3 = vertex_array[i+2]
        v1 = [ a1,a2,a3]

        b1 = vertex_array[i+3]      # second vertex.
        b2 = vertex_array[i+4]
        b3 = vertex_array[i+5]
        v2 = [ b1,b2,b3]

        c1 = vertex_array[i+6]      # third vertex.
        c2 = vertex_array[i+7]
        c3 = vertex_array[i+8]
        v3 = [ c1,c2,c3]

        vec_norm = unit_normals(v1, v2, v3)
        norm_array.append(vec_norm)                     # Set stride to 0 to match each face to a normal.
        norm_array.append(vec_norm)
        norm_array.append(vec_norm)
    norm_array = list(itertools.chain(*norm_array))     # Ensure the array has been flattened.

    return norm_array

#========================================================
# Cube planet made of triangles. 36 faces.
cube_triangles_1_faces = len(cube_triangles_1)/3
print ('cube_triangles_1_faces: ', cube_triangles_1_faces)
cube_triangles_1_norm = array_triangle_normals(cube_triangles_1)
#========================================================
def InitGL(Width, Height):
    """ Initialize and setup the Graphics Software/Hardware pipeline.
    """
    glClearColor(1.0, 1.0, 1.0, 0.0)
    # ∧∧∧∧∧∧∧∧∧∧∧∧∧∧∧∧∧∧∧∧∧∧∧∧∧∧∧∧∧∧∧∧∧
    glEnable(GL_NORMALIZE)
    glEnable(GL_COLOR_MATERIAL)
    glEnable(GL_LIGHTING)
    glEnable(GL_LIGHT0)
    glLightfv(GL_LIGHT0, GL_POSITION, light0_position)
    glLightfv(GL_LIGHT0, GL_DIFFUSE,   diffuse_lite_kula_white)
    #∧∧∧∧∧∧∧∧∧∧∧∧∧∧∧∧∧∧∧∧∧∧∧∧∧∧∧∧∧∧∧∧∧∧
    glEnable(GL_DEPTH_TEST)
    glMatrixMode(GL_PROJECTION)
    glLoadIdentity()
    gluPerspective(45.0, float(Width)/float(Height), 0.1, 100.0)
    glMatrixMode(GL_MODELVIEW)

def draw_planet(num_vertices, vertex_array, norm_array, kula):
    glColor3f(kula[0], kula[1], kula[2] )
    glEnableClientState(GL_VERTEX_ARRAY)
    glEnableClientState(GL_NORMAL_ARRAY)
    glVertexPointer(3, GL_FLOAT, 0, vertex_array)       # (size, type, stride, pointer)
    glNormalPointer(GL_FLOAT, 0, vertex_array)          # (type, stride, pointer).
    glDrawArrays(GL_TRIANGLES, 0, num_vertices)         # (primitive type, starting index, number of indices
(vertices?) to be rendered)

    glColor3f(kula[0], kula[1], kula[2])
    glVertexPointer(3, GL_FLOAT, 0, vertex_array)
    glNormalPointer(GL_FLOAT, 0, norm_array)
```

```
        glDrawArrays(GL_TRIANGLES, 0, num_vertices)

        glDisableClientState(GL_VERTEX_ARRAY)
        glDisableClientState(GL_NORMAL_ARRAY)


def DrawGLScene():
    """ Test each primitive. For each primitive to be tested, un-comment the relevant line.
    Ensure all the others are commented out to keep the situation simple.
    """
    global rotation_orbit, rotation_spin
    glClear(GL_COLOR_BUFFER_BIT | GL_DEPTH_BUFFER_BIT)

    # Sun - 1
    glLoadIdentity()
    glTranslatef(0.0,  0.0,  -18.0)
    glRotatef(-rotation_spin*20.0, 0.0, 0.0, 1.0)
    glScale(1.0,  1.0,  1.0)
    draw_planet(24, cube_triangles_1,cube_triangles_1, yellow_k)

    # 2: Earth Cube.
    glLoadIdentity()
    glRotatef(rotation_orbit*16.0, 0.0, 0.0, 1.0)  # Orbital rotation.
    glTranslatef(5.0,  0.0,  -18.0)
    glRotatef(-rotation_spin*120.0, 0.0, 0.0, 1.0) # Axis spin.
    glScale(0.5,  0.5,  0.5)
    draw_planet(36, cube_triangles_1, cube_triangles_1, blue_k)

    # 2.2: Moon Cube. note order of execution is 1st translate then rotate (counterintuitive to instruction order
    #      This is because it is achieved through matrix multiplication.
    glRotatef(rotation_orbit*64.0, 0.0, 0.0, 1.0) # Orbital rotation moon orbits earth 4 times per solar year.
    glTranslatef(4.0,  0.0,  0.0)
    #glRotatef() # Axis spin - same as earth -> earth always sees te same side of the moon.
    glScale(0.5,  0.5,  0.5)
    draw_planet(36, cube_triangles_1, cube_triangles_1, moon_blue_k)

    # Lunar module 1 orbiting around the moon.
    glRotatef(rotation_orbit*128.0, 0.0, 0.0, 1.0)
    glTranslatef(2.5,  0.0,  0.0)
    glScale(0.5,  0.5,  0.5)
    draw_planet(36, cube_triangles_1, cube_triangles_1, red_k)

    # Lunar module 2 on opposite side of the moon.
    glTranslatef(-9.5,  0.0,  0.0)
    glRotatef(180.0, 0.0, 0.0, 1.0)
    glScale(0.8,  0.8,  0.8)
    draw_planet(36, cube_triangles_1, cube_triangles_1, green_k)

    rotation_orbit -= 0.01
    rotation_spin += 0.003
    glutSwapBuffers()

def main():
    ''' Main Program.
    '''
    glutInit(sys.argv)
    glutInitWindowSize(600,600)    #  W,H. Line gets scaled to the window.
```

```
glutCreateWindow('OpenGL Vertex Arrays from Primitive Triangles: Sun, Planets and Spacecraft')
InitGL(600, 600)
glutIdleFunc(DrawGLScene)      # Update the frames when processor has spare time.
glutMainLoop()

main()
```

Construct Symmetrical Objects from Small Chunks

Here we construct a relatively complex object by assembling it, at runtime, from a simpler component. Our simple object is a four sided portion of an enclosed 32-sided solid.

There are two important things the constructing programmer must ensure.

The first and most important is that the octant (one-eigth portion) is located so that it requires no translation operations to rotate it into place in order for its edges to align precisely with its neighbours. Secondly we need to keep track of exactly which rotation transformations are applied. We do not want a situation where we have increasingly long sequences of operations that are difficult to fault find. The simplest way to achieve this is by starting from the beginning with each of the eight segments. This is achieved simply by placing *glLoadIdentity()* at the start of each separate octant positioning operation.

The price we pay for this clarity of operation is that there is redundancy of instructions as well as of operation. With each rendering operation for each frame, every single octant is translated, sized and rotated afresh. This requires around 40 matrix multiplications. The number of multiplications could possibly be reduced to about 10 if the process were optimized. However we want to emphasize clarity, simplicity and ease of understanding as far as possible.

The octant (eigth portion) of a solid enclosed with 32 triangles.

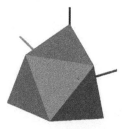

The initial position allows the other seven components to enclose the figure by applying only rotation transformations.

An exploded view of eight components.

Start Off with Good Position of the Octant

Good positioning means that pure rotations, without translations, will place each one of the 8 octants into position without any further adjustmnet required. This is achieved by careful positioning of the object in Blender when the object is originally being created.

The wireframe octant. The initial position allows the other seven components to enclose the figure by applying only rotation about the principal axes.

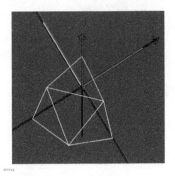

'''''

Program name: opengl_3D_soctet4tri_separate_1.py
Objective: Construct an enclosed solid from an one-eighth segment using symmetry.

Keywords: OpenGL, triangle, sphere, octets, separate, normals, lighting.
===79
Comments: Each octet-sector is derived from the same vertex array and is positioned, scaled and rotated independently from the others.

Tested on: Python 2.6, Python 2.7.3, Python 3.2.3
Author: Mike Ohlson de Fine
=====================================
'''''

```python
from OpenGL.GL import *
from OpenGL.GLUT import *
from OpenGL.GLU import *
import vector_2d3d_ops

rotation_y = 0.0
rotation_x = 0.0

octet4tri = [
-0.0, 0.7, 0.7,    -0.0, 1.0, 0.0,    -0.7, 0.7, 0.0,   # 1st triangle
-0.7, 0.0, 0.7,    -0.0, 0.7, 0.7,    -0.7, 0.7, 0.0,   # 2nd triangle
-0.0, 0.7, 0.7,    -0.7, 0.0, 0.7,    -0.0, 0.0, 1.0,   # 3rd triangle
-1.0, 0.0, 0.0,    -0.7, 0.0, 0.7,    -0.7, 0.7, 0.0 ] # 4th triangle

#================================================================
octet4tri_faces = len(octet4tri)/3
print ( 'octet4tri_faces: ', octet4tri_faces)
octet4tri_norm =vector_2d3d_ops. array_triangle_normals(octet4tri)
#================================================================
def InitGL(Width, Height):
    """ Initialize and setup the Graphics Software/Hardware pipeline.
    """

    # Note -  the value of the fourth parameter is immaterial for diffuse light.
    diffuse_lite_kula_white  = [1.0, 1.0, 1.0, 0.0]
    light0_position  = [ 5.0, 1.0, 5.0, 0.0 ]
    glClearColor(0.6, 0.6, 1.0, 0.0)
    # /\/\/\/\/\/\/\/\/\/\/\/\/\/\/\/\/\/\/\/\/\/\/\/\/\
    glEnable(GL_NORMALIZE)
    glEnable(GL_COLOR_MATERIAL)
    glEnable(GL_LIGHTING)
    glEnable(GL_LIGHT0)
    glLightfv(GL_LIGHT0, GL_POSITION, light0_position)
    glLightfv(GL_LIGHT0, GL_DIFFUSE,   diffuse_lite_kula_white)
    #/\/\/\/\/\/\/\/\/\/\/\/\/\/\/\/\/\/\/\/\/\/\/\/\/\
    glEnable(GL_DEPTH_TEST)
    glMatrixMode(GL_PROJECTION)
    glLoadIdentity()
    gluPerspective(45.0, float(Width)/float(Height), 0.1, 100.0)
    glMatrixMode(GL_MODELVIEW)

def Octocapsule():
    """ Draw an enclose eight segmented solid by suitably rotating the
        same segment into position using matrix operations.
    """

    global rotation_y, rotation_x
    glClear(GL_COLOR_BUFFER_BIT | GL_DEPTH_BUFFER_BIT)

    # Enable vertex arrays
    glEnableClientState(GL_VERTEX_ARRAY)
    glEnableClientState(GL_NORMAL_ARRAY)

    # 1 first octant of Vertex arrays
    glLoadIdentity()
    glTranslatef(0.0,  0.4,  -5.0)
    glRotatef(rotation_y, 0.0, 1.0, 0.0)
    glScale(1.0,  1.0,  1.0)
    glColor3f(1.0, 0.0, 0.0)                # Red
```

```
glVertexPointer(3, GL_FLOAT, 0, octet4tri)        # (size, type, stride, pointer) .
glNormalPointer(GL_FLOAT, 0, octet4tri_norm)   # (type, stride, pointer).
glDrawArrays(GL_TRIANGLES, 0, 12) # (primitive type, starting index, number of indices (vertices?) to be
rendered).

# 2 - second octant
glLoadIdentity()
glTranslatef(-0.0,  0.4,  -5.0)
glRotatef(rotation_y, 0.0, 1.0, 0.0)
glRotatef(90.0, 0.0, 1.0, 0.0)
glScale(1.0,  1.0,  1.0)
glColor3f(0.0, 0.0, 1.0)                # Blue
glVertexPointer(3, GL_FLOAT, 0, octet4tri)
glNormalPointer(GL_FLOAT, 0, octet4tri_norm)
glDrawArrays(GL_TRIANGLES, 0, 12)

# 3 - third octant
glLoadIdentity()
glTranslatef(-0.0,  0.4,  -5.0)
glRotatef(rotation_y, 0.0, 1.0, 0.0)
glRotatef(180.0, 0.0, 1.0, 0.0)
glScale(1.0,  1.0,  1.0)
glColor3f(1.0, 0.0, 1.0)                # Purple
glVertexPointer(3, GL_FLOAT, 0, octet4tri)
glNormalPointer(GL_FLOAT, 0, octet4tri_norm)
glDrawArrays(GL_TRIANGLES, 0, 12)

# 4 - fourth octant
glLoadIdentity()
glTranslatef(-0.0,  0.4,  -5.0)
glRotatef(rotation_y, 0.0, 1.0, 0.0)
glRotatef(-90.0, 0.0, 1.0, 0.0)
glScale(1.0,  1.0,  1.0)
glColor3f(0.0, 1.0, 0.0)                # Green
glVertexPointer(3, GL_FLOAT, 0, octet4tri)
glNormalPointer(GL_FLOAT, 0, octet4tri_norm)
glDrawArrays(GL_TRIANGLES, 0, 12)

# 5 - fifth octant
glLoadIdentity()
glTranslatef(-0.0,  0.4,  -5.0)
glRotatef(rotation_y, 0.0, 1.0, 0.0)
glRotatef(90.0, 0.0, 1.0, 0.0)
glRotatef(-180.0, 0.0, 0.0, 1.0)
glScale(1.0,  1.0,  1.0)
glColor3f(0.0, 1.0, 1.0)                # Lilac
glVertexPointer(3, GL_FLOAT, 0, octet4tri)
glNormalPointer(GL_FLOAT, 0, octet4tri_norm)
glDrawArrays(GL_TRIANGLES, 0, 12)

# 6 - sixth octant
glLoadIdentity()
glTranslatef(-0.0,  0.4,  -5.0)
glRotatef(rotation_y, 0.0, 1.0, 0.0)
glRotatef(180.0, 0.0, 1.0, 0.0)
glRotatef(-180.0, 0.0, 0.0, 1.0)
glScale(1.0,  1.0,  1.0)
```

```
glColor3f(1.0, 1.0, 0.0)                # Yellow
glVertexPointer(3, GL_FLOAT, 0, octet4tri)
glNormalPointer(GL_FLOAT, 0, octet4tri_norm)
glDrawArrays(GL_TRIANGLES, 0, 12)

# 7 - seventh octant
glLoadIdentity()
glTranslatef(-0.0,  0.4,  -5.0)
glRotatef(rotation_y, 0.0, 1.0, 0.0)
glRotatef(-180.0, 0.0, 0.0, 1.0)
glScale(1.0,  1.0,  1.0)
glRotatef(-270.0, 0.0, 1.0, 0.0)
glColor3f(1.0, 0.6, 0.0)                # Orange
glVertexPointer(3, GL_FLOAT, 0, octet4tri)
glNormalPointer(GL_FLOAT, 0, octet4tri_norm)
glDrawArrays(GL_TRIANGLES, 0, 12)

# 8 - eigth octant
glLoadIdentity()
glTranslatef(-0.0,  0.4,  -5.0)
glRotatef(rotation_y, 0.0, 1.0, 0.0)
glRotatef(-180.0, 0.0, 0.0, 1.0)
glScale(1.0,  1.0,  1.0)
glColor3f(1.0, 1.0, 1.0)                # Grey-white
glVertexPointer(3, GL_FLOAT, 0, octet4tri)
glNormalPointer(GL_FLOAT, 0, octet4tri_norm)
glDrawArrays(GL_TRIANGLES, 0, 12)

# Disable vertex arrays.
glDisableClientState(GL_VERTEX_ARRAY)
glDisableClientState(GL_NORMAL_ARRAY)

rotation_y += 0.1
rotation_x += 0.05
glutSwapBuffers()


def main():
    ''' Main Program.
    '''
    glutInit(sys.argv)
    glutInitWindowSize(600,600)    # Width, Height. Line gets scaled to the window.
    glutCreateWindow(b'OpenGL Vertex Arrays from Primitive Triangles: PsuedoSphere. 144 vertices')
    InitGL(600, 600)
    glutIdleFunc(Octocapsule)      # During idle time redraw the frame.
    glutMainLoop()

main()
```

The Result

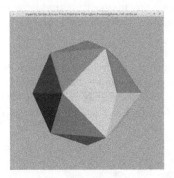

A Model is a World within a World

The complete secret to constructing and controlling the behaviour of objects within a common world or model and then to control that world within larger worlds is simply about executing three matrix multiplications in the appropriate sequence. The three matrix multiplications are those which result in the scaling, rotation and translation of a point in 3D coordinate space. That is all. The trick is to understand sequence.

A group of points or vertices can represent a flower. The flower can be positioned on a surface that will become a field. The field can be filled with other flowers and the field can be placed in a landscape. The landscape can be on a planet that is one of many orbiting a star and so on forever. This can all be achieved by a sequence of matrix multiplications that represent scaling, rotation and translation transformations.

An Articulated Hand as a Model

We now explore how to place objects in models and how to control these models by animation. We shall try to keep the model sufficiently simple so the we will not lose our bearings. We need to come out of this with a clear mental picture of how to assemble more than one object, each inside its own separate object space, into a common model space. We must be able to manipulate the model space as if it was just another object and make it simply one of many components belonging to a larger model.

We shall use the example of an articulated human hand. We simplify the hand by assembling it from simple geometric 'bones'. The three primary matrix transformations will be used to arrange a single bone into a representation of all the bones of the four fingers and a thumb of a human hand. In object oriented terminology we define a bone and then creates many instances of that bone in order to make the other bones. We shall then articulate the movement on the fingers and move the whole hand as a unit.

I apologize in advance for the length of the Python code that follows but it has been made so in order that the detailed design can be easily followed – compactness has been sacrificed to enhance clarity. It is possible to reduce the length with more cunning programming but that strategy has been left to the example on Push and Pop that follows this one.

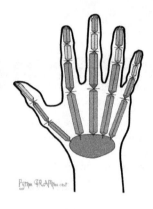

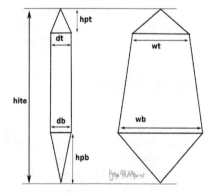

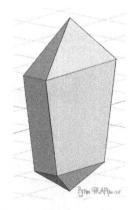

The bones of the model hand are represented by a rectangular box with pyramid end caps. We will call this is a capped beam.

The local object coordinates for the bone have the origin at the lowermost tip of one pyramid.

We want a 3D data structure that is general and flexible.
Here is the Python function that will furnish the 16 triangles making up the capped
beam that will be used for each one of the 19 bones for the articulated hand. The
particular argument parameters that make one bone differenct from the other are
passed as the list called **beam.**

```
def capped_beam(beam):
    ''' Draw a tapered tube with capped endpieces, from triangles.
        Arguments: origin (bottom center), botton width (wb),  bottom z-depth(db), height of bottom pyramid(hbp)
                   top width (wt), top z-depth (dt), height of top pyramid hPT) , total height (hite).
    '''
    hite = beam[0]
    wb = beam[1]
    db = beam[2]
    hpb = beam[3]
    wt = beam[4]
    dt = beam[5]
    hpt = beam[6]

    # Vertices
    vt1 = [      0,  0,        0.0 ]
    vt2 = [ -wb/2.0,  hpb,       db ]
    vt3 = [ -wb/2.0,  hpb,      -db ]
    vt4 = [  wb/2.0,  hpb,      -db ]
    vt5 = [  wb/2.0,  hpb,       db ]
    vt6 = [ -wt/2.0,  hite-hpt,  dt ]
    vt7 = [ -wt/2.0,  hite-hpt, -dt ]
    vt8 = [  wt/2.0,  hite-hpt, -dt ]
    vt9 = [  wt/2.0,  hite-hpt,  dt ]
    vt10 = [      0,  hite,      0.0 ]

    # 1 - 2 - 5 etc. Bottom cap.
    tri1 = [ vt1, vt2, vt5 ]
    tri2 = [ vt1, vt2, vt3 ]
    tri3 = [ vt1, vt3, vt4 ]
    tri4 = [ vt1, vt4, vt5 ]

    # 10 - 6 - 9 etc. Top cap.
    tri5 = [ vt10, vt6, vt9 ]
    tri6 = [ vt10, vt6, vt7 ]
    tri7 = [ vt10, vt7, vt8 ]
    tri8 = [ vt10, vt8, vt9 ]

    # Front
    tri9  = [ vt2, vt9, vt5 ]
    tri10 = [ vt2, vt6, vt9 ]
    # Back
    tri11 = [ vt3, vt8, vt4 ]
    tri12 = [ vt3, vt7, vt8 ]
    # Right side
    tri13 = [ vt2, vt7, vt3 ]
    tri14 = [ vt2, vt6, vt7 ]
```

```
# Left side
tri15 = [ vt5, vt8, vt4 ]
tri16 = [ vt5, vt9, vt8 ]

   return tri1, tri9,  tri10, tri5,  tri2, tri13, tri14, tri6, tri3, tri11, tri12, tri7, tri4, tri15, tri16, tri8
```

For each finger a common ratio of bone length relative to the longest bone has been used:

```
# beam = [ hite, wb, db,  hpb,  wt,  dt,  hpt]  - construction note.

a_fbone = [ 1.0, 0.15, 0.12, 0.2, 0.12, 0.1, 0.2 ]          # The longest bone in the finger.
b_fbone = [ length*0.75 for length in a_fbone]              # The Second longest bone.
c_fbone = [ length*0.4 for length in a_fbone]               # The Third longest bone.
d_fbone = [ length*0.35 for length in a_fbone]              # The shortest bone.
e_thumbone =  [ length*0.78 for length in a_fbone]          # The thumb base bone.
```

and to make an instance of each prototype finger bone:

```
bone_1 = capped_beam(a_fbone)
bone_2 = capped_beam(b_fbone)
bone_3 = capped_beam(c_fbone)
bone_4 = capped_beam(d_fbone)
thum_bone = capped_beam(e_thumbone)
```

The drawing and animation of the hand clenching and unclenching is:

```
def all_displays():
   ''' A  Five Fingered hand that clenches and unclenches while simultaneously rotating around the wrist.
   '''

   global shift_1, shift_2, shift_3, shift_4, shift_5
   global rotate_angle_1, rotate_axis_1, rotation_speed_1
   global rotate_angle_2, rotation_speed_2,  rotate_angle_3, rotation_speed_3

   glClear(GL_COLOR_BUFFER_BIT|GL_DEPTH_BUFFER_BIT) # Clear the colour and depth buffer
   glEnableClientState(GL_VERTEX_ARRAY)
   glEnableClientState(GL_NORMAL_ARRAY)


   #=========================================================
   # First Finger
   #=========================================================
   glLoadIdentity()                              # Clear matrix stack
   glTranslate( shift_1[0], shift_1[1], shift_1[2])      # Each object's origin.
   glRotate(rotate_angle_3, 0.0, 1.0, 0.0)        # Common rotation around wrist (y-axis).
   glScale(0.91, 0.91, 0.91)                      # Relative size of each finger (wrt longest finger).
   glScale(3.0, 3.0, 3.0)                         # Overall amplification applied to all fingers.
   #glColor(0.5, 0.5,  0.5)

   # Bone_1
   glColor(0.8, 0.0,  0.0)
   for i in range(0,len(bone_1)):
      glVertexPointer(3, GL_FLOAT, 0, bone_1[i])
      glNormalPointer(GL_FLOAT, 0, bone_1[i])   #Arguments: (type, stride, pointer).
      glDrawArrays(GL_TRIANGLES, 0, 4 ) # 16 = number of triangles.

   # Bone_2
   glTranslate(0.0, 1.0, 0.0)                    # Each object's origin.
   glRotate(rotate_angle_2, 1.0, 0.0, 0.0)       # Rotate joint relative to previous - an additive process.
```

```
glColor(0.0, 0.0,  0.8)
for i in range(0,len(bone_1)):
   glVertexPointer(3, GL_FLOAT, 0, bone_2[i])
   glNormalPointer(GL_FLOAT, 0, bone_2[i])        #Arguments:  (type, stride, pointer).
   glDrawArrays(GL_TRIANGLES, 0, 4 )              # 16 = number of triangles.

# Bbone_3
glTranslate(0.0, 0.75, 0.0)                       # Each object's origin.
glRotate(rotate_angle_2, 1.0, 0.0, 0.0)          # Rotate joint relative to previous.
glColor(0.0, 0.8,  0.0)
for i in range(0,len(bone_1)):
   glVertexPointer(3, GL_FLOAT, 0, bone_3[i])
   glNormalPointer(GL_FLOAT, 0, bone_3[i])        # Arguments:  (type, stride, pointer).
   glDrawArrays(GL_TRIANGLES, 0, 4 )              # 16 = number of triangles.

# Bone_4
glTranslate(0.0, 0.40, 0.0)                       # Each object's origin.
glRotate(rotate_angle_2, 1.0, 0.0, 0.0)          #Rotate joint relative to previous.
glColor(0.6, 0.0,  0.6)
for i in range(0,len(bone_1)):
   glVertexPointer(3, GL_FLOAT, 0, bone_4[i])
   glNormalPointer(GL_FLOAT, 0, bone_4[i])        # Arguments:  (type, stride, pointer).
   glDrawArrays(GL_TRIANGLES, 0, 4 )              # 16 = number of triangles.


#================================================================
# Second Finger
#================================================================
glLoadIdentity()                                  # Clear matrix stack and start afresh.
glTranslate(0.0, 0.0, shift_2[2])                 # Each object's origin.
glRotate(rotate_angle_3, 0.0, 1.0, 0.0)          # common rotation around wrist (y-axis).
glTranslate(shift_2[0],shift_2[1], 0.0)
glRotate(-3.0, 0.0,  0.0, 1.0)                    # Splay the finger slightly  - 3 degrees.
glScale(3.0, 3.0, 3.0)                            # Overall amplification applied to all fingers.

glColor(0.8, 0.0,  0.0)
# bone_1
for i in range(0,len(bone_1)):
   glVertexPointer(3, GL_FLOAT, 0, bone_1[i])
   glNormalPointer(GL_FLOAT, 0, bone_1[i])   #Arguments:  (type, stride, pointer).
   glDrawArrays(GL_TRIANGLES, 0, 4 ) # 16 = number of triangles.

# bone_2
glTranslate(0.0, 1.0, 0.0)                        # Each object's origin.
glRotate(rotate_angle_2, 1.0, 0.0, 0.0)          # rotate joint relative to previous.
glColor(0.0, 0.0,  0.8)
for i in range(0,len(bone_1)):
   glVertexPointer(3, GL_FLOAT, 0, bone_2[i])
   glNormalPointer(GL_FLOAT, 0, bone_2[i])
   glDrawArrays(GL_TRIANGLES, 0, 4 )

# bone_3
glTranslate(0.0, 0.75, 0.0)                       # Each object's origin.
glRotate(rotate_angle_2, 1.0, 0.0, 0.0)          # Rotate joint relative to previous.
glColor(0.0, 0.8,  0.0)
for i in range(0,len(bone_1)):
   glVertexPointer(3, GL_FLOAT, 0, bone_3[i])
```

```
  glNormalPointer(GL_FLOAT, 0, bone_3[i])
  glDrawArrays(GL_TRIANGLES, 0, 4 )

# bone_4
glTranslate(0.0, 0.40, 0.0)                    # Each object's origin.
glRotate(rotate_angle_2, 1.0, 0.0, 0.0)        # rotate joint relative to previous.
glColor(0.6, 0.0,  0.6)
for i in range(0,len(bone_1)):
  glVertexPointer(3, GL_FLOAT, 0, bone_4[i])
  glNormalPointer(GL_FLOAT, 0, bone_4[i])

  glDrawArrays(GL_TRIANGLES, 0, 4 )

#===========================================================
# Third Finger
#===========================================================
glLoadIdentity()                       # Clear matrix stack
glTranslate(0.0, 0.0, shift_3[2])      # Each object's origin.
glRotate(rotate_angle_3, 0.0, 1.0, 0.0)        # common rotation around wrist (y-axis).
glTranslate(shift_3[0],shift_3[1], 0.0)
glRotate(-6.0, 0.0,  0.0, 1.0)  # Splay the finger slightly.
glScale(3.0, 3.0, 3.0)
glScale(0.93, 0.93, 0.93)

# bone_1
glColor(0.8, 0.0,  0.0)
for i in range(0,len(bone_1)):
  glVertexPointer(3, GL_FLOAT, 0, bone_1[i])
  glNormalPointer(GL_FLOAT, 0, bone_1[i])
  glDrawArrays(GL_TRIANGLES, 0, 4 )

# bone_2
glTranslate(0.0, 1.0, 0.0)
glRotate(rotate_angle_2, 1.0, 0.0, 0.0)
glColor(0.0, 0.0,  0.8)
for i in range(0,len(bone_1)):
  glVertexPointer(3, GL_FLOAT, 0, bone_2[i])
  glNormalPointer(GL_FLOAT, 0, bone_2[i])
  glDrawArrays(GL_TRIANGLES, 0, 4 )

# bone_3
glTranslate(0.0, 0.75, 0.0)
glRotate(rotate_angle_2, 1.0, 0.0, 0.0)
glColor(0.0, 0.8,  0.0)
for i in range(0,len(bone_1)):
  glVertexPointer(3, GL_FLOAT, 0, bone_3[i])
  glNormalPointer(GL_FLOAT, 0, bone_3[i])
  glDrawArrays(GL_TRIANGLES, 0, 4 )

# bone_4
glTranslate(0.0, 0.40, 0.0)
glRotate(rotate_angle_2, 1.0, 0.0, 0.0)
glColor(0.6, 0.0,  0.6)
for i in range(0,len(bone_1)):
  glVertexPointer(3, GL_FLOAT, 0, bone_4[i])
  glNormalPointer(GL_FLOAT, 0, bone_4[i])
  glDrawArrays(GL_TRIANGLES, 0, 4 )
```

```
#===============================================================
# Fourth Finger
#===============================================================
glLoadIdentity()
glTranslate(0.0, 0.0, shift_4[2])
glRotate(rotate_angle_3, 0.0, 1.0, 0.0)
glTranslate(shift_4[0],shift_4[1], 0.0)
glRotate(-9.0, 0.0,  0.0, 1.0)
glScale(3.0, 3.0, 3.0)
glScale(0.78, 0.78, 0.78)

# bone_1
glColor(0.8, 0.0,  0.0)
for i in range(0,len(bone_1)):
   glVertexPointer(3, GL_FLOAT, 0, bone_1[i])
   glNormalPointer(GL_FLOAT, 0, bone_1[i])
   glDrawArrays(GL_TRIANGLES, 0, 4 )

# bone_2
glTranslate(0.0, 1.0, 0.0)          # Each object's origin.
glRotate(rotate_angle_2, 1.0, 0.0, 0.0)       # rotate joint relative to previous.
glColor(0.0, 0.0,  0.8)
for i in range(0,len(bone_1)):
   glVertexPointer(3, GL_FLOAT, 0, bone_2[i])
   glNormalPointer(GL_FLOAT, 0, bone_2[i])
   glDrawArrays(GL_TRIANGLES, 0, 4 )

# bone_3
glTranslate(0.0, 0.75, 0.0)
glRotate(rotate_angle_2, 1.0, 0.0, 0.0)
glColor(0.0, 0.8,  0.0)
for i in range(0,len(bone_1)):
   glVertexPointer(3, GL_FLOAT, 0, bone_3[i])
   glNormalPointer(GL_FLOAT, 0, bone_3[i])
   glDrawArrays(GL_TRIANGLES, 0, 4 )

# bone_4
glTranslate(0.0, 0.40, 0.0)
glRotate(rotate_angle_2, 1.0, 0.0, 0.0)
glColor(0.6, 0.0,  0.6)
for i in range(0,len(bone_1)):
   glVertexPointer(3, GL_FLOAT, 0, bone_4[i])
   glNormalPointer(GL_FLOAT, 0, bone_4[i])
   glDrawArrays(GL_TRIANGLES, 0, 4 )

#===============================================================
# Thumb
#===============================================================
glLoadIdentity()
glTranslate(0.0, 0.0, shift_5[2])
glRotate(rotate_angle_3, 0.0, 1.0, 0.0)
glTranslate(shift_5[0],shift_5[1], 0.0)
glRotate(20.0, 0.0,  0.0, 1.0)        # Splay the thumb by 30 degrees from the fingers.
glRotate(-30.0, 0.0,  1.0,  0.0)      # Angle thumb toward palm (Rotate about y).
glScale(3.0, 3.0, 3.0)
glScale(0.78, 0.78, 0.78)
```

```
# bone_1
glColor(0.8, 0.0,  0.0)
for i in range(0,len(bone_1)):
    glVertexPointer(3, GL_FLOAT, 0, bone_1[i])
    glNormalPointer(GL_FLOAT, 0, bone_1[i])
    glDrawArrays(GL_TRIANGLES, 0, 4 )

# bone_2
glTranslate(0.0, 1.0, 0.0)
glRotate(rotate_angle_2, 1.0, 0.0, 0.0)
glColor(0.0, 0.0,  0.8)
for i in range(0,len(bone_1)):
    glVertexPointer(3, GL_FLOAT, 0, bone_2[i])
    glNormalPointer(GL_FLOAT, 0, bone_2[i])
    glDrawArrays(GL_TRIANGLES, 0, 4 )

# bone_3
glTranslate(0.0, 0.75, 0.0)
glRotate(rotate_angle_2, 1.0, 0.0, 0.0)
glColor(0.0, 0.8,  0.0)
for i in range(0,len(bone_1)):
    glVertexPointer(3, GL_FLOAT, 0, bone_3[i])
    glNormalPointer(GL_FLOAT, 0, bone_3[i])
    glDrawArrays(GL_TRIANGLES, 0, 4 )

glDisableClientState(GL_VERTEX_ARRAY)
glDisableClientState(GL_NORMAL_ARRAY)

glFlush() # Makes sure that we output the model to the graphics card
glutSwapBuffers()
glutPostRedisplay()

rotate_angle_1 += rotation_speed_1
rotate_angle_3 += rotation_speed_3
if rotate_angle_2 >= 90.0 or rotate_angle_2 <= -5.0 : rotation_speed_2 = - rotation_speed_2
rotate_angle_2 += rotation_speed_2
```

For Completeness here are the other parts of the program:

```
def InitGL(Width, Height):
    """ Initialize and setup the state of Graphics Software/Hardware pipeline.
    """
    diffuse_lite_kula_white  = [1.0, 1.0, 1.0, 0.0]
    light0_position  = [  0.0, 1.0, 5.0, 0.0 ]
    glClearColor(0.8, 0.8, 0.8, 0.0)
    # /\/\/\/\/\/\/\/\/\/\/\/\/\/\/\/\/\/\/\/\/\/\/\/\/\
    glEnable(GL_NORMALIZE)
    glEnable(GL_COLOR_MATERIAL)
    glEnable(GL_LIGHTING)
    glEnable(GL_LIGHT0)
    glLightfv(GL_LIGHT0, GL_POSITION, light0_position)
    glLightfv(GL_LIGHT0, GL_DIFFUSE,  diffuse_lite_kula_white)
    #/\/\/\/\/\/\/\/\/\/\/\/\/\/\/\/\/\/\/\/\/\/\/\/\/\
    glEnable(GL_DEPTH_TEST)
    glMatrixMode(GL_PROJECTION)
```

```
glLoadIdentity()
gluPerspective(45.0, float(Width)/float(Height), 0.1, 100.0)
glMatrixMode(GL_MODELVIEW)


def update(a):
    """ Animation frame rate control.
        glutTimerFunc(frame-rate, update, 0). Frame-rate is in milliseconds.
    """
    all_displays()
    glutTimerFunc(50, update, 0)

def main():
    ''' Main Program.
    '''
    glutInit(sys.argv)
    glutInitWindowSize(1000,1000)
    glutCreateWindow('OpenGL Transform Sequence: Finger Flexing')
    InitGL(1000, 1000)
    glutTimerFunc(1,update,0)        # Control re-draw with timed interrups.
    glutMainLoop()

main()
```

How can we make Python-OpenGL code more compact?

The previous program can be made significantly shorter. But will we lose readability and intelligibility if we do? The answer is that we should only shorten such programs if it improves intelligibility. That is, if it makes the code easier to read and understand.

What is tedious and irritating in the above program is the repitition of the sequence:

```
glLoadIdentity()
glTranslate(0.0, 0.0, shift_4[2])
glRotate(rotate_angle_3, 0.0, 1.0, 0.0)
glTranslate(shift_4[0],shift_4[1], 0.0)
glScale(3.0, 3.0, 3.0)
```

It is repeated five times, once for each finger. In the next section we see how to avoid this and end up with better looking code at the same time.

The Smartness of Push and Pop

We want to assemble a model in a simple and logical way - a way that helps us to understand clearly what is happening. We shall use the example of assembling a family of dogs on a patch of ground as shown here.

To create this model we will use two vertex arrays. One is the vertex array for the patch of ground and the other is the vertex array for the dog. For the purpose of illustration we use a vertex array of a dog that is inherently at an unsuitable angle and position as shown below. This is the program called "opengl_pushpop_vertex_arrays_1.py" in Github, in the repository Python_3D_Graphics

Here we see the transforms that create each dog that will become part of the model.

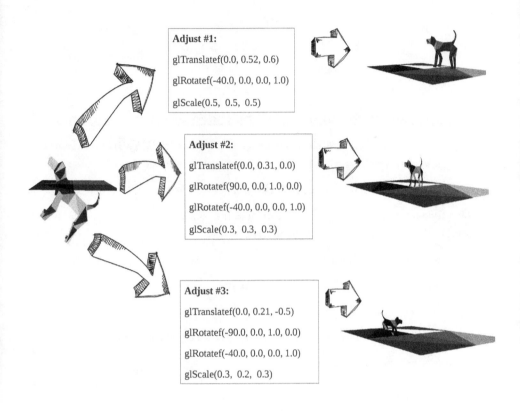

Adjust #1:

glTranslatef(0.0, 0.52, 0.6)

glRotatef(-40.0, 0.0, 0.0, 1.0)

glScale(0.5, 0.5, 0.5)

Adjust #2:

glTranslatef(0.0, 0.31, 0.0)

glRotatef(90.0, 0.0, 1.0, 0.0)

glRotatef(-40.0, 0.0, 0.0, 1.0)

glScale(0.3, 0.3, 0.3)

Adjust #3:

glTranslatef(0.0, 0.21, -0.5)

glRotatef(-90.0, 0.0, 1.0, 0.0)

glRotatef(-40.0, 0.0, 0.0, 1.0)

glScale(0.3, 0.2, 0.3)

Each sequence of scale/rotate/translate matrices transform the vertices of badly positioned, incorrectly sized yellow dog on the left into the correctly sized, oriented, colored instance of each dog on the right.

So we now have the family of three dogs grouped nicely on the square patch of ground to produce our model. Now we need to be able to move the complete model as a single unit. In our demonstaration we want to rotate the model around the y-axis, allowing us to view it from all sides. To achieve this model rotation we use the following transformtion sequence:

Model Position and Rotate:
```
glLoadIdentity()                          # Clear the Modelview stack .
glTranslatef(0.0, -0.5,-8.0)              # Shift entire model to a convenient view position.
glRotatef(rot_grande*3.0, 0.0, 1.0, 0.0) # Continuous animated rotation of the whole model, including dogs.
glScale(3.0,  3.0,  2.0)                  # Scale-up x2 of the entire model, including dogs.
```

The sequence of actions we need executed will be as follows:

1. Adjust # 1
2. Model Position and Rotate.
3. Adjust # 2
4. Model Position and Rotate.
5. Adjust # 3
6. Model Position and Rotate.

OpenGL Matrix operations must be coded in reverse sequence.

Why? Because of the way matrix operations work. Say we have the position vector of a vertex **Vert1**, which we want to rotate using a matrix **Mrotate1**.

The desired transformation will be **MTransform1 = Mrotate1 x Vertertex1**

Some time after this we may want to translate the rotated vertex to a new location by multiplying it with **MTranslate1** matrix.

The new complete transformation will be:

MTransform2 = MTranslate1 x MTransform1

This is same as **MTransform2 = MTranslate1 x Mrotate1 x Vertex1**

Expressing this as OpenGL code we get:

```
glTranslatef(parameters for translation)
glRotatef(parameters for rotation)
Vertex1
```

The important thing to note is that the matrix at the **top** (ie. glTranslate) is the **LAST** one executed. Normal Python instructions are the reverse of this - the last instruction in a column of Python instructions is in fact the last one executed by the CPU.

Because of way OpenGL operates the sequence of matrix multiplications the instructions need to appear inside the Python program in the following sequence:

1. Model Position and Rotate. - Last matrix executed.
2. Adjust # 3
3. Model Position and Rotate.

4. Adjust # 2
5. Model Position and Rotate.
6. Adjust # 1   -   First matrix executed.

This sequence seems unnecessarily complicated because we repeat the :"Model Position and Rotate" transformation three times. We need a way to copy and reuse this transformation. This is where glPushMatrix() is useful.

glPushMatrix()

glPushMatrix() saves a copy of the current matrix transformations that have just been executed. It saves this copy on the glModel *stack*. This stack is a portion of memory kept particulary for the purpose of re-using transformations. The current matrix is still in effect - only a copy is placed on the stack. This stack can save up to 32 separate transformations. Each new glPushMatrix() pushes all the other transformations on the stack down one position.

glPopMatrix()

glPopMatrix() discards the matrix on the top of the stack. It makes the next one the current matrix.
So it effectively restores the state of the stack to its condition prior to the most recent push.

Using the Push/Pop instructions to assemble the above three-dog model we would do the following:

1. Model Position and Rotate.   -   Last matrix executed.
2. glPushMatrix()   -   creates the first copy onto the stack.
3. glPushMatrix()   -   creates the second copy onto the stack, the first moves down.
4. glPushMatrix()   -   creates the third copy onto the stack, all others move down.
5. Adjust # 3
6. glPopMatrix()   -   discards the top of the stack, all others move up.
7. Adjust # 2
8. glPopMatrix()   -   discards the top of the stack, all others move up
9. Adjust # 1   -   First matrix executed.

Here is the Python code that achieves this.

```python
def DrawGLScene():
    """ Test each primitive. For each primitive to be tested, un-comment the relevant line.
        Ensure all the others are commented out to keep the situation simple.
    """
    global rot_grande
    glClear(GL_COLOR_BUFFER_BIT | GL_DEPTH_BUFFER_BIT)

    glEnableClientState(GL_VERTEX_ARRAY)      # Enable Vertex Array.
    glEnableClientState(GL_NORMAL_ARRAY)      # Enable Normals Array.

    # Final Transform. This needs to be applied to each dog, after the dog has been positiond correctly.
```

```
glLoadIdentity()                              # Clear the Modelview stack .
glTranslatef(0.0, -0.5,-8.0)                  # Shift entire model to a convenient view position.
glRotatef(rot_grande*3.0, 0.0, 1.0, 0.0);     # Continuous animated rotation of the whole model.
glScale(3.0,  3.0,  2.0)                       # Scale-up x2 of the entire model, including dogs.
```

```
# Why are there 2 Pushes?
''' There are three dogs that have to be placed on the same patch of earth, but in different positions.
    Once in place they must each be operated of the same three transformations above.
    So we preserve three "clean" copies.
    As soon as each dog has been sized, rotated and translated into position,
    the transformation matrix that was used must be discarded and replaced by the 'Final Transform' that
    must be applied to each.
    The unwanted transformations are deleted by each glPopMatrix() which happens after the dog has been
positioned.
    '''
```

```
glPushMatrix()                                # Preserve the common patch transform.
glPushMatrix()                                # Preserve a second copy of the common patch.
```

```
# GROUND PATCH - No extra positioning transformations needed.
''' Base floor vertex array - not to be altered.
    The three dogs will be placed on this platform.
    '''
```

```
glEnableClientState(GL_COLOR_ARRAY)           # Enable COLOR Array.
glColorPointer(4, GL_FLOAT, 0, kula)          # (type, stride, pointer).
glVertexPointer(3, GL_FLOAT, 0, base_patch)   # (size, type, stride, pointer) .
glNormalPointer(GL_FLOAT, 0, flat_base_norm)  # (type, stride, pointer).
glDrawArrays(GL_TRIANGLES, 0, 24) # (primitive type, starting index, number of vertices to be
rendered).
glDisableClientState(GL_COLOR_ARRAY)
```

```
# DOG 1 - Old Yaller
'''  tilt the dog up by 40 degrees, scale him down by 50%, shift him forward by 0.5.
```

```
glTranslatef(0.0, 0.52, 0.6)                  # Shift the dog 1 up and forward.
glRotatef(-40.0, 0.0, 0.0, 1.0)               # Tilt the dog 1 to make it horizontal.
glScale(0.5,  0.5,  0.5)                       # Scale the yellow dog to 50% of full size.
```

```
glColor3f(0.8, 0.8, 0.1)                       # Yellow.
glVertexPointer(3, GL_FLOAT, 0, dog3_world.dog40tiltz)
glNormalPointer(GL_FLOAT, 0, dog40tiltz_norm)
glDrawArrays(GL_TRIANGLES, 0, 174)
```

```
glPopMatrix()    # Pop No.1
# DOG 2 - Rufus
glTranslatef(0.0, 0.31, 0.0)                   # Shift the dog 2 up.
glRotatef(90.0, 0.0, 1.0, 0.0)                 # Rotate the dog 2 to point down the z-axis.
glRotatef(-40.0, 0.0, 0.0, 1.0)                # Tilt the dog 2 to make it horizontal.
glScale(0.3,  0.3,  0.3)                        # Scale the yellow dog 2 to 30% of full size.
```

```
glColor3f(0.8, 0.2, 0.1)                        # Rufus coloring.
glVertexPointer(3, GL_FLOAT, 0, dog3_world.dog40tiltz)
glNormalPointer(GL_FLOAT, 0, dog40tiltz_norm)
glDrawArrays(GL_TRIANGLES, 0, 174)
```

```
glPopMatrix()    # Pop No.2
# DOG 3 - Bluey
```

```
glTranslatef(0.0, 0.21, -0.5)          # Shift the dog 3 up and back.
glRotatef(-90.0, 0.0, 1.0, 0.0);       # Rotate the dog 3 to face dog 2.
glRotatef(-40.0, 0.0, 0.0, 1.0);       # Tilt the dog 3 to make it horizontal.
glScale(0.3,  0.2,  0.3)               # Scale the same as the red dog but with shorter legs.

glColor3f(0.3, 0.3, 0.8)               # Blue.
glVertexPointer(3, GL_FLOAT, 0, dog3_world.dog40tiltz)
glNormalPointer(GL_FLOAT, 0, dog40tiltz_norm)
glDrawArrays(GL_TRIANGLES, 0, 174)

glDisableClientState(GL_VERTEX_ARRAY)  # disable the Vertex Array.
glDisableClientState(GL_NORMAL_ARRAY)  # disable the Normal Array.
rot_grande += 0.01
glutSwapBuffers()


def main():
    glutInit(sys.argv)
    glutInitWindowSize(1000,1000)
    glutCreateWindow(b'OpenGL: Three dog family model.')
    InitGL(1000, 1000)
    glutIdleFunc(DrawGLScene)
    glutMainLoop()
main()
```

The complete program is called "opengl_pushpop_dog_family_1.py" in Github.

Deprecation – the "D" word

Push and Pop, along with glBegin and glEnd are *deprecated*. This is a way of saying that they are regarded as old fashioned by Khronos group who manage the OpenGL specification. However almost all versions up to version 3.2, released in 2009, have a *compatibility profile* which retains the ability to execute old code. The newer versions since 3.2 are designed to be able to use features of the increasingly sophisticated cutting-edge GPU technology that is a feature of the GPU arms race that is going on.

A fairly good explanation of the old and new OpenGL landscape given by David C. Bishop can be found at (http://www.davidbishop.org/oglmeta#old-vs).

12

OpenGL: Texture Coverings

"As computers have become more powerful, computer graphics have advanced to the point where it's possible to create photo-realistic images. The bottleneck wasn't, 'How do we make pixels prettier?' It was, 'How do we engage with them more?' Jefferson Han.

"I am inspired by anything beautiful. Sometime it's a pair of eyes or flowing gorgeous hair, other times it's the sky or a sunset. I've been inspired by supple skin or the texture of a soft shirt." Nadine Velazquez

Topics covered in this chapter are:

- **OpenGL Frame Buffers and Depth Buffers.**
- **What is Texture Mapping**
- **The Basic Principle of Texture Mapping**
- **The Six Permutations of a Rectangular Mapping**
- **Distortionless Texture Mapping**

- **Mapping onto Triangles**
- **Dynamic Transformations of Texture Maps**
- **Animating Images with Texture Maps**
- **Multiple Image Animations**

Now we explore how to cover objects with pictures, called *texture* by the OpenGL folk, using OpenGL and Python.
Covering an object with a *texture* gives it a kind of solidity and reality. If we wanted to make arealistic looking Panda bear we would cover the object with a patterned Panda bear picture as a texture. We are able to see the effects of the perspective matrix and the depth buffer. The key strategy in creating realistic virtual worlds hinges on depth buffering. This is simply the technique that causes only those pixels nearest the "camera" or "eye" to be drawn on the computer screen while ignoring any that are obscured. The other objects in the scene are not discarded, they are just temporarily ignored for the purpose of assembling pixels for the next frame to be rendered.

OpenGL Framebuffers and Depth Buffers.

The basic requirement of the hardware is that it should contain a graphics frame buffer. A framebuffer or frame store is a section of RAM memory that stores a complete pixel-for-pixel replica of the computer screen. This complete picture intended for the screen can be sent out with a single 'refresh' command. Each computer, tablet or cellphone automatically sends frames to its display screen at the rate decided by the hardware designers. Typical values are 30 or 60 frames per second. This means that a new frame has to be available for rendering every 33 milliseconds or 16 milliseconds. Whatever collection of pixels is available in the framebuffer will get rendered onto the screen of the device. Software and the GPU have the task of populating the framebuffer with fresh pixels.

Every pixel needs to have red, green and blue values stored as well as other information like optical surface properties, lighting and relative geometric position.

What is Texture Mapping?

Up till now every 3D surface was filled with a solid color or a shaded blend of simple colors determined by light direction and the color assigned to vertices. Texture mapping gives us a method of gluing photographic or artist painted pictures onto objects. A texture is an OpenGL Object that contains one or more images that all have the same image format. Texture mapping ensures the image behaves correctly when surface geometry is transformed by translation, rotation and perspective.

Textures are just rectangular arrays of data. The data represents image pixels, surface color, the color of light and transparency (alpha) data. What makes texture mapping seemingly unpredictable is how a rectangular image needs to be mapped onto a non-rectangular region like a triangle. The texture has to be distorted to fit the target shape. The term used for a tiny texture element is a *texel*. If a whole bunch of texels have to be sqeezed onto one pixel then all the color and light data associated with each texel has to be averaged down to a single pixel.

The critical step in texture mapping is to apply the right geometry coordinates for the texture to be mapped onto. The corners of a rectangular texture-image are mapped onto nominated vertexes of a geometry surface as demonstrated in all the examples following below.

The connection of each corner of the rectangular texture map to a particular vertex is done with an instruction sequence like:

```
""" Rectangle 1 - Texture mapping """
    glBegin(GL_QUADS)
        glTexCoord2f(0.0, 0.0); glVertex3f( 0.0, 0.0,  0.0)
        glTexCoord2f(1.0, 0.0); glVertex3f( 1.0, 0.0,  0.0)
        glTexCoord2f(1.0, 1.0); glVertex3f( 1.0, 1.0,  0.0)
        glTexCoord2f(0.0, 1.0); glVertex3f( 0.0, 1.0,  0.0)
        glEnd()
```

The Basic Principle of Texture Mapping

In the next example we apply the texture-image shown below to a rectangular OpenGL primitive. Then we show all the different ways a rectangular texture can be mapped onto the same rectangular surface and what the resulting image looks like.

We need to use a function from the Python Image Library (PIL) to convert .jpg format images into a flat data format.

These examples are best understood by hacking, where hacking means experimenting. For instance we can try the following.
- Try to prepare and place your own image onto a rectangle,
- Try to fit a rectangular image onto a triangle,
- Make a kaleidoscope image using triangles arranges as a hexagon.

RECT_test_pattern, an image to test the result of various texture mapping configurations.

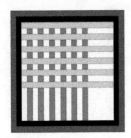

Warning: The original PIL (Python Imaging Library) does not work with Python versions3.x. We have to install "Pillow" to modernize PIL. See the Appendix for instructions.

```
"""
Program name: textured_rectangle_1.py
Objective: Experiment with different texture mappings settings.

keywords: opengl, transparency, ball textures, animation
==================================================================================79
Comments: A texture binding created with glBindTexture remains active until a new or
different texture is bound to the same target, or until the bound texture is
deleted with glDeleteTextures.

Warning on Python version 3.x:
We have to have Pillow ( A more modern version of PIL) for the imaging functions of PIL.
See the appendix on how to install Pillow for Python 3.x
Also helpful are:
1. http://askubuntu.com/questions/427358/install-pillow-for-python-3 (installation instrucetions).
2. https://pillow.readthedocs.org/handbook/concepts.html (a user manual for Pillow).
3. http://www.pythonforbeginners.com/modules-in-python/how-to-use-pillow/ ( A good tutorial).

Tested on: Python 2.6, Python 2.7.3, Python 3.2.3
Author:      Mike Ohlson de Fine
"""
from OpenGL.GL import *
from OpenGL.GLUT import *
from OpenGL.GLU import *
from PIL import Image

texture_1 = 0   # An integer label associated with the texture.

def texture_setup(image_name, texture_num, ix, iy):
    """ Assign texture attributes to specific images.
    """
    glBindTexture(GL_TEXTURE_2D, texture_1)
    glTexEnvf(GL_TEXTURE_ENV, GL_TEXTURE_ENV_MODE, GL_MODULATE)
    glTexParameterf(GL_TEXTURE_2D, GL_TEXTURE_MIN_FILTER, GL_NEAREST)
    glTexParameterf(GL_TEXTURE_2D, GL_TEXTURE_WRAP_S, GL_CLAMP)
    glTexParameterf(GL_TEXTURE_2D, GL_TEXTURE_WRAP_T, GL_CLAMP)
```

```
glTexParameterf(GL_TEXTURE_2D, GL_TEXTURE_WRAP_S, GL_REPEAT)
glTexParameterf(GL_TEXTURE_2D, GL_TEXTURE_WRAP_T, GL_REPEAT)
glTexParameterf(GL_TEXTURE_2D, GL_TEXTURE_MAG_FILTER, GL_NEAREST)
glTexParameterf(GL_TEXTURE_2D, GL_TEXTURE_WRAP_S, GL_REPEAT)
glPixelStorei(GL_UNPACK_ALIGNMENT,1)
glEnable(GL_TEXTURE_2D)
glTexImage2D(GL_TEXTURE_2D, 0, 3, ix, iy, 0, GL_RGBA, GL_UNSIGNED_BYTE, image_name)

def LoadTextures():
    """ Open texture images and convert them to "raw" pixel maps and
        bind or associate each image with and integer refernece number.
    """
    image_1 = Image.open("/home/mikeodf/constr/images_opengl/RECT_test_pattern.jpg")
    ix = image_1.size[0]                    # image.size is a PIL function.
    iy = image_1.size[1]
    print ('ix:', ix)                       # Just checking.
    print ('iy:', iy)
    image_1 = image_1.tostring("raw", "RGBX", 0, -1)   # Convert jpg to the 'string' for textures.
    texture_setup(image_1, 0, ix, iy)

def InitGL(Width, Height):
    """ A general OpenGL initialization function.  Sets all of the initial parameters.
        We call this right after our OpenGL window is created.
    """
    glClearColor(0.0, 0.0, 0.0, 0.0)                        # Clear the background color to black.
    glMatrixMode(GL_PROJECTION)
    glLoadIdentity()                                        # Reset The Projection Matrix.
    gluPerspective(30.0, float(Width)/float(Height), 0.1, 100.0) # Aspect Ratio Of The Window, makes it resizable.
    glMatrixMode(GL_MODELVIEW)

#================================================================
def make_rectangle_1(texture):
    """ A generic rectangle.
    """
    glBindTexture(GL_TEXTURE_2D,texture)
    # Rectangle Face (Each texture's corner is matched a quad's corner.)
    glBegin(GL_QUADS)
    glTexCoord2f(0.0, 0.0), glVertex3f(-1.0, -1.0,  1.0)  # Bottom Left Of The Texture and Quad.
    glTexCoord2f(1.0, 0.0), glVertex3f( 1.0, -1.0,  1.0)  # Bottom Right Of The Texture and Quad.
    glTexCoord2f(1.0, 1.0), glVertex3f( 1.0,  1.0,  1.0)  # Top Right Of The Texture and Quad.
    glTexCoord2f(0.0, 1.0), glVertex3f(-1.0,  1.0,  1.0)  # Top Left Of The Texture and Quad.
    glEnd()


def DrawFrontFace():
    """ A texture binding created with glBindTexture remains active until a different texture
        is bound to the same target, or until the bound texture is deleted with glDeleteTextures.
    """
    glClear(GL_COLOR_BUFFER_BIT | GL_DEPTH_BUFFER_BIT) # Clear the screen and Depth buffer
    glLoadIdentity()        # Reset the geometry matrix.
    glTranslatef(0.0, 0.0, -5.0)
    make_rectangle_1(texture_1)
    glutSwapBuffers()

def main():
    glutInit("")
    glutInitDisplayMode(GLUT_RGBA | GLUT_DOUBLE | GLUT_ALPHA | GLUT_DEPTH)
```

```
glutInitWindowSize(650, 650)
window = glutCreateWindow(b"Textured rectangle.")
LoadTextures()
glutDisplayFunc(DrawFrontFace)
InitGL(650, 650)          # Initialize our window.
glutMainLoop()            # Start the event processing engine.

main()
```

The Six Permutations of Rectangular Mapping

Texture mapping 1

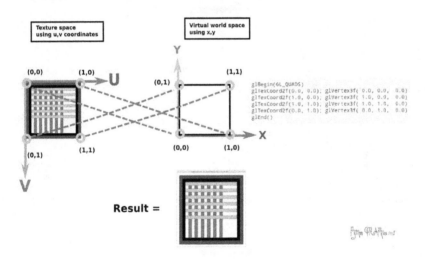

Texture Mapping 2

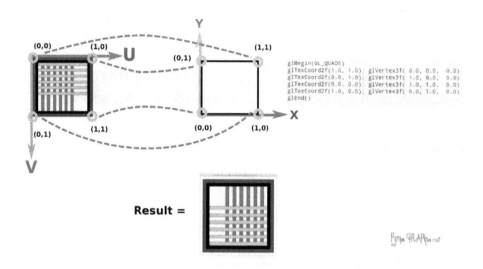

```
glBegin(GL_QUADS)
glTexCoord2f(1.0, 1.0); glVertex3f( 0.0, 0.0, 0.0)
glTexCoord2f(0.0, 1.0); glVertex3f( 1.0, 0.0, 0.0)
glTexCoord2f(0.0, 0.0); glVertex3f( 1.0, 1.0, 0.0)
glTexCoord2f(1.0, 0.0); glVertex3f( 0.0, 1.0, 0.0)
glEnd()
```

Result =

Texture Mapping 3

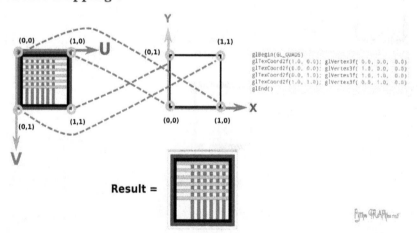

```
glBegin(GL_QUADS)
glTexCoord2f(1.0, 0.0); glVertex3f( 0.0, 0.0, 0.0)
glTexCoord2f(0.0, 0.0); glVertex3f( 1.0, 0.0, 0.0)
glTexCoord2f(0.0, 1.0); glVertex3f( 1.0, 1.0, 0.0)
glTexCoord2f(1.0, 1.0); glVertex3f( 0.0, 1.0, 0.0)
glEnd()
```

Result =

Texture Mapping 4

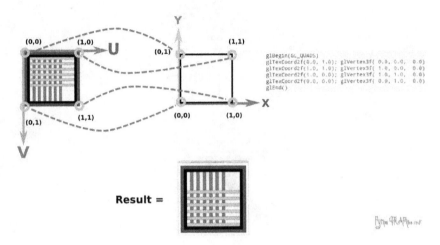

```
glBegin(GL_QUADS)
glTexCoord2f(0.0, 1.0); glVertex3f( 0.0, 0.0,  0.0)
glTexCoord2f(1.0, 1.0); glVertex3f( 1.0, 0.0,  0.0)
glTexCoord2f(1.0, 0.0); glVertex3f( 1.0, 1.0,  0.0)
glTexCoord2f(0.0, 0.0); glVertex3f( 0.0, 1.0,  0.0)
glEnd()
```

Result =

Texture Mapping 5

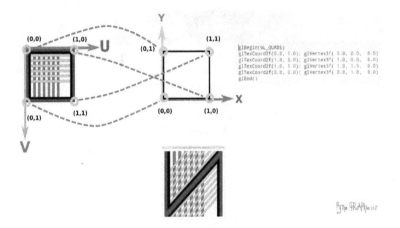

```
glBegin(GL_QUADS)
glTexCoord2f(0.0, 1.0); glVertex3f( 0.0, 0.0,  0.0)
glTexCoord2f(1.0, 0.0); glVertex3f( 1.0, 0.0,  0.0)
glTexCoord2f(1.0, 1.0); glVertex3f( 1.0, 1.0,  0.0)
glTexCoord2f(0.0, 0.0); glVertex3f( 0.0, 1.0,  0.0)
glEnd()
```

Texture Mapping 6

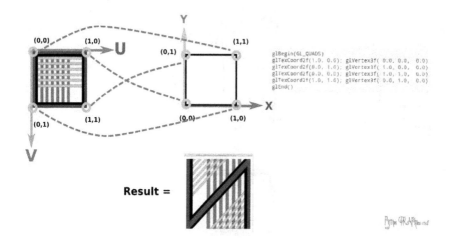

Result =

Python GRAPHics

Distortionless Texture Mappings

From the foregoing trials we have the following texture mapping schemes that do not distort the image but only rotate it or invert it horizontally or vertically. This is for images with the same aspect ratio as the target rectangle (quad). Where the width-to-height ratio of the image and the target rectangle are different the image will naturally be squashed or stretched to fit.

1. No change in geometry.

```
glBegin(GL_QUADS)
glTexCoord2f( 0,  0) , glVertex3f( 0,  0,  0)
glTexCoord2f( 1,  0) , glVertex3f( 1,  0,  0)
glTexCoord2f( 1,  1) , glVertex3f( 1,  1,  0)
glTexCoord2f( 0,  1) , glVertex3f( 0,  1,  0)
glEnd
```

2. Vertical and Horizontal Flip (inversion)

```
glBegin(GL_QUADS)
glTexCoord2f( 1,  1) , glVertex3f( 0,  0,   0)
glTexCoord2f( 0,  1) , glVertex3f( 1,  0,   0)
glTexCoord2f( 0,  0) , glVertex3f( 1,  1,   0)
glTexCoord2f( 1,  0) , glVertex3f( 0,  1,   0)
glEnd
```

3. Horizontal Flip (Lateral Inversion)

```
glBegin(GL_QUADS)
glTexCoord2f( 1,  0) , glVertex3f( 0,  0,   0)
glTexCoord2f( 0,  0) , glVertex3f( 1,  0,   0)
glTexCoord2f( 0,  1) , glVertex3f( 1,  1,   0)
glTexCoord2f( 1,  1) , glVertex3f( 0,  1,   0)
glEnd
```

4. Vertical Flip (Vertical Inversion)

```
glBegin(GL_QUADS)
glTexCoord2f( 0,  1) , glVertex3f( 0,  0,   0)
glTexCoord2f( 1,  1) , glVertex3f( 1,  0,   0)
glTexCoord2f( 1,  0) , glVertex3f( 1,  1,   0)
glTexCoord2f( 0,  0) , glVertex3f( 0,  1,   0)
glEnd
```

Mapping onto Non-Rectangular Areas like Triangles

If we see a triangle as a type of rectangle where two of the vertices are placed together onto the same point then we can map rectangular images onto triangluar areas in our 3D display window. In the example following we use this idea to create a kaliedoscopic image. The basic triangle is composed of two triangles that result if we vertically cut an equilateral triangle in two. An equilateral triangle has all sides the same length and the sides are at 60 degrees to each other.

A kaliedoscopic pattern ceated from the image **poppies_30.jpg**

```
"""
Program name: textured_hexagonal_kaliedoscope_1.py
Objective: Experiment with triangular texture mappings settings.

keywords: opengl, kaliedoscope, triangle, animation
================================================================================79
Comments:

Tested on: Python 2.6, Python 2.7.3, Python 3.2.3
Author:      Mike Ohlson de Fine
"""
from OpenGL.GL import *
from OpenGL.GLUT import *
from OpenGL.GLU import *
from PIL import Image

texture_1 = 0

def texture_setup(image_name, texture_num, ix, iy):
    """ Assign texture attributes to specific images.
    """
    glBindTexture(GL_TEXTURE_2D, texture_1)
    glTexEnvf(GL_TEXTURE_ENV, GL_TEXTURE_ENV_MODE, GL_MODULATE)
    glTexParameterf(GL_TEXTURE_2D, GL_TEXTURE_MIN_FILTER, GL_NEAREST)
    glTexParameterf(GL_TEXTURE_2D, GL_TEXTURE_WRAP_S, GL_CLAMP)
    glTexParameterf(GL_TEXTURE_2D, GL_TEXTURE_WRAP_T, GL_CLAMP)
    glTexParameterf(GL_TEXTURE_2D, GL_TEXTURE_WRAP_S, GL_REPEAT)
    glTexParameterf(GL_TEXTURE_2D, GL_TEXTURE_WRAP_T, GL_REPEAT)
    glTexParameterf(GL_TEXTURE_2D, GL_TEXTURE_MAG_FILTER, GL_NEAREST)
    glTexParameterf(GL_TEXTURE_2D, GL_TEXTURE_WRAP_S, GL_REPEAT)
    glPixelStorei(GL_UNPACK_ALIGNMENT,1)
    glEnable(GL_TEXTURE_2D)
    glTexImage2D(GL_TEXTURE_2D, 0, 3, ix, iy, 0, GL_RGBA, GL_UNSIGNED_BYTE, image_name)

def LoadTextures():
    """ Open texture images and convert them to "raw" pixel maps and
```

bind or associate each image with and integer refernece number.
"""

```
image_1 = Image.open("/home/mikeodf/constr/images_opengl/poppies_30.jpg")
ix = image_1.size[0]                    # image.size is a PIL function.
iy = image_1.size[1]
print ('ix:', ix)                        # Just checking.
print ('iy:', iy)
image_1 = image_1.tostring("raw", "RGBX", 0, -1)  # Convert jpg to the 'string' for textures.
texture_setup(image_1, 0, ix, iy)
```

```
def InitGL(Width, Height):
    """ A general OpenGL initialization function.  Sets all of the initial parameters.
    Called immediately after the OpenGL window is created.
    """

    glClearColor(0.0, 0.0, 0.0, 0.0) # Clear the background color to black.
    glMatrixMode(GL_PROJECTION)
    glLoadIdentity()             # Reset The Projection Matrix.
    gluPerspective(30.0, float(Width)/float(Height), 0.1, 100.0) # Aspect Ratio Of The Window, makes it
resizable.
    glMatrixMode(GL_MODELVIEW)
```

```
def make_triangular_rectangle_1(texture):
    """  Two Triangluar areas composed of two halves of an equilateral triangle.
    The second triangle will displat a horizontally inverted copy of the same image on the first triangle.
    The apex of both triangles are on the ( 0, 0, 0 ) position in 3d space. This simplifies positioning
    after rotation.
    """

    glBindTexture(GL_TEXTURE_2D,texture)
    # Rectangle Face (Each texture's corner is matched a quad's corner.)
    glBegin(GL_QUADS)
    glTexCoord2f(0.0, 0.0), glVertex3f( -1.0, -1.732,  0.0)# Bottom Left Of The Texture and Quad
    glTexCoord2f(1.0, 0.0), glVertex3f(  0.0, -1.732,  0.0)# Bottom Right Of The Texture and Quad
    glTexCoord2f(1.0, 1.0), glVertex3f(  0.00, 0.0,  0.0)  # Texture Top Right to Quad-narrow end.
    glTexCoord2f(0.0, 1.0), glVertex3f(  0.00, 0.0,  0.0)  # Texture Top Left to Quad-narrow end.
    glEnd()

    glBegin(GL_QUADS)
    glTexCoord2f(1.0, 0.0), glVertex3f(  0.0, -1.732,  0.0)
    glTexCoord2f(0.0, 0.0), glVertex3f(  1.0, -1.732,  0.0)
    glTexCoord2f(0.0, 1.0), glVertex3f(  0.00, 0.0,  0.0)
    glTexCoord2f(1.0, 1.0), glVertex3f(  0.00, 0.0,  0.0)
    glEnd()
```

```
def DrawFrontFace():
    """  A texture binding created with glBindTexture remains active until a different texture
    is bound to the same target, or until the bound texture is deleted with glDeleteTextures.
    """

    glClear(GL_COLOR_BUFFER_BIT | GL_DEPTH_BUFFER_BIT)
    glLoadIdentity()
    glTranslatef(0.0, 0.0, -5.0)
    glScalef(0.6, 0.6, 0.6)
    make_triangular_rectangle_1(texture_1)
    glRotatef(60.0, 0.0, 0.0, 1.0)
    make_triangular_rectangle_1(texture_1)
    glRotatef(60.0, 0.0, 0.0, 1.0)
    make_triangular_rectangle_1(texture_1)
```

```
        glRotatef(60.0, 0.0, 0.0, 1.0)
        make_triangular_rectangle_1(texture_1)
        glRotatef(60.0, 0.0, 0.0, 1.0)
        make_triangular_rectangle_1(texture_1)
        glRotatef(60.0, 0.0, 0.0, 1.0)
        glRotatef(60.0, 0.0, 0.0, 1.0)
        make_triangular_rectangle_1(texture_1)

        glutSwapBuffers()
#=====================================================================
def main():
        glutInit("")
        glutInitDisplayMode(GLUT_RGBA | GLUT_DOUBLE | GLUT_ALPHA | GLUT_DEPTH)
        glutInitWindowSize(650, 650)
        window = glutCreateWindow(b"Textured rectangle: Kaleidoscopic 60 degree rotations.")
        LoadTextures()
        glutDisplayFunc(DrawFrontFace)
        InitGL(650, 650)          # Initialize our window.
        glutMainLoop()            # Start the event processing engine

main()
```

Dynamic Transformations of Texture Maps

Now we discover how to place texture images on each of the six sides of a rotating cubes.

```
"""
Program name: textured_cubes_rotation_1.py
Objective: Fully cover two cubes with photo images.
Observe the result of ignoring pixel depth.
```

```
keywords: opengl, polygon, color control
==================================================================================79
comments: There are six 256 x 256 bmp images on the faces of a cube.
Usable image types:    bmp  and jpg work fine, but png does not.
Attempting to use png we get: "SystemError: unknown raw mode"

Tested on: Python 2.6, Python 2.7.3, Python 3.2.3
Author:        Mike Ohlson de Fine
"""
from OpenGL.GL import *
from OpenGL.GLUT import *
from OpenGL.GLU import *
from PIL import Image

# Rotation angles for each cube.
xrot1 = yrot1 = zrot1 = 0.0
xrot2 = yrot2 = zrot2 = 0.0
#==============================================================================
texture_1 = 0, 1, 2, 3, 4, 5, 6, 7, 8, 9, 10, 11
image_proto = Image.open("/home/mikeodf/constr/images_opengl/firesky_6821.jpg")
ix = image_proto.size[0]       # image.size is a PIL function.
iy = image_proto.size[1]
print( 'ix:', ix)                    # Just checking.
print ('iy:', iy )


def texture_setup(image_name, texture_num, ix, iy):
    """ Assign texture attributes to specific images.
    """
    glBindTexture(GL_TEXTURE_2D, texture_1[texture_num])
    glTexEnvf(GL_TEXTURE_ENV, GL_TEXTURE_ENV_MODE, GL_MODULATE)
    glTexParameterf(GL_TEXTURE_2D, GL_TEXTURE_MIN_FILTER, GL_NEAREST)
    glTexParameterf(GL_TEXTURE_2D, GL_TEXTURE_WRAP_S, GL_CLAMP)
    glTexParameterf(GL_TEXTURE_2D, GL_TEXTURE_WRAP_T, GL_CLAMP)
    glTexParameterf(GL_TEXTURE_2D, GL_TEXTURE_WRAP_S, GL_REPEAT)
    glTexParameterf(GL_TEXTURE_2D, GL_TEXTURE_WRAP_T, GL_REPEAT)
    glTexParameterf(GL_TEXTURE_2D, GL_TEXTURE_MAG_FILTER, GL_NEAREST)
    glTexParameterf(GL_TEXTURE_2D, GL_TEXTURE_WRAP_S, GL_REPEAT)
    glPixelStorei(GL_UNPACK_ALIGNMENT,1)
    glEnable(GL_TEXTURE_2D)
    glTexImage2D(GL_TEXTURE_2D, 0, 3, ix, iy, 0, GL_RGBA, GL_UNSIGNED_BYTE, image_name)

def LoadTextures():
    """ Open texture images and convert them to "raw" pixel maps and
        bind or associate each image with and integer refernece number.
    """
    image_12 = Image open("/home/mikeodf/constr/images_opengl/tree_7723.jpg")
    image_11 = Image open("/home/mikeodf/constr/images_opengl/sea_0049.jpg")
    image_10 = Image open("/home/mikeodf/constr/images_opengl/realowl_7958.jpg")
    image_9 = Image open("/home/mikeodf/constr/images_opengl/owl_1070.jpg")
    image_8 = Image open("/home/mikeodf/constr/images_opengl/blusset_0036.jpg")
    image_7 = Image open("/home/mikeodf/constr/images_opengl/green_0986.jpg")

    image_6 = Image open("/home/mikeodf/constr/images_opengl/weaver_1047.jpg")
    image_5 = Image open("/home/mikeodf/constr/images_opengl/watson_6202.jpg")
    image_4 = Image open("/home/mikeodf/constr/images_opengl/mount_morn1.jpg")
```

```
image_3 = Image open("/home/mikeodf/constr/images_opengl/marys_1026.jpg")
image_2 = Image open("/home/mikeodf/constr/images_opengl/rainbow_6754adj.jpg")
image_1 = Image open("/home/mikeodf/constr/images_opengl/firesky_6821.jpg")

image_1 = image_1.tostring("raw", "RGBX", 0, -1)  # convert bmp to the type needed for textures
image_2 = image_2.tostring("raw", "RGBX", 0, -1)
image_3 = image_3.tostring("raw", "RGBX", 0, -1)
image_4 = image_4.tostring("raw", "RGBX", 0, -1)
image_5 = image_5.tostring("raw", "RGBX", 0, -1)
image_6 = image_6.tostring("raw", "RGBX", 0, -1)


image_7  = image_7.tostring( "raw", "RGBX", 0, -1)   # convert bmp to the type needed for textures
image_8  = image_8.tostring( "raw", "RGBX", 0, -1)
image_9  = image_9.tostring( "raw", "RGBX", 0, -1)
image_10 = image_10.tostring("raw", "RGBX", 0, -1)
image_11 = image_11.tostring("raw", "RGBX", 0, -1)
image_12 = image_12.tostring("raw", "RGBX", 0, -1)


glGenTextures(11, texture_1)   # Create texture number and names and sizw.
#====================================
texture_setup(image_1, 0, ix, iy)
texture_setup(image_2, 1, ix, iy)
texture_setup(image_3, 2, ix, iy)
texture_setup(image_4, 3, ix, iy)
texture_setup(image_5, 4, ix, iy)
texture_setup(image_6, 5, ix, iy)


texture_setup(image_7, 6, ix, iy)
texture_setup(image_8, 7, ix, iy)
texture_setup(image_9, 8, ix, iy)
texture_setup(image_10, 9, ix, iy)
texture_setup(image_11, 10, ix, iy)
texture_setup(image_12, 11, ix, iy)


def InitGL(Width, Height):
    """ A general OpenGL initialization function.  Sets all of the initial parameters.
    We call this right after our OpenGL window is created.
    """

    glClearColor(0.0, 0.0, 0.0, 0.0)        # Clear the background color to black.
    glClearDepth(1.0)                       # Clear the Depth buffer.
    glDepthFunc(GL_LESS)                    # The type Of depth test to do.
    glEnable(GL_DEPTH_TEST)                 # Leave this Depth Testing and observe the visual weirdness.
    glMatrixMode(GL_PROJECTION)
    glLoadIdentity()                        # Reset The Projection Matrix.
    gluPerspective(45.0, float(Width)/float(Height), 0.1, 100.0) # Aspect ratio. Make window resizable.
    glMatrixMode(GL_MODELVIEW)


#=============================================================================
def make_cube_1(texture, texture_index):
    """ A generic cube. A texture binding created with glBindTexture remains active until a different
        texture is bound to the same target, or until the bound texture is deleted with glDeleteTextures.
    """

    glBindTexture(GL_TEXTURE_2D,texture[texture_index])
    # Front Face (Each texture's corner is matched a quad's corner.)
    glBegin(GL_QUADS)
        glTexCoord2f(0.0, 0.0); glVertex3f(-1.0, -1.0,  1.0)        # Bottom Left of The Texture and Quad
```

```python
glTexCoord2f(1.0, 0.0); glVertex3f( 1.0, -1.0,  1.0)      # Bottom Right of The Texture and Quad
glTexCoord2f(1.0, 1.0); glVertex3f( 1.0,  1.0,  1.0)      # Top Right of The Texture and Quad
glTexCoord2f(0.0, 1.0); glVertex3f(-1.0,  1.0,  1.0)      # Top Left of The Texture and Quad
glEnd();

glBindTexture(GL_TEXTURE_2D,texture[texture_index+1])
    # Back Face
    glBegin(GL_QUADS)
    glTexCoord2f(1.0, 0.0); glVertex3f(-1.0, -1.0, -1.0)      # Bottom Right
    glTexCoord2f(1.0, 1.0); glVertex3f(-1.0,  1.0, -1.0)      # Top Rightn
    glTexCoord2f(0.0, 1.0); glVertex3f( 1.0,  1.0, -1.0)      # Top Left
    glTexCoord2f(0.0, 0.0); glVertex3f( 1.0, -1.0, -1.0)      # Bottom Left
    glEnd()

glBindTexture(GL_TEXTURE_2D,texture[texture_index+2])
    # Top Face
    glBegin(GL_QUADS)
    glTexCoord2f(0.0, 1.0); glVertex3f(-1.0,  1.0, -1.0)      # Top Left
    glTexCoord2f(0.0, 0.0); glVertex3f(-1.0,  1.0,  1.0)      # Bottom Left
    glTexCoord2f(1.0, 0.0); glVertex3f( 1.0,  1.0,  1.0)      # Bottom Right
    glTexCoord2f(1.0, 1.0); glVertex3f( 1.0,  1.0, -1.0)      # Top Right
glEnd();

glBindTexture(GL_TEXTURE_2D,texture[texture_index+3])
# Bottom Face
    glBegin(GL_QUADS)
    glTexCoord2f(1.0, 1.0); glVertex3f(-1.0, -1.0, -1.0)      # Top Right
    glTexCoord2f(0.0, 1.0); glVertex3f( 1.0, -1.0, -1.0)      # Top Left
    glTexCoord2f(0.0, 0.0); glVertex3f( 1.0, -1.0,  1.0)      # Bottom Left
    glTexCoord2f(1.0, 0.0); glVertex3f(-1.0, -1.0,  1.0)      # Bottom Right
    glEnd();

glBindTexture(GL_TEXTURE_2D,texture[texture_index+4])
    # Right face
    glBegin(GL_QUADS)
    glTexCoord2f(1.0, 0.0); glVertex3f( 1.0, -1.0, -1.0)      # Bottom Right
    glTexCoord2f(1.0, 1.0); glVertex3f( 1.0,  1.0, -1.0)      # Top Right
    glTexCoord2f(0.0, 1.0); glVertex3f( 1.0,  1.0,  1.0)      # Top Left
    glTexCoord2f(0.0, 0.0); glVertex3f( 1.0, -1.0,  1.0)      # Bottom Left
    glEnd();

glBindTexture(GL_TEXTURE_2D,texture[texture_index+5])
    # Left Face
    glBegin(GL_QUADS)
    glTexCoord2f(0.0, 0.0); glVertex3f(-1.0, -1.0, -1.0)      # Bottom Left
    glTexCoord2f(1.0, 0.0); glVertex3f(-1.0, -1.0,  1.0)      # Bottom Right
    glTexCoord2f(1.0, 1.0); glVertex3f(-1.0,  1.0,  1.0)      # Top Right
    glTexCoord2f(0.0, 1.0); glVertex3f(-1.0,  1.0, -1.0)      # Top Left
glEnd();


def DrawFrontFace():
    """ A texture binding created with glBindTexture remains active until a different texture
    is bound to the same target, or until the bound texture is deleted with glDeleteTextures.
    """

    global xrot1, yrot1, zrot1, xrot2, yrot2, zrot2
    glClear(GL_COLOR_BUFFER_BIT | GL_DEPTH_BUFFER_BIT) # Clear the screen and Depth buffer
```

```
# First textured cube.
    glLoadIdentity()                              # Reset The View
    glTranslatef(-2.0,0.0,-5.0)                   # Shift cube left and back.
    glRotatef(xrot1,1.0,0.0,0.0)                  # Rotate the cube on It's X axis.
    glRotatef(yrot1,0.0,1.0,0.0)                  # Rotate the cube on It's Y axis.
    glRotatef(zrot1,0.0,0.0,0.0)                  # Rotate the cube on It's Z axis.
    make_cube_1(texture_1, 0)    # "0" is the first index no. of a six member sequence - images.
    xrot1 = xrot1 + 0.2          # X rotation of first cube.
    yrot1 = yrot1 - 0.1          # Y rotation
    zrot1 = zrot1 + 0.1          # Z rotation

# Second textured cube.
    glLoadIdentity()                              # Reset The view
    glTranslatef(1.5,0.0,-5.0)                    # Shift cube right and back.
    glRotatef(xrot2,1.0,0.0,0.0)                  # Rotate the cube on It's X axis.
    glRotatef(yrot2,0.0,1.0,0.0)                  # Rotate the cube on It's Y axis.
    glRotatef(zrot2,0.0,0.0,0.0)                  # Rotate the cube on It's Z axis
    make_cube_1(texture_1, 6)  # "6" is the first index no. of a different six member sequence - images.
    xrot2 = xrot2 - 0.1          # X rotation of second cube.
    yrot2 = yrot2 + 0.2          # Y rotation
    zrot2 = zrot2 + 0.4          # Z rotation

    glutSwapBuffers()
#================================================================================#
def main():
 glutInit("")
 glutInitDisplayMode(GLUT_RGBA | GLUT_DOUBLE | GLUT_ALPHA | GLUT_DEPTH)
 glutInitWindowSize(1000, 480)
 window = glutCreateWindow(b"Textured rotating cubes")
 LoadTextures()
 glutDisplayFunc(DrawFrontFace)
 glutIdleFunc(DrawFrontFace)       # When we are doing nothing, redraw the scene.
 InitGL(1000, 480)                 # Initialize our window.
 glutMainLoop()                    # Start the event processing engine

main()
```

Some experiments to try

Replace images on a rotating cube on the face that is out of sight.
Set up a wall of blocks that each show part of an image.
Rotate each block in the wall. Control six giant images that way.
Make flower with 3D petals made of wedge-shaped blocks.

Animating Images with Texture Maps

Now we explore how far we can go in simulating the effect of textured balls. With the image placed on a black background we create the illusion that we have mapped a detaile texture onto a spherical surface.

The **steel_ball3.jpg** image.

```
"""
Program name: bouncing_square_1.py
Objective: Animate a square covered with a steel ball texture..
OpenGL will not accept .gif images.

keywords: opengl, square, animation
==============================================================================79
comments:

Tested on: Python 2.6, Python 2.7.3, Python 3.2.3
Author:      Mike Ohlson de Fine
"""
from OpenGL.GL import *
from OpenGL.GLUT import *
from OpenGL.GLU import *
from PIL import Image

# Position and Velocity of the cube.
# ball_1
xpos_1 = ypos_1 = 0.0
zpos_1 = -10.0
xvel_1 = 0.02
yvel_1 = 0.03
zvel_1 = 0.01
#================================================================
texture_1 = 0, 1, 2, 3, 4, 5
image_proto = Image. open("/home/mikeodf/constr/images_opengl/steel_ball3.jpg")
ix = image_proto.size[0]      # image.size is a PIL function.
iy = image_proto.size[1]
print ( 'ix:', ix)           # Just checking.
print ('iy:', iy )

def texture_setup(image_name, texture_num, ix, iy):
    """ Assign texture attributes to specific images.
    """
    glBindTexture(GL_TEXTURE_2D, texture_1[texture_num])
```

```
glTexEnvf(GL_TEXTURE_ENV, GL_TEXTURE_ENV_MODE, GL_MODULATE)
glTexParameterf(GL_TEXTURE_2D, GL_TEXTURE_MIN_FILTER, GL_NEAREST)
glTexParameterf(GL_TEXTURE_2D, GL_TEXTURE_WRAP_S, GL_CLAMP)
glTexParameterf(GL_TEXTURE_2D, GL_TEXTURE_WRAP_T, GL_CLAMP)
glTexParameterf(GL_TEXTURE_2D, GL_TEXTURE_WRAP_S, GL_REPEAT)
glTexParameterf(GL_TEXTURE_2D, GL_TEXTURE_WRAP_T, GL_REPEAT)
glTexParameterf(GL_TEXTURE_2D, GL_TEXTURE_MAG_FILTER, GL_NEAREST)
glTexParameterf(GL_TEXTURE_2D, GL_TEXTURE_WRAP_S, GL_REPEAT)
glPixelStorei(GL_UNPACK_ALIGNMENT,1)
glEnable(GL_TEXTURE_2D)
glTexImage2D(GL_TEXTURE_2D, 0, 3, ix, iy, 0, GL_RGBA, GL_UNSIGNED_BYTE, image_name)

def LoadTextures():
    """ Open texture images and convert them to "raw" pixel maps and
        bind or associate each image with and integer refernece number.
    """
    image_1 = Image.open("/home/mikeodf/constr/images_opengl/steel_blue_ball3.jpg")
    image_1 = image_1.tostring("raw", "RGBX", 0, -1)  # convert bmp to the type needed for textures
    glGenTextures(11, texture_1)  # Create texture number and names and size.
    texture_setup(image_1, 0, ix, iy)

def InitGL(Width, Height):
    """ A general OpenGL initialization function.  Sets all of the initial parameters.
        We call this right after our OpenGL window is created.
    """
    glClearColor(0.0, 0.0, 0.0, 0.0) # Clear the background color to black.
    glClearDepth(1.0)                # Clear the Depth buffer.
    glDepthFunc(GL_LESS)             # The type Of depth test to do.
    glEnable(GL_DEPTH_TEST)          # Leave this Depth Testing and observe the visual weirdness.
    glMatrixMode(GL_PROJECTION)
    glLoadIdentity()                 # Reset The Projection Matrix.
    gluPerspective(30.0, float(Width)/float(Height), 0.1, 100.0) # Aspect Ratio Of The Window, makes it resizable.
    glMatrixMode(GL_MODELVIEW)


#=================================================================
def make_cube_1(texture, texture_index):
    """ A generic swuare. A texture binding created with glBindTexture remains active until
        a different texture is bound to the same target, or until the bound texture is
        deleted with glDeleteTextures.
    """
    glBindTexture(GL_TEXTURE_2D,texture[texture_index])
    # Front Face (Each texture's corner is matched a quad's corner.)
    glBegin(GL_QUADS)
    glTexCoord2f(0.0, 0.0); glVertex3f(-1.0, -1.0,  1.0)    # Bottom Left Of The Texture and Quad
    glTexCoord2f(1.0, 0.0); glVertex3f( 1.0, -1.0,  1.0)    # Bottom Right Of The Texture and Quad
    glTexCoord2f(1.0, 1.0); glVertex3f( 1.0,  1.0,  1.0)    #  Top Right Of The Texture and Quad
    glTexCoord2f(0.0, 1.0); glVertex3f(-1.0,  1.0,  1.0)    # Top Left Of The Texture and Quad
    glEnd();


def DrawFrontFace():
    """ A texture binding created with glBindTexture remains active until a different texture
        is bound to the same target, or until the bound texture is deleted with glDeleteTextures.
    """
    global xpos_1, ypos_1, zpos_1, xvel_1, yvel_1, zvel_1
    glClear(GL_COLOR_BUFFER_BIT | GL_DEPTH_BUFFER_BIT)
    #The textured square.
```

```
glLoadIdentity()                                          # Reset The View
glTranslatef(xpos_1, ypos_1, zpos_1)                # Shift cube left and back.
make_cube_1(texture_1, 0)  # "0" is the first index no. of a six member sequence - images.
# Ball_1 - blue
xpos_1 = xpos_1 + xvel_1
ypos_1 = ypos_1 + yvel_1
zpos_1 = zpos_1 + zvel_1
if xpos_1 >= 3.0 or xpos_1 <= -2.0:
    xvel_1 = -xvel_1
if ypos_1 >= 3.0 or ypos_1 <= -3.0:
    yvel_1 = -yvel_1
 if zpos_1 >= -5.01 or zpos_1 <= -30.0:
    zvel_1 = -zvel_1
  glutSwapBuffers()
#===========================================================================
def main():
 glutInit("")
 glutInitDisplayMode(GLUT_RGBA | GLUT_DOUBLE | GLUT_ALPHA | GLUT_DEPTH)
 glutInitWindowSize(500, 500)
 window = glutCreateWindow(b"Textured rectangle bouncing")
 LoadTextures()
 glutDisplayFunc(DrawFrontFace)
 glutIdleFunc(DrawFrontFace)          # When we are doing nothing, redraw the scene.
 InitGL(500, 500)                     # Initialize our window.
 glutMainLoop()                       # Start the event processing engine

main()
```

Can we extend the bouncing ball effect to multiple balls?

In the next example we explore this possibility.

Multiple Ball Image Animations

Here we experiment with multiple bouncing balls in a three dimensional volume
where the effect of perspective creates the impression of moving backwards and
forwards. The flaw that breaks the complete illusion is when the black corners of any
of the images moves across any colored area of another image. What we would like to
be able to do would be to cover a disk shaped object with texture-images or somehow
make portions of the image transparent. Although it is possible to make images
transparent with alpha channel color values of zero, it is not possible to apply this to
selected portions of images. It is the whole image or none.

Animated control of steel_ball3.jpg,

steel_green_ball3.jpg, steel_red_ball3.jpg, steel_blue_ball3.jpg.

To keep the program below to a reasonable length we have eliminated lines of code that are identical to sections in the previous example. We indicate these sections with line in blue text like: {{ code identical to previous example (bouncing_square_1.py) }}

```
"""
Program name: multiple_bouncing_balls_1.py
etc.
Author:        Mike Ohlson de Fine
"""

from OpenGL.GL import *
from OpenGL.GLUT import *
from OpenGL.GLU import *
from PIL import Image

# Starting position and Velocity of the cube.
# ball_1
xpos_1 = ypos_1 = 0.0
zpos_1 = -10.0
xvel_1 = 0.02
yvel_1 = 0.03
zvel_1 = 0.01

# ball_2
xpos_2 = ypos_2 = 0.0
zpos_2 = -10.0
xvel_2 = -0.025
yvel_2 = -0.03
zvel_2 = -0.01

# ball_3
xpos_3 = ypos_3 = 0.0
zpos_3 = -20.0
xvel_3 = 0.015
yvel_3 = 0.02
zvel_3 = 0.02
```

```python
# ball_4
xpos_4 = ypos_4 = 0.0
zpos_4 = -15.0
xvel_4 = -0.02
yvel_4 = -0.025
zvel_4 = -0.015


#====================================================================
texture_1 = 0, 1, 2, 3, 4, 5
image_proto = Image.open("/home/mikeodf/constr/images_opengl/steel_ball3.jpg")
ix = image_proto.size[0]     # image.size is a PIL function.
iy = image_proto.size[1]
print ('ix:', ix )
print '(iy:', iy)


def texture_setup(image_name, texture_num, ix, iy):
    """ Assign texture attributes to specific images.
    """
    {{ code identical to previous example (bouncing_square_1.py ) }}


def LoadTextures():
    """ Open texture images and convert them to "raw" pixel maps and
        bind or associate each image with and integer refernece number.
    """
    image_1 = Image. open("/home/mikeodf/constr/images_opengl/steel_ball3.jpg")
    image_2 = Image .open("/home/mikeodf/constr/images_opengl/steel_green_ball3.jpg")
    image_3 = Image .open("/home/mikeodf/constr/images_opengl/steel_blue_ball3.jpg")
    image_4 = Image .open("/home/mikeodf/constr/images_opengl/steel_red_ball3.jpg")

    image_1 = image_1.tostring("raw", "RGBX", 0, -1)   # Convert bmp to the type needed for textures .
    image_2 = image_2.tostring("raw", "RGBX", 0, -1)
    image_3 = image_3.tostring("raw", "RGBX", 0, -1)
    image_4 = image_4.tostring("raw", "RGBX", 0, -1)
    glGenTextures(3, texture_1)                         # Create texture number and names and size.

    texture_setup(image_1, 0, ix, iy)
    texture_setup(image_2, 1, ix, iy)
    texture_setup(image_3, 2, ix, iy)
    texture_setup(image_4, 3, ix, iy)


def InitGL(Width, Height):
    """ A general OpenGL initialization function. Sets all of the initial parameters.
        We call this right after our OpenGL window is created.
    """
    {{ code identical to previous example (bouncing_square_1.py ) }}


def DrawFrontFace():
    """ A texture binding created with glBindTexture remains active until a different texture
        is bound to the same target, or until the bound texture is deleted with glDeleteTextures.
    """
    global xpos_1, ypos_1, zpos_1, xvel_1, yvel_1, zvel_1
    global xpos_2, ypos_2, zpos_2, xvel_2, yvel_2, zvel_2
    global xpos_3, ypos_3, zpos_3, xvel_3, yvel_3, zvel_3
    global xpos_4, ypos_4, zpos_4, xvel_4, yvel_4, zvel_4
```

```
glClear(GL_COLOR_BUFFER_BIT | GL_DEPTH_BUFFER_BIT)

    # Textured cube 1 (grey).
    glLoadIdentity()                        # Reset the view.
    glTranslatef(xpos_1, ypos_1, zpos_1)         # Shift cube incrementally.
    make_cube_1(texture_1, 0)  # "0" is the first index no. of a four member sequence - images.

    # Textured cube 2 (green).
    glLoadIdentity()                        # Reset the view.
    glTranslatef(xpos_2, ypos_2, zpos_2)         # Shift cube incrementally.
    make_cube_1(texture_1, 1)  # "1" is the second index no. of a four member sequence - images.

    # Textured cube 3 (blue).
    glLoadIdentity()                        # Reset the view.
    glTranslatef(xpos_3, ypos_3, zpos_3)         # Shift cube incrementally.
    make_cube_1(texture_1, 2)  # "2" is the third index no. of a four member sequence - images.

    # Textured cube 4 (red).
    glLoadIdentity()                        # Reset the view.
    glTranslatef(xpos_4, ypos_4, zpos_4)         # Shift cube incrementally.
    make_cube_1(texture_1, 3)  # "3" is the fourth index no. of a four member sequence - images.

# Ball_1 - grey : crude bounce simulation.
xpos_1 = xpos_1 + xvel_1
ypos_1 = ypos_1 + yvel_1
zpos_1 = zpos_1 + zvel_1
if xpos_1 >= 3.0 or xpos_1 <= -2.0:
    xvel_1 = -xvel_1
if ypos_1 >= 3.0 or ypos_1 <= -3.0:
    yvel_1 = -yvel_1
if zpos_1 >= -5.01 or zpos_1 <= -30.0:
    zvel_1 = -zvel_1

# Ball_2 - green : crude bounce simulation.
xpos_2 = xpos_2 + xvel_2
ypos_2 = ypos_2 + yvel_2
zpos_2 = zpos_2 + zvel_2
if xpos_2 >= 3.0 or xpos_2 <= -2.0:
    xvel_2 = -xvel_2
if ypos_2 >= 3.0 or ypos_2 <= -3.0:
    yvel_2 = -yvel_2
if zpos_2 >= -5.01 or zpos_2 <= -30.0:
    zvel_2 = -zvel_2

# Ball_3 - blue : crude bounce simulation.
xpos_3 = xpos_3 + xvel_3
ypos_3 = ypos_3 + yvel_3
zpos_3 = zpos_3 + zvel_3
if xpos_3 >= 3.0 or xpos_3 <= -2.0:
    xvel_3 = -xvel_3
if ypos_3 >= 3.0 or ypos_3 <= -3.0:
    yvel_3 = -yvel_3
if zpos_3 >= -5.01 or zpos_3 <= -30.0:
    zvel_3 = -zvel_3

# Ball_4 - red : crude bounce simulation.
```

```
    xpos_4 = xpos_4 + xvel_4
    ypos_4 = ypos_4 + yvel_4
    zpos_4 = zpos_4 + zvel_4
    if xpos_4 >= 3.0 or xpos_4 <= -2.0:
        xvel_4 = -xvel_4
    if ypos_4 >= 3.0 or ypos_4 <= -3.0:
        yvel_4 = -yvel_4
    if zpos_4 >= -5.01 or zpos_4 <= -30.0:
        zvel_4 = -zvel_4

    glutSwapBuffers()
#-----------------------------------------------------------------
def main():
    {{ code identical to previous example (bouncing_square_1.py ) }}
main()
```

13

OpenGL: Fog and Transparency.

"The fog comes on little cat feet. It sits looking over harbor and city on silent haunches and then moves on. " Carl Sandberg.

"Distance fog is a technique used in 3D computer graphics to enhance the perception of distance by simulating fog." Wikipedia.

The topics in this chapter we deal with fog as a visual control effect. It's artistic value is not so much to suggest minute water droplets hanging in the air but rather the fact that objects are paler in color when far away. Fog enhances perspective.

Topics covered in this chapter are:

- **The purpose of Fog**
- **Fog Color Calculations**
- **Fog Color Graphs**
- **Linear Fog**
- **Exponential Fog**
- **Colored Fog**
- **Tranparency**
- **Dynamic Control of Transparency**

OpenGL can do so many things – it is *powerful* as they say. It is highly complex and consequently very difficult to start learning. A lot of the examples and tutorials on the web are written for C and C++ programmers. The examples that are for Python users are adaptions of C code. However, despite these difficulties, it is well worth the trouble to learn to use OpenGL with Python.

Particular effects like fog, transparency, lighting and light reflection from surfaces offer unlimited choices. OpenGL does a good job of simplifying these special effects but using them well will take an enormous amount of trial and error, experience and artistic insight. Although comprehensive treatment of these topics is well beyond the scope of this book we will work through examples that are designed to give us a boost that enables us to understand and harvest the vast number of hints and examples on the web.

So the plan now is to try some examples that can serve as a launching pad for deeper expertise.

Fog – The Purpose

Leonardo da Vinci, the artist genius, understood that the dimming and color paling effect of fog was vital to enhancing the sense of depth and distance in an image. He said

*"The divisions of Perspective are 3, as used in drawing; of these, the first includes the diminution in size of opaque objects; the second treats of the diminution and loss of outline in such opaque objects; **the third, of the diminution and loss of colour at long distances.**"*

If we want make an outdoor scene, with distant features like mountains, valleys or cities then these features look more real if they are made dimmer using some kind of fog effect.

This is demonstrated in the landscape images below. The main thing to notice is how features become paler as they are more distant. The second noteworthy attribute is how the color of the fog influences the mood and apparent temperature of the scene.

These observations introduce the ideas of fog density-distance curve and fog color, both of which we can control using OpenGL.

OpenGL tries to simulate real fog by combining the inherent colors of objects in a scene together with the color of the fog. Typically fog is grey but we can make it any color we want. Real fog has a density which is a measure of how difficult it would be to see objects in the fog. OpenGL uses three equations to calculate how dense (opaque) the fog should be. This "density" is called fog-factor f and is used to combine fog color with the color of objects in a scene.

Fog Density-rate Calculations

Fog *density-rate* (or density-distance rate) describes how fast the fog density grows for objects that are further away. Fog density is the amount of fog between the viewer and the object being viewed.

The expression "the fog was so dense I could not see my hand at the end of my arm" describes a fog density that completely hides any object at a distance of about one meter (yard). As mentioned above, there are three equations that we can use to control the fog density-with-distance rate that OpenGL applies fog to our model. Roughly speaking there is linear density-distance rate which is the slowest. We can see furthest in linear fog. Then there is exponential fog which gets dense fast. Finally there is exponential-squared which is the fastest. We can specify at which distances the fog must start and end. The variable *density* controls how dense the fog is to start with. The equations used are given below. It may be easier to vizualize the effect of the different equations using the graph shown below.

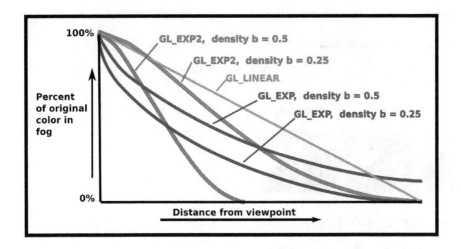

The three fog equations.

They each determine how dense the fog is by means of calculating a fog factor f.

Linear Fog is the simplest fog equation. It blends the fog color with original color based on the distance between the viewer and the object in the scene. We need two parameters to create this function. The first one is the *fogStart* parameter or minimum distance where we need to provide information where the fog should start to blend, and of course the second one is the *fogEnd* or the maximum distance where the fog color will block (cover) the original color from the viewer.

We call f the fogFactor and this value should give a value between 0.0 and 1.0 to get a correct mix between original color and fog color, so we need to clamp it between 0.0 and 1.0.

> ## Linear fogFactor:
>
> $$f = \frac{fogEnd - vertexViewDistance}{fogEnd - fogStart}$$

The images below are the result of applying various fogStart and fogEnd distances.

The OpenGL instructions controlling this are:
glFogi(GL_FOG_MODE, GL_LINEAR)   # Linear Fog settings: GL_LINEAR.
glFogf(GL_FOG_START, 1.0)   # Near distance in the fog equation: f = (near-c)/(near-far)
glFogf(GL_FOG_END, 17.0)   # Far distance in the fog equation:

An OpenGL array of colored balls with no fog applied to the image:

glFogf(GL_FOG_DENSITY, 0.125)

glFogf(GL_FOG_DENSITY, 0.25)

glFogf(GL_FOG_DENSITY, 0.5)

glFogf(GL_FOG_DENSITY, 1.0)

Exponential Fog

Exponential fog expressions are best described by demonstrating their influence on object at various distances as shown below.

Exponential fogFactor

$$f = \frac{1}{e^{d*b}}$$

where d = vertex distance
b = attenuation factor

Exponential Squared fogFactor

$$f = \frac{1}{e^{(d*b)^2}}$$

Attenuation factor b in above equations.

```
glFogf(GL_FOG_DENSITY, 1.0)      - very dense fog.
glFogf(GL_FOG_DENSITY, 0.5)
glFogf(GL_FOG_DENSITY, 0.25)
glFogf(GL_FOG_DENSITY, 0.125)    - low density fog.
```

OpenGl instruction to use exponential or exponential-squared:

glFogi(GL_FOG_MODE, GL_EXP)   **glFogi(GL_FOG_MODE, GL_EXP2)**

238

Exponential fog factor.   **Exponential-squared fog factor.**

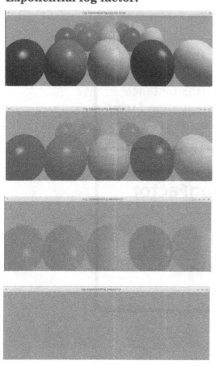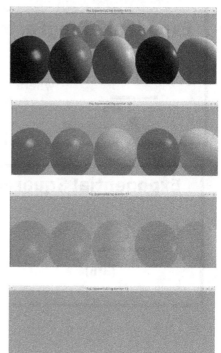

The Python program below will allow us to experiment with the complete range of fog control variables. We just need to un-comment the equations we want to apply while commenting out those we want to have no influence. As the code stands it enables linear fog. If we wanted exponential-squared fog then we would alter the fog equation instructions to:

```
#glFogi(GL_FOG_MODE, GL_LINEAR)      # Linear Fog settings: GL_LINEAR.
#glFogf(GL_FOG_START, 1.0)           # Near distance in the fog equation: f =  (near-c)/(near-far)
#glFogf(GL_FOG_END, 17.0)            # Far distance in the fog equation:

#glFogi(GL_FOG_MODE, GL_EXP)         # Exponential fog
glFogi(GL_FOG_MODE, GL_EXP2)         # Exponential squared fog
glFogf(GL_FOG_DENSITY, 0.5)          # Fog density exponent for both GL_EXP and GL_EXP2
```

For pure exponential fog then the last section would be:

```
glFogi(GL_FOG_MODE, GL_EXP)          # Exponential fog
#glFogi(GL_FOG_MODE, GL_EXP2)         # Exponential squared fog
glFogf(GL_FOG_DENSITY, 0.5)          # Fog density exponent for both GL_EXP and GL_EXP2
```

```
"""
Program name: opengl_fog_material_lighting_1.py
Objective: Explore fog design.

keywords: opengl, fog, lighting, materials, sphere, icosahedron.
==============================================================================================79
Comments: Experimentation with fog.

fog properties:
  glFogi(GL_FOG_MODE, GL_LINEAR)        # Fog linear gradient calculated using (Near-Far)
  glFogf(GL_FOG_START, 1.0);            # Near distance in the fog equation: f =  (Near-c)/(Near-Far)
  glFogf(GL_FOG_END, 17.0);            # Far distance in the fog equation

  glFogi(GL_FOG_MODE, GL_EXP)          # f = 1/e**(distance*density)
  glFogi(GL_FOG_MODE, GL_EXP2)         # f = 1/(e**(distance*density))**2
  glFogf(GL_FOG_DENSITY, 0.5)          # Exponent multiplier in fog equation f = 1/e**(distance*density)

Tested on: Python 2.6
 Python 2.7.3
Test failed with Python 3.2.3
Author:  Mike Ohlson de Fine
"""
from OpenGL.GL import *
from OpenGL.GLUT import *
from OpenGL.GLU import *
import math

# material colors.
kula_red      = [ 1.0,0.0, 0.0 ]     # Red
kula_green    = [ 0.0,1.0, 0.0 ]     # Green
kula_blue     = [ 0.0,0.0, 1.0 ]     # Blue
kula_white    = [ 1.0,1.0,1.0 ]      # White
kula_charcoal = [ 0.1,0.1,0.1 ]      # Dark charcoal

# Lighting Parameters.
```

```
light_specular = [ 1.0, 1.0, 1.0, 1.0 ]
light_position_1 = [ 10.0, 5.0, 5.0, 1.0 ]

# Material Parmeters.
material_specular   = [ 1.0, 1.0, 1.0, 1.0 ]
high_shininess = [ 127.0 ]

def InitGL(Width, Height):          # Set OpenGL up in the required state .
    glClearColor(0.6, 0.6, 0.6, 1.0)    # Set the background color to Black .
    glClearDepth(1.0)                   # Clear the Depth buffer .
    glDepthFunc(GL_LESS)                # Type of depth test.
    glEnable(GL_DEPTH_TEST)             # Enable depth testing .
    #-----------------------------
    # Lighting and materials
    glEnable(GL_LIGHT0)
    glEnable(GL_NORMALIZE)
    glEnable(GL_COLOR_MATERIAL)
    glEnable(GL_LIGHTING)

    glLightfv(GL_LIGHT0, GL_SPECULAR, light_specular)
    glLightfv(GL_LIGHT0, GL_POSITION, light_position_1)
    glMaterialfv(GL_FRONT, GL_SPECULAR,  material_specular)
    glMaterialfv(GL_FRONT, GL_SHININESS, high_shininess)
    ######### FOG  parameters start ###############################################
    # Fog Parameters
    glEnable(GL_FOG)                          # Enable fog
    fogColor=(0.6, 0.6, 0.6, 1.0)            # fog color
    glFogfv(GL_FOG_COLOR, fogColor)          # Set fog color (grey).

    glFogi(GL_FOG_MODE, GL_LINEAR)           # Linear Fog settings: GL_LINEAR.
    glFogf(GL_FOG_START, 1.0)                # Near distance in the fog equation: f =  (near-c)/(near-far)
    glFogf(GL_FOG_END, 17.0)                 # Far distance in the fog equation:

    #glFogi(GL_FOG_MODE, GL_EXP)             # Exponential fog
    #glFogi(GL_FOG_MODE, GL_EXP2)            # Exponential squared fog
    #glFogf(GL_FOG_DENSITY, 0.5)             # Fog density exponent for both GL_EXP and GL_EXP2
    ######### FOG  parameters end ###############################################
    glShadeModel(GL_SMOOTH)
    glMatrixMode(GL_PROJECTION)
    glLoadIdentity()
    gluPerspective(40.0, float(Width)/float(Height), 1.0, 30.0)
    glMatrixMode(GL_MODELVIEW)
#=========================================================
# Planetary parameters and Controls
#==================================
sun_location   = [0.0, 1.0, -9.0 ] # Position of the Sun.
sun_earth = 6.0                    # Distances between planet and sun.
earth_orbit_angle = 0              # Planet orbit position in path around sun.

def orbit_yz_plane(radius, angle):
    """ GetrRelative coordinates wrt sun due to orbital rotation.
       Distance of planet = radius, angle = radian distance around orbit.
    """
    yy = radius * math.cos(angle)
    zz = radius * math.sin(angle)
    return [yy, zz]
```

```
def add_vectors(loc1, loc2):
    """ Vector addition of 3D vectors.
        Solar system position is sum af sun's position
        added to position relative to the sun.
    """
    xx = loc1[0] + loc2[0]
    yy = loc1[1] + loc2[1]
    zz = loc1[2] + loc2[2]
    return [ xx, yy, zz ]
#===========================================================
# Rows of Spheres
#===================
rradius = 0.5
sslices = 30
sstacks = 30
shape = [ rradius, sslices, sstacks ] # Shape of sphere

def sphereic(xx, yy, zz, x_incr, y_incr, z_incr, kula):
    """ Draw a group of four spheres in a row formation.
        The position and color parameters are supplied as arguments.
    """
    glLoadIdentity()
    glColor(kula[0], kula[1], kula[2] )
    xyz = [ xx+x_incr,  yy+y_incr,  zz+z_incr ]
    glTranslatef(xyz[0], xyz[1], xyz[2] )
    glutSolidSphere(shape[0], shape[1], shape[2])

def row_spheres( xx, yy, zz, x_incr, y_incr, z_incr):
    """ Draw a row of five colored spheres.
        Charcoal, red, green, blue, white.
    """
    xx = -1.0
    yy = -3.0
    zz = -4.0
    sphereic(xx, yy, zz, x_incr, y_incr, z_incr, kula_charcoal)
    x_incr = 0.0
    sphereic(xx, yy, zz, x_incr, y_incr, z_incr, kula_red)
    x_incr = 1.0
    sphereic(xx, yy, zz, x_incr, y_incr, z_incr, kula_green)
    x_incr = 2.0
    sphereic(xx, yy, zz, x_incr, y_incr, z_incr, kula_blue)
    x_incr = 3.0
    sphereic(xx, yy, zz, x_incr, y_incr, z_incr, kula_white)

# The main drawing function.
def DrawGLScene():
    global sun_location, sun_earth, earth_orbit_angle

    glLightfv(GL_LIGHT0, GL_POSITION, light_position_1 )
    glClear(GL_COLOR_BUFFER_BIT | GL_DEPTH_BUFFER_BIT)  # Clear Screen and Depth buffer

    xx = -1.0
    yy = -3.0
    zz = -4.0
    row_spheres( xx, yy, zz, -1.0, 2.0, 0.0)      # First row.
    row_spheres( xx, yy, zz, -1.0, 2.0, -4.0)     # Second row.
    row_spheres( xx, yy, zz, -1.0, 2.0, -8.0)     # Third row.
```

```
   row_spheres( xx, yy, zz, -1.0, 2.0, -12.0)        # Fourth row.

   # Draw Icosahedron - Planet
   glLoadIdentity()
   earth_orbit_angle += 0.01
   new_zx = orbit_yz_plane(sun_earth, earth_orbit_angle)
   temp_earth_loc = [0.0, new_zx[0], new_zx[1] ]        # New planet position relative to sun.
   temp_earth_loc = add_vectors(sun_location, temp_earth_loc)
   glTranslatef(temp_earth_loc[0], temp_earth_loc[1], temp_earth_loc[2])
   glColor(1.0,0.2, 0.2)  # Reddish.
   glutSolidIcosahedron()

   glutSwapBuffers()

def main():
   glutInit(sys.argv)
   glutInitDisplayMode(GLUT_RGBA | GLUT_DOUBLE | GLUT_DEPTH)
   glutInitWindowSize(1000, 600)
   glutInitWindowPosition(0, 0)
   window = glutCreateWindow("Fog. linear:color: grey(0.6, 0.6, 0.6, 1.0). start-end:1-17 ")
   glutDisplayFunc(DrawGLScene)
   glutIdleFunc(DrawGLScene)
   InitGL(1000, 600)
   glutMainLoop()

main()
```

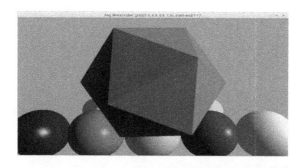

Colored Fog

When colored fog is used, the color of objects is dominated more and more by the fog color as the objects are placed further away from the view point.

White Fog:

Red Fog

Green Fog

Blue Fog

Yellow Fog

The OpenGL instructions we use are:

```
fogColor=(0.0, 0.0, 0.2, 1.0)      # Fog color (dark blue).
  glEnable(GL_FOG)                          # Enable fog
  glFogi(GL_FOG_MODE, GL_LINEAR)            # Fog settings: GL_LINEAR, GL_EXP, or GL_EXP2.
  glFogfv(GL_FOG_COLOR, fogColor);          # Set fog color (blue).
  glFogf(GL_FOG_DENSITY, 1.0);              # Set fog density
  glFogf(GL_FOG_START, 0.2);                # Near distance in the fog equation: f = (near-c)/(near-far)
  glFogf(GL_FOG_END, 5.0);                  # Far distance in the fog equation.
```

We can vary fog density between 0.0 (no fog) to 1.0 (maximum fog) and we can control how the fog intensity varies with the different GL_LINEAR, GL_EXP, or GL_EXP2 settings in the GL_FOG_MODE instruction.

```
"""
Program name: opengl_foggy_moon_1.py
Objective: Demonstrate fog.

keywords: opengl, cube, moon, fog
===============================================================================79
Comments: Fog blends a fog color with each rasterized pixel.
          The fog is applied an top of the texture image.
          The fog "density" is controlled by a blending factor f.
          Factor f is computed in one of three ways,
          depending on the fog mode (linear or exponentials).
          Let c be either the distance in eye coordinate from the origin, then
          the equation for GL_LINEAR fog is f = (near-c)/(near-far).

Tested on: Python 2.7.3
Test failed with Python 3.2.3 - problem using Image.py module.
Author:      Mike Ohlson de Fine
"""
from OpenGL.GL import *
from OpenGL.GLUT import *
from OpenGL.GLU import *
from PIL import Image
xrot = yrot = zrot = 0.0       # Rotations for cube.
fogColor=(0.0, 0.0, 0.2, 1.0)  # Fog color (dark blue).

def LoadTextures():
    image = Image.open("/home/mikeodf/constr/images_opengl/Moon.jpg")
    ix = image.size[0]
    iy = image.size[1]
    image = image.tostring("raw", "RGBX", 0, -1)

    # Create Texture
    glBindTexture(GL_TEXTURE_2D, glGenTextures(1))  # 2D texture.
    glPixelStorei(GL_UNPACK_ALIGNMENT,1)
    glTexImage2D(GL_TEXTURE_2D, 0, 3, ix, iy, 0, GL_RGBA, GL_UNSIGNED_BYTE, image)
    glTexParameterf(GL_TEXTURE_2D, GL_TEXTURE_WRAP_S, GL_CLAMP)
    glTexParameterf(GL_TEXTURE_2D, GL_TEXTURE_WRAP_T, GL_CLAMP)
    glTexParameterf(GL_TEXTURE_2D, GL_TEXTURE_WRAP_S, GL_REPEAT)
    glTexParameterf(GL_TEXTURE_2D, GL_TEXTURE_WRAP_T, GL_REPEAT)
    glTexParameterf(GL_TEXTURE_2D, GL_TEXTURE_MAG_FILTER, GL_NEAREST)
    glTexParameterf(GL_TEXTURE_2D, GL_TEXTURE_MIN_FILTER, GL_NEAREST)
    glTexEnvf(GL_TEXTURE_ENV, GL_TEXTURE_ENV_MODE, GL_DECAL)
```

```python
def InitGL(Width, Height):          # OpenGL initialization function.
    LoadTextures()
    glEnable(GL_TEXTURE_2D)
    glClearDepth(1.0)                       # Clear the Depth buffer.
    glDepthFunc(GL_LESS)                # Type Of Depth test.
    glEnable(GL_DEPTH_TEST)         # Enable Depth testing
    glMatrixMode(GL_PROJECTION)
    glLoadIdentity()                    # Reset The projection Matrix
    gluPerspective(45.0, float(Width)/float(Height), 0.1, 100.0)
    glMatrixMode(GL_MODELVIEW)


def DrawGLScene(): # The main drawing function.
    global xrot, yrot, zrot, texture

    glClear(GL_COLOR_BUFFER_BIT | GL_DEPTH_BUFFER_BIT) # Clear screen and Depth buffer.
    glLoadIdentity()                                                    # Reset The View
    glClearColor(0.0,0.0,0.1,1.0)                                      # Background color. Dark blue

    glEnable(GL_FOG)                            # Enable fog
    glFogi(GL_FOG_MODE, GL_LINEAR)       # Fog settings: GL_LINEAR, GL_EXP, or GL_EXP2.
    glFogfv(GL_FOG_COLOR, fogColor)        # Set fog color (blue).
    glFogf(GL_FOG_DENSITY, 1.0)            # Set fog density
    glFogf(GL_FOG_START, 0.2)             # Near distance in the fog equation: f = (near-c)/(near-far)
    glFogf(GL_FOG_END, 5.0)               # Far distance in the fog equation.

    glTranslatef(0.0,0.0,-4.8)          # Move cube into the screen - negative z-direction.
    glRotatef(xrot,1.0,0.0,0.0)         # Rotate The Cube On It's X Axis
    glRotatef(yrot,0.0,1.0,0.0)         # Rotate The Cube On It's Y Axis
    glRotatef(zrot,0.0,0.0,1.0)         # Rotate The Cube On It's Z Axis

    glBegin(GL_QUADS)  # Three faces of a cube.
    # Front Face. The texture's corners have to match the quad's corners .
    glTexCoord2f(0.0, 0.0); glVertex3f(-1.0, -1.0,  1.0)   # Bottom Left Of The Texture and Quad
    glTexCoord2f(1.0, 0.0); glVertex3f( 1.0, -1.0,  1.0)   # Bottom Right Of The Texture and Quad
    glTexCoord2f(1.0, 1.0); glVertex3f( 1.0,  1.0,  1.0)   # Top Right Of The Texture and Quad
    glTexCoord2f(0.0, 1.0); glVertex3f(-1.0,  1.0,  1.0)   # Top Left Of The Texture and Quad

    # Top Face
    glTexCoord2f(0.0, 1.0); glVertex3f(-1.0,  1.0, -1.0)   # Top Left Of The Texture and Quad
    glTexCoord2f(0.0, 0.0); glVertex3f(-1.0,  1.0,  1.0)   # Bottom Left Of The Texture and Quad
    glTexCoord2f(1.0, 0.0); glVertex3f( 1.0,  1.0,  1.0)   # Bottom Right Of The Texture and Quad
    glTexCoord2f(1.0, 1.0); glVertex3f( 1.0,  1.0, -1.0)   # Top Right Of The Texture and Quad

    # Right face
    glTexCoord2f(1.0, 0.0); glVertex3f( 1.0, -1.0, -1.0)   # Bottom Right Of The Texture and Quad
    glTexCoord2f(1.0, 1.0); glVertex3f( 1.0,  1.0, -1.0)   # Top Right Of The Texture and Quad
    glTexCoord2f(0.0, 1.0); glVertex3f( 1.0,  1.0,  1.0)   # Top Left Of The Texture and Quad
    glTexCoord2f(0.0, 0.0); glVertex3f( 1.0, -1.0,  1.0)   # Bottom Left Of The Texture and Quad.
    glEnd();

    xrot = xrot + 0.2       # X rotation
    yrot = yrot + 0.1       # Y rotation
    zrot = zrot + 0.1       # Z rotation

    glutSwapBuffers()
```

```
def main():
    glutInit(sys.argv)
    glutInitDisplayMode(GLUT_RGBA | GLUT_DOUBLE | GLUT_DEPTH) # Select display mode.
    glutInitWindowSize(640, 480)
    glutInitWindowPosition(0, 0)
    window = glutCreateWindow(b"Blue Moon and Fog")
    glutDisplayFunc(DrawGLScene)
    glutIdleFunc(DrawGLScene)
    InitGL(640, 480)
    glutMainLoop()

main()
```

Transparency

A fully transparent object is invisible - light reflecting off objects behind it passes through unhindered. If on the the other hand, the object is partially transparent or translucent, as if it were made of colored glass – some of the light from behind gets through it but not all and the color is changed to some degree. Ultimately a single pixel can only be one color so partial transparency is simulated by mixing or blending colors.

We understand how the primary colors of red, green and blue are mixed and combined to give any intended color. In computer graphics there is the fourth dimension to color known as **alpha.** Alpha is just another word for opacity-transparency. OpenGL uses the alpha channel value to modulate the color of a pixel by adding in a portion of an underlying color. This underlying color is the color of the pixel on a polygon that is further away from the camera. There is a portion of graphic memory hardware that keeps track of the distance from the camera/viewer of every polygon called the depth buffer.

The computational process by which transparency is handled is known as blending. In OpengGL blending must be enabled by **glEnable(GL_BLEND).** Transparency is complicated by the fact that the sequence in which the graphic hardware presents pixels affects the combined color of transparent objects.

Four full opacity colored images:

blue_moon256.jpg, red_moon256.jpg, green_moon256.jpg, white_moon256.jpg,

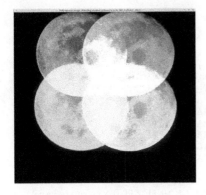 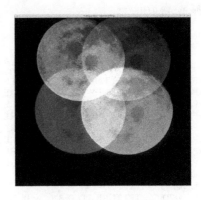

High opacity

Low opacity

```
"""
Program name: opengl_transparency_moons_1.py
Objective: Vary transparency on colored moon images.

keywords: opengl, transparency, opacity, moon, alpha, animation
==============================================================================79
Comments: Transparency achieved through blending.
        Blending combines the color of a pixel that is about to be drawn
        with the color of the pixel that is already on the screen.

Tested on: Python 2.6, Python 2.7.3
Test failed with Python 3.2.3
Author:       Mike Ohlson de Fine
"""
from OpenGL.GL import *
from OpenGL.GLUT import *
from OpenGL.GLU import *
from PIL import Image


#======================================================
texture_1 = 0, 1, 2, 3
image_proto = Image.open("/home/mikeodf/constr/images_opengl/blue_moon256.jpg")
ix = image_proto.size[0]        # image.size is a PIL function.
iy = image_proto.size[1]
print ('ix:', ix)               # Just checking.
print ('iy:', iy)

# Make four independent opacity variables.
opacity_full = 1.0   # Initialization - zero transparency.
opacity_1 = 1.0
delta_opacity_1 = 0.01
opacity_2 = 0.01
delta_opacity_2 = -0.001
opacity_3 = 0.7
delta_opacity_3 = -0.001
opacity_4 = 0.3
```

```
delta_opacity_4 = 0.001

def texture_setup(image_name, texture_num, ix, iy):
    """ Map jpg images to a square.
    """
    glBindTexture(GL_TEXTURE_2D, texture_1[texture_num])
    glTexEnvf(GL_TEXTURE_ENV, GL_TEXTURE_ENV_MODE, GL_MODULATE)
    glTexParameterf(GL_TEXTURE_2D, GL_TEXTURE_MIN_FILTER, GL_NEAREST)
    glTexParameterf(GL_TEXTURE_2D, GL_TEXTURE_WRAP_S, GL_CLAMP)
    glTexParameterf(GL_TEXTURE_2D, GL_TEXTURE_WRAP_T, GL_CLAMP)
    glTexParameterf(GL_TEXTURE_2D, GL_TEXTURE_WRAP_S, GL_REPEAT)
    glTexParameterf(GL_TEXTURE_2D, GL_TEXTURE_WRAP_T, GL_REPEAT)
    glTexParameterf(GL_TEXTURE_2D, GL_TEXTURE_MAG_FILTER, GL_NEAREST)
    glTexParameterf(GL_TEXTURE_2D, GL_TEXTURE_WRAP_S, GL_REPEAT)
    glPixelStorei(GL_UNPACK_ALIGNMENT,1)
    glEnable(GL_TEXTURE_2D)
    glTexImage2D(GL_TEXTURE_2D, 0, 3, ix, iy, 0, GL_RGBA, GL_UNSIGNED_BYTE, image_name)

def LoadTextures():
    """ Open texture images and convert them to "raw" pixel maps and
        bind or associate each image with and integer refernece number.
    """
    image_1 =Image. open("/home/mikeodf/constr/images_opengl/blue_moon256.jpg")
    image_2 = Image.open("/home/mikeodf/constr/images_opengl/red_moon256.jpg")
    image_3 = Image.open("/home/mikeodf/constr/images_opengl/green_moon256.jpg")
    image_4 = Image.open("/home/mikeodf/constr/images_opengl/white_moon256.jpg")

    image_1 = image_1.tostring("raw", "RGBX", 0, -1)   # convert jpg to the type needed for textures .
    image_2 = image_2.tostring("raw", "RGBX", 0, -1)
    image_3 = image_3.tostring("raw", "RGBX", 0, -1)
    image_4 = image_4.tostring("raw", "RGBX", 0, -1)

    glGenTextures(4, texture_1)               # Create texture index numbers and array name.

    texture_setup(image_1, 0, ix, iy)         # Map image (texture) to a square shape.
    texture_setup(image_2, 1, ix, iy)
    texture_setup(image_3, 2, ix, iy)
    texture_setup(image_4, 3, ix, iy)


def InitGL(Width, Height):
    """ A general OpenGL initialization function.  Sets all of the initial parameters.
        glEnable(GL_BLEND) - important for transparency .
    """
    glClearColor(0.0, 0.0, 0.0, 0.0)          # Set the background color to black.
    glClearDepth(1.0)                         # Clear the Depth buffer.
    glDepthFunc(GL_LESS)                      # Type of depth test to do.
    glEnable(GL_DEPTH_TEST)                   # Cancel this Depth Testing and observe the visual weirdness.

    glColor4f(1.0,1.0,1.0,opacity_full)       # Full Brightness, Alpha will be varied later.
    glEnable(GL_BLEND)
    glBlendFunc(GL_SRC_ALPHA,GL_ONE)          # Blending function for translucency.

    glMatrixMode(GL_PROJECTION)
    glLoadIdentity()                          # Reset The Projection Matrix.
    gluPerspective(30.0, float(Width)/float(Height), 0.1, 100.0) # Aspect ratio.
    glMatrixMode(GL_MODELVIEW)
```

```
#==========================================================================
def make_square(texture, texture_index):
    """  A generic square.
        A texture binding created with glBindTexture remains active
        until a different texture is bound to the same target,
        or until the bound texture is deleted with glDeleteTextures.
    """

    glBindTexture(GL_TEXTURE_2D,texture[texture_index])
    # Front Face (Each texture's corner is matched a quad's corner.)
    glBegin(GL_QUADS)
        glTexCoord2f(0.0, 0.0), glVertex3f(-1.0, -1.0,  1.0)    # Bottom Left Of The Texture and Quad .
        glTexCoord2f(1.0, 0.0), glVertex3f( 1.0, -1.0,  1.0)    # Bottom Right Of The Texture and Quad.
        glTexCoord2f(1.0, 1.0), glVertex3f( 1.0,  1.0,  1.0)    # Top Right Of The Texture and Quad.
        glTexCoord2f(0.0, 1.0), glVertex3f(-1.0,  1.0,  1.0)    # Top Left Of The Texture and Quad.
    glEnd()

def DrawFrontFace():
    """  Repeated Shape drawing function.
        Includes opacity control.
    """

        #global opacity, delta_opacity
    # We need the valuse of opacity to persist between graphic image update cycles.
    global opacity_1, delta_opacity_1
    global opacity_2, delta_opacity_2
    global opacity_3, delta_opacity_3
    global opacity_4, delta_opacity_4

    glClear(GL_COLOR_BUFFER_BIT | GL_DEPTH_BUFFER_BIT) # Clear screen and Depth buffer

    # Incremental cycling of four indepencent opacity controls.
    if opacity_1 >= 1.0:
        delta_opacity_1 = -0.002
    if opacity_1 <= 0.0:
        delta_opacity_1 = 0.002
    opacity_1 = opacity_1 + delta_opacity_1

    if opacity_2 >= 1.0:
        delta_opacity_2 = -0.002
    if opacity_2 <= 0.0:
        delta_opacity_2 = 0.002
    opacity_2 = opacity_2 + delta_opacity_2

    if opacity_3 >= 1.0:
        delta_opacity_3 = -0.002
    if opacity_3 <= 0.0:
        delta_opacity_3 = 0.002
    opacity_3 = opacity_3 + delta_opacity_3

    if opacity_4 >= 1.0:
        delta_opacity_4 = -0.002
    if opacity_4 <= 0.0:
        delta_opacity_4 = 0.002
    opacity_4 = opacity_4 + delta_opacity_4

    # Moon shots
    glLoadIdentity()
```

```
  glTranslatef(-0.5, 1.0, -8.3)
   glColor4f(1.0,1.0,1.0,opacity_1)      # cycling opacity
  make_square(texture_1, 0)             # "0" is blue

  glLoadIdentity()
  glTranslatef(0.5, 1.0, -8.2)
  glColor4f(1.0,1.0,1.0,opacity_2)      # cycling  opacity
  make_square(texture_1, 1)             # "1" is red

  glLoadIdentity()
  glTranslatef(-0.5, -0.2, -8.1)
  glColor4f(1.0,1.0,1.0,opacity_3)      # cycling  opacity
  make_square(texture_1, 2)             # "2" is green

  glLoadIdentity()
  glTranslatef(0.5, -0.2, -8.0)
  glColor4f(1.0,1.0,1.0,opacity_4)      # cycling  opacity
  make_square(texture_1, 3)             # "3" is white

  glutSwapBuffers()
#==================================
def main():
 glutInit("")
 glutInitDisplayMode(GLUT_RGBA | GLUT_DOUBLE | GLUT_ALPHA | GLUT_DEPTH)
 glutInitWindowSize(1000, 1000)
 glutInitWindowPosition(0, 0)     # the window starts at the upper left corner of the screen.
 window = glutCreateWindow(b"Transparency - Opacity cycling.")
 LoadTextures()
 glutDisplayFunc(DrawFrontFace)
 glutIdleFunc(DrawFrontFace)      # Redraw the scene each frame cycle.
 InitGL(1000, 1000)              # Initialize our window.
 glutMainLoop()                  # Start the continuous event processing.

main()
```

Dynamic Control of Transparency

Here we see how transparency can be varied in real time.

```
"""
Program name: opengl_transparency_bouncing_balls_1.py
Objective: Vary transparency on the bouncing balls.

keywords: opengl, transparency, ball textures, animation
================================================================================79
Comments: Transparency achieved through blending.
         Blending combines the color of a pixel that is about to be drawn
         with the color of the pixel that is already on the screen.

Tested on: Python 2.7.3
Test failed with Python 3.2.3
Author:      Mike Ohlson de Fine
"""

from OpenGL.GL import *
```

```python
from OpenGL.GLUT import *
from OpenGL.GLU import *
from PIL import Image

# Position and Velocity of the cube.
# ball_1
xpos_1 = ypos_1 = 0.0
zpos_1 = -10.0
xvel_1 = 0.02
yvel_1 = 0.03
zvel_1 = 0.01

# ball_2
xpos_2 = ypos_2 = 0.0
zpos_2 = -10.0
xvel_2 = -0.025
yvel_2 = -0.03
zvel_2 = -0.01

# ball_3
xpos_3 = ypos_3 = 0.0
zpos_3 = -20.0
xvel_3 = 0.015
yvel_3 = 0.02
zvel_3 = 0.02

# ball_4
xpos_4 = ypos_4 = 0.0
zpos_4 = -15.0
xvel_4 = -0.02
yvel_4 = -0.025
zvel_4 = -0.015

#===================================================================
texture_1 = 0, 1, 2, 3, 4, 5
image_proto = Image.open("/home/mikeodf/constr/images_opengl/steel_ball3.jpg")
ix = image_proto.size[0]      # image.size is a PIL function.
iy = image_proto.size[1]
print ('ix:', ix)             # Just checking.
print '(iy:', iy)
opacity = 0.0
del_opacity = 0.001

def timerCB(millisec):
    glutTimerFunc(millisec, timerCB, millisec)
    glutPostRedisplay()


def texture_setup(image_name, texture_num, ix, iy):
    """ Assign texture attributes to specific images.
    """
    glBindTexture(GL_TEXTURE_2D, texture_1[texture_num])
    glTexEnvf(GL_TEXTURE_ENV, GL_TEXTURE_ENV_MODE, GL_MODULATE)
    glTexParameterf(GL_TEXTURE_2D, GL_TEXTURE_MIN_FILTER, GL_NEAREST)
    glTexParameterf(GL_TEXTURE_2D, GL_TEXTURE_WRAP_S, GL_CLAMP)
    glTexParameterf(GL_TEXTURE_2D, GL_TEXTURE_WRAP_T, GL_CLAMP)
    glTexParameterf(GL_TEXTURE_2D, GL_TEXTURE_WRAP_S, GL_REPEAT)
```

```python
glTexParameterf(GL_TEXTURE_2D, GL_TEXTURE_WRAP_T, GL_REPEAT)
glTexParameterf(GL_TEXTURE_2D, GL_TEXTURE_MAG_FILTER, GL_NEAREST)
glTexParameterf(GL_TEXTURE_2D, GL_TEXTURE_WRAP_S, GL_REPEAT)
glPixelStorei(GL_UNPACK_ALIGNMENT,1)
glEnable(GL_TEXTURE_2D)
glTexImage2D(GL_TEXTURE_2D, 0, 3, ix, iy, 0, GL_RGBA, GL_UNSIGNED_BYTE, image_name)

def LoadTextures():
    """ Open texture images and convert them to "raw" pixel maps and
        bind or associate each image with and integer refernece number.
    """
    image_1 = Image.open("/home/mikeodf/constr/images_opengl/steel_ball3.jpg")
    image_2 = Image.open("/home/mikeodf/constr/images_opengl/steel_green_ball3.jpg")
    image_3 = Image.open("/home/mikeodf/constr/images_opengl/steel_blue_ball3.jpg")
    image_4 = Image.open("/home/mikeodf/constr/images_opengl/steel_red_ball3.jpg")

    image_1 = image_1.tostring("raw", "RGBX", 0, -1)   # convert bmp to the type needed for textures
    image_2 = image_2.tostring("raw", "RGBX", 0, -1)   # convert bmp to the type needed for textures
    image_3 = image_3.tostring("raw", "RGBX", 0, -1)   # convert bmp to the type needed for textures
    image_4 = image_4.tostring("raw", "RGBX", 0, -1)   # convert bmp to the type needed for textures
    glGenTextures(11, texture_1)   # Create texture number and names and size.
    #=======================================
    texture_setup(image_1, 0, ix, iy)
    texture_setup(image_2, 1, ix, iy)
    texture_setup(image_3, 2, ix, iy)
    texture_setup(image_4, 3, ix, iy)


def InitGL(Width, Height):
    """ A general OpenGL initialization function.  Sets all of the initial parameters.
        We call this right after our OpenGL window is created.
        glEnable(GL_BLEND);
        glBlendFunc(GL_SRC_ALPHA, GL_ONE_MINUS_SRC_ALPHA);
        or glBlendFunc(GL_ONE, GL_ONE_MINUS_SRC_ALPHA)
    """
    glClearColor(0.0, 0.0, 0.0, 0.0)    # Clear the background color to black.
    glClearDepth(1.0)                   # Clear the Depth buffer.
    glDepthFunc(GL_LESS)                # The type of depth test to do.
    glEnable(GL_DEPTH_TEST)             # Leave this Depth Testing and observe the visual weirdness.

    glColor4f(1.0,1.0,1.0,opacity)      # Full Brightness, variable Alpha
    glEnable(GL_BLEND)
    glBlendFunc(GL_SRC_ALPHA,GL_ONE)    # Blending function for translucency based on source alpha value.

    glMatrixMode(GL_PROJECTION)
    glLoadIdentity()                    # Reset The Projection Matrix.
    gluPerspective(30.0, float(Width)/float(Height), 0.1, 100.0) # Aspect Ratio Of The Window, makes it resizable.
    glMatrixMode(GL_MODELVIEW)

#=====================================================================
def make_cube_1(texture, texture_index):
    """ A generic cube. A texture binding created with glBindTexture remains active
        until a different texture is bound to  the same target, or until the bound texture
        is deleted with glDeleteTextures.
    """
    glBindTexture(GL_TEXTURE_2D,texture[texture_index])
    # Front Face (Each texture's corner is matched a quad's corner.)
```

```python
glBegin(GL_QUADS)
glTexCoord2f(0.0, 0.0), glVertex3f(-1.0, -1.0,  1.0)    # Bottom Left Of The Texture and Quad.
glTexCoord2f(1.0, 0.0), glVertex3f( 1.0, -1.0,  1.0)    # Bottom Right Of The Texture and Quad.
glTexCoord2f(1.0, 1.0), glVertex3f( 1.0,  1.0,  1.0)    # Top Right Of The Texture and Quad.
glTexCoord2f(0.0, 1.0), glVertex3f(-1.0,  1.0,  1.0)    # Top Left Of The Texture and Quad.
glEnd()


def DrawFrontFace():
    """ A texture binding created with glBindTexture remains active until a different texture
        is bound to the same target, or until the bound texture is deleted with glDeleteTextures.
    """
    global xpos_1, ypos_1, zpos_1, xvel_1, yvel_1, zvel_1
    global xpos_2, ypos_2, zpos_2, xvel_2, yvel_2, zvel_2
    global xpos_3, ypos_3, zpos_3, xvel_3, yvel_3, zvel_3
    global xpos_4, ypos_4, zpos_4, xvel_4, yvel_4, zvel_4
    global opacity, del_opacity

    glClear(GL_COLOR_BUFFER_BIT | GL_DEPTH_BUFFER_BIT)
    glColor4f(1.0,1.0,1.0, opacity)        # Full Brightness Alphawill vary.
    if opacity >= 1.0:
       del_opacity = -0.001
    if opacity <= 0.0:
       del_opacity = 0.001
    opacity = opacity + del_opacity
    # Textured square.
    glLoadIdentity()                              # Reset The View
    glTranslatef(xpos_1, ypos_1, zpos_1)      # Shift cube left and back.
    make_cube_1(texture_1, 0)  # "0" is the first index no. of a four images.

    glLoadIdentity()
    glTranslatef(xpos_2, ypos_2, zpos_2)
    make_cube_1(texture_1, 1)  # "1" is the second index no. of a four images.

    glLoadIdentity()
    glTranslatef(xpos_3, ypos_3, zpos_3)
    make_cube_1(texture_1, 2)  # "2" is the third index no. of a four  images'
    glLoadIdentity()
    glTranslatef(xpos_4, ypos_4, zpos_4)
    make_cube_1(texture_1, 3)  # "3" is the fourth index no. of a four images.

    # Ball_1 - grey
    xpos_1 = xpos_1 + xvel_1
    ypos_1 = ypos_1 + yvel_1
    zpos_1 = zpos_1 + zvel_1
    if xpos_1 >= 3.0 or xpos_1 <= -2.0:
       xvel_1 = -xvel_1
    if ypos_1 >= 3.0 or ypos_1 <= -3.0:
       yvel_1 = -yvel_1
    if zpos_1 >= -5.01 or zpos_1 <= -30.0:
       zvel_1 = -zvel_1

    # Ball_2 - green
    xpos_2 = xpos_2 + xvel_2
    ypos_2 = ypos_2 + yvel_2
    zpos_2 = zpos_2 + zvel_2
    if xpos_2 >= 3.0 or xpos_2 <= -2.0:
```

254

```
      xvel_2 = -xvel_2
    if ypos_2 >= 3.0 or ypos_2 <= -3.0:
      yvel_2 = -yvel_2
    if zpos_2 >= -5.01 or zpos_2 <= -30.0:
      zvel_2 = -zvel_2

    # Ball_3 - blue
    xpos_3 = xpos_3 + xvel_3
    ypos_3 = ypos_3 + yvel_3
    zpos_3 = zpos_3 + zvel_3
    if xpos_3 >= 3.0 or xpos_3 <= -2.0:
      xvel_3 = -xvel_3
    if ypos_3 >= 3.0 or ypos_3 <= -3.0:
      yvel_3 = -yvel_3
    if zpos_3 >= -5.01 or zpos_3 <= -30.0:
      zvel_3 = -zvel_3

    # Ball_4 - red
    xpos_4 = xpos_4 + xvel_4
    ypos_4 = ypos_4 + yvel_4
    zpos_4 = zpos_4 + zvel_4
    if xpos_4 >= 3.0 or xpos_4 <= -2.0:
      xvel_4 = -xvel_4
    if ypos_4 >= 3.0 or ypos_4 <= -3.0:
      yvel_4 = -yvel_4
    if zpos_4 >= -5.01 or zpos_4 <= -30.0:
      zvel_4 = -zvel_4
      glutSwapBuffers()
#================================================================
def main():
  glutInit("")
  glutInitDisplayMode(GLUT_RGBA | GLUT_DOUBLE | GLUT_ALPHA | GLUT_DEPTH)
  glutInitWindowSize(1000, 1000)
  glutInitWindowPosition(0, 0)      # the window starts at the upper left corner of the screen
  window = glutCreateWindow(b"Textured rectangles bouncing")
  LoadTextures()
  glutDisplayFunc(DrawFrontFace)
  glutIdleFunc(DrawFrontFace)       # Redraw the scene each cycle.
  InitGL(1000, 1000)                # Initialize our window.
  glutMainLoop()                    # Start the event processing engine.

main()
```

14

OpenGL: Lighting and Materials.

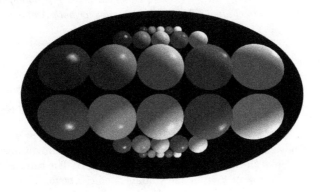

"I'm a firm believer that lighting affects mood, and twinkly lights on strings bring something magical to occasions ranging from concerts to weddings, though I'm fond of using them as year-round home decor. There's a reason why they're sometimes called fairy lights. When the night is right, there aren't any strings at all." Erin Morgenstern.

The topics in this chapter deal with the interaction of light and matter.
- **The difficulty of lighting**
- **Lighting and Materials**
- **Basic Properties of OpenGL Light Sources**
- **Begin Simply**
- **Diffuse Light**
- **Light Position**
- **Diffuse Light Color**

- **Emissive Light**
- **Ambient Light**
- **Specular Lighting**
- **Spotlights**
- **Spotlight Distance**
- **Spotlight Direction**
- **Overlapping Spotlights**
- **Lighting Summary**

OpenGL can do so many things with it's lighting instructions that it is overwhelmingly confusion for a beginner. One of the chief difficulties is that many of the instruction directives interact with each other and consequently it is diffult to understand lighting effects in a systematic way. Specifying material color is an example. Consider the following quotation from a web tutorial: " *glColorMaterial - This is without doubt the most confusing thing about OpenGL lighting - and the biggest cause of problems for beginners. You frequently need to change glMaterial properties for both Ambient and Diffuse to identical values.*

You cannot change glMaterial settings with many of the more advanced polygon rendering techniques such as Vertex arrays and glDrawElements.

For these reasons, OpenGL has a feature that allows you do drive the glMaterial colours using the more flexible glColor command (which is not otherwise useful when lighting is enabled)."

Very, very confusing! The above quotation does not lead to understanding or insight. It is not the author's fault. He is merely stating some hard won facts. The tutorial from which this is quoted is actually well written and valuable and can be found at http://www.sjbaker.org/steve/omniv/opengl_lighting.html.

So in this chapter we are going to make an effort to simplify and separate lighting controls. As part of this effort we will not attempt to control color by using the glMaterial. We will however demonstrate the effect of a colored lamp shining out from the inside (emissive lighting) of a 3D object because this effect is valuable and cannot be achieved any other way.

Particular effects like fog, transparency, lighting and light reflection from surfaces offer unlimited variations and choices. OpenGL does a good job of simplifying these special effects but using them well will take an enormous amount of trial and error, experience and artistic insight. Although comprehensive treatment of these topics is well beyond the scope of this book we will work through examples that are designed to give us a boost that empowers us to understand and harvest the vast number of hints and examples on the web.

Lighting and Materials

We have created a 3D object designed to have a curved surface with eight distinct colors that are intended to allow us to see fairly easily how light color, light direction and surface emission change the appearance of the object. With these variables clearly understood a lot of potential confusion melts away.

Here are a few views of our 3D object. The object, a half sphere, shows the primary colors red, green and blue with the intermediate mixtures of yellow, lilac and purple in between. Pure black and white are also shown. It is constructed using the code below the picture.

```
"""
Program name: opengl_3D_compact_shield_1.py
Objective: Construct an enclosed solid from an 11.25 degree strip
using symmetry.

Keywords: OpenGL, triangle, hemi-sphere, strip, separate, normals, lighting.
====================================================================================79
Comments: Each 32nd angular portion is derived from the same vertex array
and is positioned,scaled and rotated in a single Python loop.

Tested on: Python 2.6, Python 2.7.3, Python 3.2.3
Author:  Mike Ohlson de Fine
====================================
"""

from OpenGL.GL import *
from OpenGL.GLUT import *
from OpenGL.GLU import *

rotation_y = 0.0
rotation_x = 0.0

# Hemisphere object
hemi_strip =    [
  0.0031, 0.9522, 0.2684,   -0.1051, 0.8312, 0.5407,   -0.0499, 0.9522, 0.2632,
 -0.1051, 0.8311,0.54073,    0.0031, 0.9522, 0.2684,    0.0031, 0.8312, 0.5514,
  0.0031, 0.8312, 0.5514,   -0.1475, 0.6358, 0.754,    -0.1051, 0.8312, 0.5407,
  0.0031, 0.3846, 0.9136,   -0.1757, 0.3846, 0.8959,   -0.1475, 0.6358,   0.754,
 -0.1475, 0.6358,  0.754,    0.0031, 0.8314, 0.5514,    0.0031, 0.6358, 0.7688,
```

```
-0.1475, 0.6358,  0.754,    0.0031, 0.6358, 0.7688,    0.0031, 0.3846, 0.9136,
 0.0031, 0.3846, 0.9136,   -0.1951,    0.0, 0.9808,  -0.1757, 0.3846,   0.896,
   -0.0,     0.0,    1.0,   -0.1951,    0.0, 0.9808,    0.0031, 0.3846, 0.9136 ]

# Object color strips
kula_1 = [
[1.0 , 0.0, 0.0], [1.0 , 0.0, 0.0], # red
[1.0 , 1.0, 0.0], [1.0 , 1.0, 0.0], # yellow
[0.0 , 1.0, 0.0], [0.0 , 1.0, 0.0], # green
[0.0 , 1.0, 1.0], [0.0 , 1.0, 1.0], # lilac
[0.0 , 0.0, 1.0], [0.0 , 0.0, 1.0], # blue
[1.0 , 0.0, 1.0], [1.0 , 0.0, 1.0], # purple
[1.0 , 1.0, 1.0], [1.0 , 1.0, 1.0], # white
[0.0 , 0.0, 0.0], [0.0 , 0.0, 0.0], # black
[1.0 , 0.0, 0.0], [1.0 , 0.0, 0.0], # red
[1.0 , 1.0, 0.0], [1.0 , 1.0, 0.0], # yellow
[0.0 , 1.0, 0.0], [0.0 , 1.0, 0.0], # green
[0.0 , 1.0, 1.0], [0.0 , 1.0, 1.0], # lilac
[0.0 , 0.0, 1.0], [0.0 , 0.0, 1.0], # blue
[1.0 , 0.0, 1.0], [1.0 , 0.0, 1.0], # purple
[1.0 , 1.0, 1.0], [1.0 , 1.0, 1.0], # white
[0.0 , 0.0, 0.0], [0.0 , 0.0, 0.0]] # black


#=====================================================================
hemi_strip_faces = len(hemi_strip)/3
print 'hemi_strip_faces: ', hemi_strip_faces
#=====================================================================
def InitGL(Width, Height):
    """ Initialize and setup the Graphics Software/Hardware pipeline.
    """
    # Experimental colors and light position.
    diffuse_lite_kula  = [ 1.0, 1.0, 1.0, 0.0 ]
    light0_position    = [-1.0, 3.0, 1.0, 0.0 ]
    emissive_kula      = [ 0.0, 0.0, 0.0, 0.0 ]
    # /\/\/\/\/\/\/\/\/\/\/\/\/\/\/\/\/\/\/\/\/\/\/\/\
    glEnable(GL_NORMALIZE)
    glEnable(GL_COLOR_MATERIAL
    glEnable(GL_LIGHTING)

    glEnable(GL_LIGHT0)
    glLightfv(GL_LIGHT0, GL_POSITION, light0_position)
    glLightfv(GL_LIGHT0, GL_DIFFUSE,  diffuse_lite_kula)
    #/\/\/\/\/\/\/\/\/\/\/\/\/\/\/\/\/\/\/\/\/\/\/\/\/\
    glEnable(GL_DEPTH_TEST)
    glMatrixMode(GL_PROJECTION)
    glLoadIdentity()
    gluPerspective(45.0, float(Width)/float(Height), 0.1, 100.0)
    glMatrixMode(GL_MODELVIEW)

def draw32segments(seg_angle, kula):
    """ Generate hemisphere from the vertical strip object hemi_strip.
    """
    for i in range(32):
      glLoadIdentity()
      glTranslatef(0.0, 0.0, -4.0)
      glRotatef(90.0, 1.0, 0.0, 0.0)
      glRotatef(rotation_x, 0.0, 0.0, 1.0)
```

```
glRotatef(i*seg_angle, 0.0, 1.0, 0.0)
glScale(1.0,  1.0,  1.0)
glColor3f(kula[i][0], kula[i][1], kula[i][2])
glVertexPointer(3, GL_FLOAT, 0, hemi_strip)      # (size, type, stride, pointer) .
glNormalPointer(GL_FLOAT, 0, hemi_strip)       # (type, stride, pointer) - smoothed normals.
glDrawArrays(GL_TRIANGLES, 0, 24) # (primitive, start index, number of indices.

def Octocapsule():
    """ Draw an enclose eight segmented solid by suitably rotating the
        same segment into position using matrix operations.
    """
    global rotation_x
    glClear(GL_COLOR_BUFFER_BIT | GL_DEPTH_BUFFER_BIT)
    glEnableClientState(GL_VERTEX_ARRAY)  # Enable vertex arrays
    glEnableClientState(GL_NORMAL_ARRAY)
    draw32segments(11.25, kula_1)  # 11.25 is the angular width of the strip.
    rotation_x += 0.1
    glutSwapBuffers()

def main():
    ''' Main Program.
    '''
    glutInit(sys.argv)
    glutInitWindowSize(600,600)   # Width, Height. Line gets scaled to the window.
    glutCreateWindow('OpenGL Lighting: Emissive color = black')
    InitGL(600, 600)
    glutIdleFunc(Octocapsule)    # During idle time redraw the frame.
    glutDisplayFunc(Octocapsule)
    glutMainLoop()

main()
```

Basic Properties of OpenGL Light Sources

OpenGL does a very rough approximation of representing how light affects objects in a
scene. It is a good compromise, given today's technology, between the desire for
realism and the cost of complexity. The lighting model in OpenGL specifies light in
terms of various independent *components*, each described as RGB triples. Each
component describes how light that's been scattered in a certain way is colored. The
continuum of possible real-world light paths is simplified into four components, listed
here from most directional to least directional.

Specular light comes from a particular direction, and reflects off surfaces toward a
given particular direction. Shiny materials have a big specular component. A focused
beam of light bouncing off of a polished metal ball has a very high specular component
that forms a bright spot on the surface that is called a highlight.

Diffuse light comes from one direction, but scatters equally in all directions as it bounces off of the surface of an object. If the surface is facing directly at the light source, the surface color of the object is at its brightest. That is, the diffuse *component* reflected from the surface will be brightest. If the surface is pointing in another direction, it will will be darker.

Spotlight is light that has position, direction, intensity and beam width. It is like a stage light that lights up a small area while its surroundings are darker.

Ambient light is direction-less. It is light that has been scattered so many times that it does not come from a particular direction. So it appears equally bright from all directions. A room with white walls has a lot of ambient light. If the walls were black and did not reflect any light then there would be no ambient light.

Emissive lighting is the glow that comes from the inside of a translucent object that has a source of light inside it. A typical domestic light fitting with a milky-white glass cover over it is a typical example of an emissive source. The emissive light has it's own color and this is added to the color of the surface of the object enclosing it. It is light that only reaches your eye if you're looking directly at the object. This is used for modeling objects that are light sources themselves.

Begin Simply

In the previous five chapters we have been using a set of lighting instructions without explanation because we wanted to focus on other things like creating objects, positioning them and transforming their surroundings. Now we examine how to control lighting.
We have been inserting the following few lighting instructions in the *InitGL(Width, Height)* functionthat we use to set up the initial graphic state of our display environment.

```
# ∧∧∧∧∧∧∧∧∧∧∧∧∧∧∧∧∧∧∧∧∧∧∧∧∧∧∧∧∧∧∧∧∧∧∧∧
# The 6 lines below create the lighting (from a single light "LIGHT0") in the model scene.
glEnable(GL_NORMALIZE)
glEnable(GL_COLOR_MATERIAL)
glEnable(GL_LIGHTING)

glEnable(GL_LIGHT0)
glLightfv(GL_LIGHT0, GL_POSITION, light0_position)
glLightfv(GL_LIGHT0, GL_DIFFUSE,  diffuse_lite_kula)
#∧∧∧∧∧∧∧∧∧∧∧∧∧∧∧∧∧∧∧∧∧∧∧∧∧∧∧∧∧∧∧∧∧∧∧∧∧∧
```

The first three instructions 'switch-on' or enable the OpenGL graphics lighting functions needed for displaying 3D objects. GL_NORMALIZE causes the calculation of light paths to happen. This is how the software is able to determine how dark or light to make pixels to create a sense of three dimensionality. GL_COLOR_MATERIAL enables the use of colors. Disable it and objects become grey and not colored. GL_LIGHTING allows lighting to be controlled – color, direction and other features we shall see.

The instruction glEnable(GL_LIGHT0) turns on the first of eight separate light sources that the use of OpenGL allows. "GL_LIGHT0" is the label we use to refer to this first light. This light is placed in a particular position given by *light0_position* = *[x, y, z]* position coordinates. GL_DIFFUSE with *diffuse_lite_kula* = [1.0, 1.0, 1.0] makes the color of GL_LIGHT0 a white light. If it was red it would be [1.0, 0.0, 0.0] .

Diffuse Light

In computer graphics a diffuse light combines independent properties:
1. Position. A source of light placed in a particular position in our 3D object space.
2. Color. Light that has a particular color.

Light bounces or reflects of the surfaces of all objects inside the object space it belongs to. The word diffuse implies the bouncing and reflecting from the surface of the illuminated object.
We can never see the actual light source. It does not exist as a graphic object. All OpenGL lets us see is the reflected or diffuse light that is scattered by the illuminated surfaces of objects.

There are three instructions that control a diffuse light:
glEnable(GL_LIGHTING) - This turns lighting on.
glLightfv(GL_LIGHT0, GL_POSITION, light_position) - The position in 3D space.
glLightfv(GL_LIGHT0, GL_DIFFUSE, light_color) – The color of the light.

The variables *light_position* and *light_color* are the names of position and color vectors.

Colors always mix in OpenGL

An object with a pure blue or green surface will appear black if illuminated by a pure red light. A yellow light, which is a combination of green and red, will reflect green from a green object and red from a red object.

Light Position

Variations of light position in the instruction

glLightfv(GL_LIGHT0, GL_POSITION, light_position) :

Light to the right and front
light0_position = [5, 1, 5, 0]

Light to the left and front
light0_position = [-5, 1, 5, 0]

Light to the left and behind
light0_position = [-5, 1, -5, 0]

Light in the middle and front
light0_position = [0, 0, 0, 0]

Light Types

We have said there are five types of light: specular, ambient, diffuse, emissive and spotlights. We have just looked at how diffuse lights can be positioned. Immediately below we look at the effects of different colors of diffuse light on different colored surfaces. Then we look at emissive lighting effects which is the type of light that is not reflected off the surface of an object but appears to come from inside the object and gets combined with the color of the surface of the object. The object surface acts as if it was made from semi-transparent glass and adds the two colors to each other. A red emissive light emitting through a green surface will appear yellow because the green surface is added to the red light to give a total output of yellow.

Diffuse Light Color

Diffuse light color: white
diffuse_lite_kula = [1, 1, 1, 0]

Diffuse light color: red
diffuse_lite_kula = [1, 0, 0, 0]

Diffuse light color: green
diffuse_lite_kula = [0, 1, 0, 0]

Diffuse light color: blue
diffuse_lite_kula = [0, 0, 1, 0]

Diffuse light color: purple
diffuse_lite_kula = [1, 0, 1, 0]

Diffuse light color: yellow
diffuse_lite_kula = [1, 1, 0, 0]

Diffuse light color: lilac
diffuse_lite_kula = [0, 1, 1, 0]

Emissive Light

Emissive light color is added to the color of the object surface:

GL_EMISSION

black
emissive_kula = [0, 0, 0, 0]

red
emissive_kula = [1, 0, 0, 0]

yellow
emissive_kula = [1, 1, 0, 0]

green
emissive_kula = [0, 1, 0, 0]

lilac
emissive_kula = [0, 1, 1, 0]

blue
emissive_kula = [0, 0, 1, 0]

purple
emissive_kula = [1, 0, 1, 0]

white
emissive_kula = [1, 1, 0, 0]

Ambient Light

Ambient light is light that doesn't come from any particular direction. Because it does not come from a particular light source, it has a low intensity – it is not bright. It is light that has been scattered so many times that it comes from all directions in equal amounts. We cannot control it's direction. All the objects in your scene will be lit up by the ambient light.

The ambient intensity of a light in OpenGL is added to the general level of ambient light.
This ambient light interacts with the ambient color of a material, and this interaction has no dependence on the position of any light source. So, a particular light source like GL_LIGHT0 doesn't have be enabled to shine on an object for the object's ambient color to be affected by the light source; the light source just has to be turned on with an instruction like glLightModelfv(GL_LIGHT_MODEL_AMBIENT, ambient_green) .

```
ambient_black    = [ 0.0, 0.0, 0.0, 1.0 ]
ambient_white    = [ 1.0, 1.0, 1.0, 1.0 ]
ambient_green    = [ 0.0, 1.0, 0.0, 1.0 ]
kula_ambient     = [ 0.0, 0.0, 0.0, 1.0 ] # red, green, blue, Alpha channels.
# ∧∧∧∧∧∧∧∧∧∧∧∧∧∧∧∧∧∧∧∧∧∧∧∧∧∧∧∧∧∧∧∧∧∧∧∧
glClearColor(0.0, 0.0, 0.0, 0.0)                 # Set the background color To Black
glLightModelfv(GL_LIGHT_MODEL_AMBIENT, ambient_green)
#glEnable(GL_NORMALIZE)                  # Redundant for ambient light only.
glEnable(GL_COLOR_MATERIAL)
glEnable(GL_LIGHTING)                    # Without this there is no shading.
glEnable(GL_LIGHT0)                      # Without this - no light at all.
#glLightfv(GL_LIGHT0, GL_AMBIENT,  kula_ambient) # Redundant.
#∧∧∧∧∧∧∧∧∧∧∧∧∧∧∧∧∧∧∧∧∧∧∧∧∧∧∧∧∧∧∧∧∧∧∧∧∧∧∧∧∧∧∧∧∧
```

White ambient light:

ambient_white = [1.0, 1.0, 1.0, 1.0]

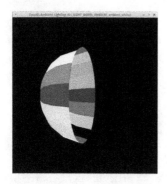

Black ambient light:
ambient_black = [0.0, 0.0, 0.0, 1.0]

Green ambient light:
ambient_green = [0.0, 1.0, 0.0, 1.0]

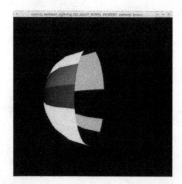

Specular Lighting

An array of balls in ambient light and three separate specular light sources - red, green and blue.

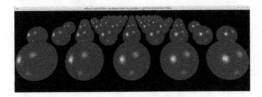

```
"""
Program name: opengl_specular_lighting_1.py
Objective: Experiment with the dynamic movement of specular lights..

keywords: opengl, lighting, specualar, source rotation..
=================================================================================79
Comments: An exercise in lighting and materials.

Tested on: Python 2.6, Python 2.7.3, Python 3.2.3
Author:  Mike Ohlson de Fine
"""

from OpenGL.GL import *
from OpenGL.GLUT import *
from OpenGL.GLU import *

# Lighting Parmeters
position_light_0   = [ 2.0, 5.0, 5.0, 0.0 ]
position_light_1   = [ 2.0, -5.0, 5.0, 0.0 ]

light_specular_red = [ 1.0, 0.0, 0.0, 1.0 ]
light_specular_blue = [ 0.0, 0.0, 1.0, 1.0 ]
material_specular   = [ 1.0, 1.0, 1.0, 1.0 ]
high_shininess = [ 128.0 ]            # Highest value.

def InitGL(Width, Height):        # Set OpenGL up in the required state .
    glClearColor(0.0, 0.0, 0.0, 0.0)  # Background color To black .
    glClearDepth(1.0)                 # Clear the Depth buffer .
    glDepthFunc(GL_LESS)              # Type of Depth test to be applied.
    glEnable(GL_DEPTH_TEST)     # Enables depth testing .
    glEnable(GL_COLOR_MATERIAL)
    #^^^^^^^^^^^^^^^^^^^^^^^^^^^^^^^^^^^^^^^^^^^^^^^^^^^^^^^^^^^^^^^^^^^^^
    # Lighting.
    glEnable(GL_LIGHT0) # First light = LIGHT0
    glEnable(GL_LIGHT1) # Second light = LIGHT1

    glEnable(GL_NORMALIZE)
    glEnable(GL_COLOR_MATERIAL)
    glEnable(GL_LIGHTING)

    glLightfv(GL_LIGHT0, GL_SPECULAR, light_specular_red) # LIGHT0
    glLightfv(GL_LIGHT0, GL_POSITION, position_light_0)
```

```
glLightfv(GL_LIGHT1, GL_SPECULAR, light_specular_blue) # LIGHT1
glLightfv(GL_LIGHT1, GL_POSITION, position_light_1)

glMaterialfv(GL_FRONT, GL_SPECULAR,  material_specular)
glMaterialfv(GL_FRONT, GL_SHININESS, high_shininess)
#/\/\/\/\/\/\/\/\/\/\/\/\/\/\/\/\/\/\/\/\/\/\/\/\/\/\/\/\/\/\/\/\
glMatrixMode(GL_PROJECTION)
glLoadIdentity()
gluPerspective(45.0, float(Width)/float(Height), 0.1, 100.0)
glMatrixMode(GL_MODELVIEW)
#=======================================================
# Set up the rotation parameters
angular_position = 0.0   # Position of light.
rradius = 0.5            # Radius of glutSolidSphere
sslices = 30
sstacks = 30

kula_1 = [ 0.01, 0.01, 0.01 ] # Dark charcoal.
kula_2 = [ 0.8, 0.94, 0.0 ]  # Yellow
kula_3 = [ 1.0,  1.0, 1.0 ]   # White

def group_4spheres(xx, yy, zz, kula):
    """ Draw a group of four spheres in a square formation.
        The position and color parameters are supplied as arguments.
    """
    glLoadIdentity()
    glColor(kula[0], kula[1], kula[2] )
    glTranslatef(xx, yy, zz )
    glutSolidSphere(rradius, sslices, sstacks )


def DrawGLScene():
    """"  The main drawing function.
    """
    global angular_position
    light_position = [ 2.0, 5.0, 5.0, 0.0 ]
    glLightfv(GL_LIGHT0, GL_POSITION, light_position)
    glClear(GL_COLOR_BUFFER_BIT | GL_DEPTH_BUFFER_BIT)

    group_4spheres(-1.0,  0.0, -2.0, kula_1)  # Dark charcoal.
    group_4spheres( 0.0,  0.0, -6.0, kula_2)  # Yellow.
    group_4spheres( 1.0, -1.0, -4.0, kula_3)  # White.

    glLoadIdentity()
    angular_position -= 0.4
    glRotatef(angular_position , 0.0, 1.0, 0.0 )

    glutSwapBuffers()

def main():
    glutInit(sys.argv)
    glutInitDisplayMode(GLUT_RGBA | GLUT_DOUBLE | GLUT_DEPTH)
    glutInitWindowSize(600, 300)
    window = glutCreateWindow(b"Specular Lighting Movement Test")
    glutIdleFunc(DrawGLScene)
    InitGL(600, 300)
```

glutMainLoop()

main()

Three objects illuminated with dynamically animated light sources. The red source moves with the default light source.

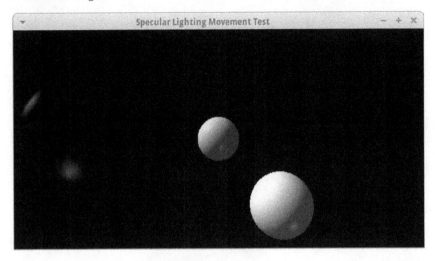

"""

Program name: opengl_spot_lighting_1.py
Objective: To demonstrate the effect of spotlight position settings.

keywords: opengl, lighting, spot, spotlight, square, quads, quadrilateral.
===79

Comments: An exercise in spot lighting.
Observe that the color of the spotlit area is dominated by the color of
diffuse light on the tiles.
Examples:
1. If the tiles are colored green and then illuminated with red spotlight,
 then the spotlight is invisible. A pure green tile is incapable of reflecting red light.
2. If the tiles are colored yellow (a mix of red and green)
 and then illuminated with red spotlight, the spotlit ares is orange (yellow with extra red).

Tested on: Python 2.6, Python 2.7.3, Python 3.2.3
Author: Mike Ohlson de Fine
"""

```
from OpenGL.GL import *
from OpenGL.GLUT import *
from OpenGL.GLU import *

kula_spotlight   = [ 1.0, 1.0, 0.0 ] # Yellow
kula_tiles = [ 0.0, 1.0, 0.0 ] # Red
x_lite = 0.0          #x_lite = -4.0
y_lite = 0.0
z_lite = -10.0
# @@@@@@@@@ Spotlight alert !!! @@@@@@@@@@@@@@@@@@@@@@@@@@@@@@
w_lite = 1.0  # NB!!! Positional: W =1.0 Directional: W = 0.0
# @@@@@@@@@@@@@@@@@@@@@@@@@@@@@@@@@@@@@@@@@@@@@@@@@@

def InitGL(Width, Height):          # Set OpenGL up in the required state
    light_position = [ x_lite, y_lite, z_lite, w_lite ]
    glClearColor(0.0, 0.0, 0.0, 0.0) # Set the background color to black .
    # ^^^^ Lighting and Materials ^^^^^^^^^^^^^^^^^^^^^^^^^^^^^
    glEnable(GL_LIGHT0)
    glEnable(GL_NORMALIZE)
    glEnable(GL_COLOR_MATERIAL)
    glEnable(GL_LIGHTING)

    glLightfv(GL_LIGHT0, GL_POSITION, light_position)
    glLightf(GL_LIGHT0, GL_SPOT_CUTOFF, 10.0)
    glLightfv(GL_LIGHT0, GL_DIFFUSE,  kula_spotlight)
    # ^^^^^^^^^^^^^^^^^^^^^^^^^^^^^^^^^^^^^^^^^^^^^^^^
    glShadeModel(GL_SMOOTH)
    glMatrixMode(GL_PROJECTION)
    glLoadIdentity()
    gluPerspective(80.0, float(Width)/float(Height), 0.1, 100.0) # last 2: near, far
    glMatrixMode(GL_MODELVIEW)


def vert_quad_1(xx, yy, zz, x_width, y_hite, z_depth, kula):
    """ Draw a VERTICAL BACK WALL (aligned with the X-axis),
        quadrilateral in a variable position.
        The shape and color parameters are supplied as arguments.
    """
    glLoadIdentity()
    glColor(kula[0], kula[1], kula[2] )
    glTranslatef(xx, yy, zz )
    glBegin(GL_QUADS)
    glVertex3f( xx    , yy, zz)
    glVertex3f(xx     , yy+y_hite, zz)
    glVertex3f(xx+x_width, yy+y_hite, zz)
```

271

```
        glVertex3f(xx+x_width,  yy, zz)
        glEnd()

def horiz_quad_1(xx, yy, zz, x_width, y_hite, z_depth, kula):
    """ Draw a HORIZONTAL (Ceiling and Floor) quadrilateral in a varaible position.
        The shape and color parameters are supplied as arguments.
    """
    glLoadIdentity()
    glColor(kula[0], kula[1], kula[2] )
    glTranslatef(xx, yy, zz )
    glBegin(GL_QUADS)
    glVertex3f( xx,       yy, zz)
    glVertex3f(xx,        yy, zz+z_depth)
    glVertex3f(xx+x_width, yy, zz+z_depth)
    glVertex3f(xx+x_width, yy, zz)
    glEnd()

def side_wall_1(xx, yy, zz, x_width, y_hite, z_depth, kula):
    """ Draw a VERTICAL quadrilateral( aligned with the Z-axis), in a varaible position.
        The shape and color parameters are supplied as arguments.
    """
    glLoadIdentity()
    glColor(kula[0], kula[1], kula[2] )
    glTranslatef(xx, yy, zz )
    glBegin(GL_QUADS)
    glVertex3f( xx, yy,  zz)
    glVertex3f(xx,  yy+y_hite, zz)
    glVertex3f(xx,  yy+y_hite, zz+z_depth)
    glVertex3f(xx,  yy     , zz+z_depth)
    glEnd()


def row_of_vert_quads(xx,yy,zz, x_incr, y_incr, z_incr):
    for i in range(12):
        vert_quad_1(xx, yy, zz, x_incr, y_incr, z_incr, kula_tiles)
        xx = xx + x_incr

def row_of_horiz_quads(xx,yy,zz, x_incr, y_incr, z_incr):
    for i in range(12):
        horiz_quad_1(xx, yy, zz, x_incr, y_incr, z_incr, kula_tiles)
        xx = xx + x_incr

def row_of_side_walls(xx,yy,zz, x_incr, y_incr, z_incr):
    for i in range(12):
        side_wall_1(xx, yy, zz, x_incr, y_incr, z_incr, kula_tiles)
        zz = zz + z_incr


# The main drawing function.
def DrawGLScene():
    """ The main drawing function.
    """

    glClear(GL_COLOR_BUFFER_BIT | GL_DEPTH_BUFFER_BIT) # Clear The Screen And The Depth Buffer

    # Left Side_wall
    xx = -5.0     # Starting position - where the tiling starts.
    yy = 3.0
```

```
zz = -17.0
x_incr = 0.0
y_incr = 1.0
z_incr = 1.0
for i in range(7):
    row_of_side_walls(xx,yy,zz, x_incr, y_incr, z_incr)
    yy -= 1.0
    zz = -17.0

# Right Side_wall
xx = 6.5
yy = 3.0
zz = -17.0
for i in range(7):
    row_of_side_walls(xx,yy,zz, x_incr, y_incr, z_incr)
    yy -= 1.0

# Horizontal Quads (Ceiling)
xx = -5.0
yy = 4.0
zz = -6.0
x_incr = 1.0
y_incr = 0.0
for i in range(12):
    row_of_horiz_quads(xx,yy,zz, x_incr, y_incr, z_incr)
    zz -= 1.0

# Horizontal Quads (Floor)
xx = -5.0
yy = -3.5
zz = -6.0
for i in range(12):
    row_of_horiz_quads(xx,yy,zz, x_incr, y_incr, z_incr)
    zz -= 1.0

# Vertical Quads (Back wall)
xx = -5.0
yy = 3.3
zz = -18.0
y_incr = 1.0
z_incr = 0.0
for i in range(8):
    row_of_vert_quads(xx,yy,zz, x_incr, y_incr, z_incr)
    yy -= 1.0

glutSwapBuffers()

def main():
    glutInit(sys.argv)
    glutInitDisplayMode(GLUT_RGBA | GLUT_DOUBLE | GLUT_DEPTH)
    glutInitWindowSize(1200, 800)
    glutInitWindowPosition(0, 0)
    window = glutCreateWindow("Spotlight. Red tiles, yrellow light")
    glutDisplayFunc(DrawGLScene)
    InitGL(1200, 800)
    glutMainLoop()
```

main()

Spotlight Distance

Spotlight distance: The closer an illuminated spotlight is to the light source, the smaller the spot.

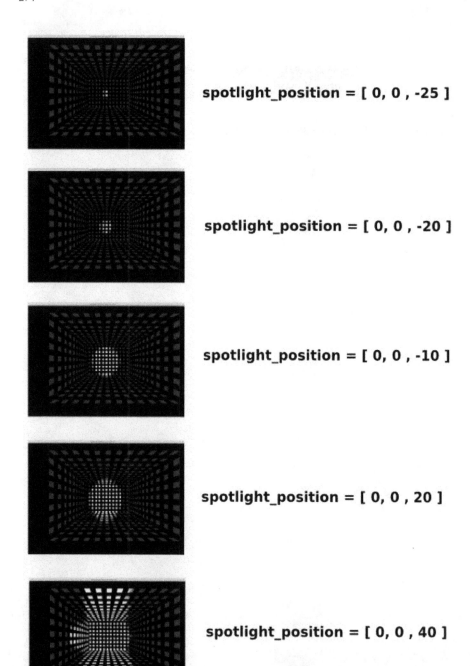

spotlight_position = [0, 0 , -25]

spotlight_position = [0, 0 , -20]

spotlight_position = [0, 0 , -10]

spotlight_position = [0, 0 , 20]

spotlight_position = [0, 0 , 40]

Spotlight Direction

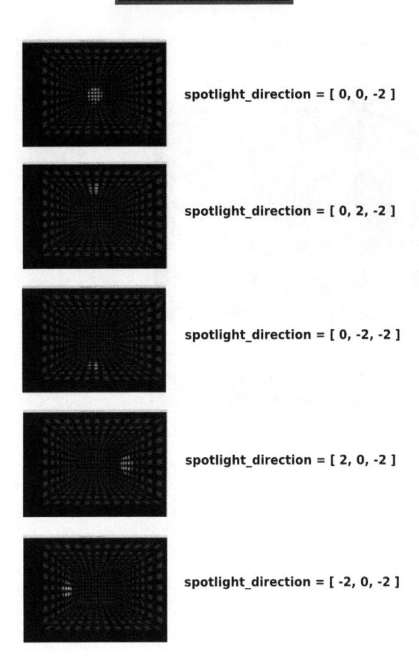

spotlight_direction = [0, 0, -2]

spotlight_direction = [0, 2, -2]

spotlight_direction = [0, -2, -2]

spotlight_direction = [2, 0, -2]

spotlight_direction = [-2, 0, -2]

Overlapping Spotlights

The effect of color mixing on spotlights composed of the primary colors red, green, blue

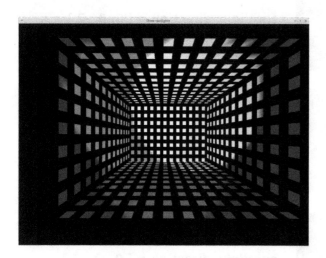

Lighting Summary

Sources

Light sources have a number of properties, such as color, position, and direction.
The command used to specify all properties of lights is **glLight()**
It takes three arguments:
1. Identity of the light whose property is being specified
2. The property being specified
3. The desired value for that property.

Light Identity.

There can be up to eight separate lights, identified as *GL_LIGHT0, GL_LIGHT1, GL_LIGHT2, GL_LIGHT3, GL_LIGHT4, GL_LIGHT5, GL_LIGHT6,* or *GL_LIGHT7*.

Light Property

The choices are *AMBIENT, DIFFUSE, SPECULAR, POSITION, SPOT_DIRECTION, SPOT_EXPONENT, SPOT_CUTOFF, CONSTANT_ATTENUATION, LINEAR_ATTENUATION, QUADRATIC_ATTENUATION.*

Examples of light creation commands are:
glLightfv(GL_LIGHT0, GL_AMBIENT, light_ambient)
glLightfv(GL_LIGHT0, GL_DIFFUSE, light_diffuse)
glLightfv(GL_LIGHT0, GL_SPECULAR, light_specular)
glLightfv(GL_LIGHT0, GL_POSITION, light_position)
glLightfv(GL_LIGHT0, GL_SPOT_DIRECTION, light_direction)
glLightfv(GL_LIGHT0, GL_SPOT_EXPONENT, 0.0)
glLightfv(GL_LIGHT0, GL_SPOT_CUTOFF, spot_cutoff_angle)
glLightfv(GL_LIGHT0, GL_CONSTANT_ATTENUATION, constant_attenuation_factor)
glLightfv(GL_LIGHT0, GL_LINEAR_ATTENUATION, linear_attenuation_factor)
glLightfv(GL_LIGHT0, GL_QUADRATIC_ATTENUATION, quadratic_attenuation_factor)

  and the default values are assigned as follows. You can change them at will.
light_ambient = [0.0, 0.0, 0.0, 1.0]   # Darkness - no ambient lightt.
light_diffuse = [1.0, 1.0, 1.0, 1.0]   # Diffuse bright white.
light_specular = [1.0, 1.0, 1.0, 1.0]   # Specular white light.
light_position = [0.0, 0.0, 1.0, 0.0]   # (x, y, z) coordinates.
light_direction = [0.0, 0.0, 1.0, 0.0]   # (x, y, z) coordinates.
spot_cutoff_angle = 180.0
constant_attenuation_factor = 1.0
linear_attenuation_factor = 0.0
quadratic_attenuation_factor = 0.0

Default values: The default values listed for GL_DIFFUSE and GL_SPECULAR apply only to one light, GL_LIGHT0. For other lights, the default value is (0.0, 0.0, 0.0, 1.0) for both GL_DIFFUSE and GL_SPECULAR.

How to turn lights on and off.

You turn on each light with *glEnable(GL_LIGHTING)*
Turn-off lighting with *glDisable(GL_LIGHTING)*

The Color given by a Light

OpenGL allows you to associate three different color-related parameters - **GL_AMBIENT, GL_DIFFUSE**, and **GL_SPECULAR** - with any particular light.

The **GL_AMBIENT** parameter refers to the light coming from the air/sky/walls and not of the surface color of the object. That is, the RGBA intensity of the ambient light that a particular light source adds to the scene. By default there is no ambient light since **GL_AMBIENT is (0.0, 0.0, 0.0, 1.0).**

The **GL_DIFFUSE** parameter is probably most similar to what we think of as "the color of a light." It defines the RGBA color of the diffuse light that a particular light source adds to a scene. By default, **GL_DIFFUSE is (1.0, 1.0, 1.0, 1.0)** for **GL_LIGHT0**, which produces a bright, white light .

The **GL_SPECULAR** parameter affects the color of the specular (shiney) highlight on an object. Typically, a real-world object such as a glass bottle has a specular highlight that's the color of the light shining on it.

Alpha Channel (the opacity/transparency)

The alpha component of these colors is not used until blending is enabled. Blending is how the color properties of polygons can be made to interact. Until blending is being used then, the alpha value can be safely ignored.

The END of the third book in the series:

Python Graphics for Games 1: Line, shape and color.

Python Graphics for Games 2: Line, shape and color.

Python Graphics for Games 3: Working in 3 Dimensions.

Appendices

1. Glossary of Computer 3D Graphics Terminology

2. How to Check Computer Hardware

3. The Matrix Transfomation Module used in this Book

4. The Vector Operation Module used in this Book

5. OpenGL and Python 3.3 Problems.

1. Glossary of Computer 3D Graphics Terminology

We encounter many new words in connection with computer graphics. Extra confusion comes in because different commercial companys choose nomenclature for marketing purposes that is not standard. This appendix tries to reduce some of the confusion and explains the names and concepts used in OpenGL particularly. OpenGL is open and not directly controlled by any single commercial interest. Because of OpenGL's growing influence the names used below are becoming a de-facto standard.

A

Alpha-Blending
Hidden-surface removal works only if the front object is totally opaque. In computer graphics, a fragment is not necessarily opaque, and could contain an alpha value specifying its degree of transparency. The alpha is typically normalized to the range of [0, 1], with 0 denotes totally transparent and 1 denotes totally opaque. If the fragment is not totally opaque, then part of its background object could show through, which is known as alpha blending. Alpha-blending and hidden-surface removal are mutually exclusive.
The order of placing the fragment is important. The fragments must be sorted from back-to-front, with the largest z-value processed first. Also, the destination alpha value is not used.

Ambient Light
A constant amount of light applied to every point of the scene. It comes from no particular direction.

Aspect Ratios of Viewport and Projection Plane
If the aspect ratio of the viewport (set via glViewport()) and the projection plane (set via gluPerspective(), glOrtho()) are not the same, the shapes will be distorted. Hence, it is important to use the same aspect ratio for the viewport and the projection plane. It is important that the aspect ratio of the projection plane is re-configure to match the viewport's aspect ratio, in order not to distort the shapes. In other words, glViewport() and gluPerpective()/glOrtho() should be issued together.

B

Back-Face Culling
While view frustum culling discard objects outside the view frustum, back-face culling discard primitives which is not facing the camera, but still inside the view volume. The Back face can be identified based on the normal vector and the vector connecting the surface and the camera.
Back-face culling will not be enabled if the object is transparent and alpha blending is enabled.

C

Color pixel Depth
The number of color-bits per pixel is called the depth (or precision) of the display. The number of rows by columns of the rectangular grid is called the resolution of the display, which can range from 640x480 (VGA), 800x600 (SVGA), 1024x768 (XGA) to 1920x1080 (FHD). As time progresses manufactureres produce higher resolution screens. The highests so far is about 4000 x 4000 (year 2015)

Coordinates
3D Graphics Coordinate Systems
OpenGL adopts the Right-Hand Coordinate System (RHS). In the RHS, the x-axis is pointing right, y-axis is pointing up, and z-axis is pointing out of the screen. With your right-hand fingers curving from the x-axis towards the y-axis, the thumb is pointing at the z-axis. RHS is counter-clockwise (CCW). The 3D Cartesian Coordinates is a RHS.

Some graphics software (such as Microsoft Direct3D) use Left-hand System (LHS), where the z-axis is inverted. LHS is clockwise (CW). In this book, we shall adopt the RHS and CCW used in OpenGL.

Coordinates Transformation

The process used to produce a 3D scene on the display in Computer Graphics is very similar to taking a photograph with a camera.
It involves four transformations:

1. Arrange the objects (or models, or avatar) in the world (Model Transformation or World transformation).

2. Position and orientation the camera (View transformation).

3. Select a camera lens (wide angle, normal or telescopic), adjust the focus length and zoom factor to set the camera's field of view (Projection transformation).

4. Print the photo on a selected area of the paper (Viewport transformation) - in rasterization stage

D

Diffuse Light
Diffuse light aims to simulate distant directional light source (such as the sun or the bright full moon). The reflected light is scattered equally in all directions, and appears the same to all viewers regardless of their positions, i.e., independent of viewer vector V. The strength of incident light depends on the angle between the light source L and the normal N, i.e., the dot product between L and N.

Double Buffering
While the display is reading from the frame buffer to display the current frame, we might be updating its contents for the next frame (not necessarily in raster-scan manner). This would result in the so-called tearing, in which the screen shows parts of the old frame and parts of the new frame.
This can be fixed by using so-called double buffering. Instead of using a single frame buffer, modern GPU uses two of them: a front buffer and a back buffer. The display reads from the front buffer, while we can write the next frame to the back buffer. When we finish, we signal to GPU to swap the front and back buffer (known as buffer swap or page flip).

E

Emissive Light
Some surfaces may emit light as if they have their own internal glow.

F

Fragment
A fragment is the data necessary to generate a single pixel's worth of a drawing primitive in the frame buffer. A fragment is 3-dimensional complex data structure, with a (x, y, z) position. The (x, y) are aligned with the 2D pixel-grid. The z-value (not grid-aligned) denotes its depth. The z-values are needed to capture the relative depth

of various primitives, so that the occluded objects can be discarded (or the alpha channel of transparent objects processed) in the output-merging stage.

Fragments are produced via interpolation of the vertices. Hence, a fragment has all the vertex's attributes such as color, fragment-normal and texture coordinates.

In modern GPU, vertex processing and fragment processing are programmable. The programs are called vertex shader and fragment shader.

Warning label: Direct3D uses the term "pixel" for "fragment".

Fragment Processing

After rasterization, we have a set of fragments for each primitive. A fragment has a position, which is aligned to the pixel-grid. It has a depth, color, normal and texture coordinates, which are interpolated from the vertices.

The fragment processing focuses on the texture and lighting, which has the greatest impact on the quality of the final image.

The operations involved in the fragment processor are:

The first operation in fragment processing is texturing.

Next, primary and secondary colors are combined, and fog calculation may be applied.

The optional scissor test, alpha test, stencil test, and depth-buffer test are carried out, if enabled.

Then, the optional blending, dithering, logical operation, and bitmasking may be performed.

Frame Buffer

The color values of the pixels are stored in a special part of graphics memory called frame buffer. The GPU writes the color value into the frame buffer. A complete screen image is called a frame. The display reads the color values from the frame buffer row-by-row, from left-to-right, top-to-bottom, and puts each of the values onto the screen. This is known as raster-scan.

G

Graphics Pipeline

A pipeline, in computing terminology, refers to a series of processing stages in which the output from one stage is fed as the input of the next stage, similar to a factory assembly line or water/oil pipe. With massive parallelism, pipeline can greatly improve the overall throughput.

GPU (Graphics Processing Unit)

A typical modern day computer has a dedicated Graphics Processing Unit (GPU) to produce images for the display, with its own graphics memory (or Video RAM or

VRAM). The GPU has massive parallel arithmetic computing hardware for fast image generation.

H

Hardware
Hardware in computers is the physical components like transistors, wires, resistors and capacitors. Software is the programmers instructions that control what the hardware is going to do. Firmware is the special software usually kept in Read-Only-Memory (ROM) and is considered as actually a form of hardware because it is not controllable by the computer user.

I

Indexed Vertices
Primitives often share vertices. Instead of repeatedly specifying the vertices, it is more efficient to create an index list of vertices, and use the indexes in specifying the primitives.

J

JavaScript
JavaScript is a programming language for web pages. JavaScript code on a web page is executed by a web browser that displays the page, and it can interact with the contents of the web page and with the user. There are JavaScript APIs for 2D and for 3D graphics

K

Keyframe Animation
An animation technique in which the position of a vertex or line is given explicitly only at certain times during the animation. The times when the quantity is specified are called keyframes. Between keyframes, the value of the quantity is obtained by interpolating between the values specified for the keyframes.

L

Lighting
Lighting refers to the handling of interactions between the light sources and the objects in the 3D scene. Lighting is one of the most important factors in producing a realistic scene.

The color that we see in the real world is the result of the interaction between the light sources and the color material surfaces. In other words, three parties are involved: viewer, light sources, and the material. When light (of a certain spectrum) from a light source strikes a surface, some gets absorbed, some is reflected or scattered. The angle of reflection depends on the angle of incidence and the surface normal. The strength of scattering depends on the smoothness of the surface and the material type of the surface. The reflected light also spans a certain color spectrum, which depends on the color spectrum of the incident light and the absorption properties of the material. The strength of the reflected light depends on the position and distance of the light source and the viewer, as well as the material. The reflected light may strike other surfaces, and some is absorbed and some is reflected again. The color that we perceived about a surface is the reflected light hitting our eye. In a 2D photograph or painting, objects appear to be three-dimensional due to some small variations in colors, known as shades.

The are two classes of lighting models:

Local illumination: Local Illumination considers only the direct lightings. The color of the surface depends on the reflectance properties of the surface and the direct lighting.

Global illumination: In the real world, objects receive indirect lighting reflected from other objects and the environment. The global illumination model considers indirect lighting reflected from other objects in the scene. A global illumination model is complex and compute intensive.

Linear Algebra
The field of mathematics that studies vector spaces and linear transformations between them. Linear algebra is part of the essential mathematical foundation of computer graphics.

Linear Transformation
A function from one vector space to another that preserves vector addition and multiplication by constants. Linear transformations can be represented by matrices. In computer graphics, they are used to implement geometric operations such as rotation and translation.

Linear Transforms
Rotation and scaling belong to a class of geometry transformations called linear transformation (by definition, a linear transformation preserves vector addition and scalar multiplication). Linear transforms and translation form the so-called affine transformations. Under an affine transformation, a straight line remains a straight line and ratios of distances between points are preserved.
In OpenGL, a vertex V at (x, y, z) is represented as a 3x1 column vector

M

Model-View Transform

In Computer Graphics, moving the objects relative to a fixed camera (Model transform), and moving the camera relative to a fixed object (View transform) produce the same image, and therefore are equivalent.

OpenGL, therefore, manages the Model transform and View transform in the same manner on a so-called Model-View matrix. Projection transformation is managed via a Projection matrix.

Material

Similar to light source, a material has reflectivity parameters for specular (GL_SPECULAR), diffuse (GL_DIFFUSE) and ambient (GL_AMBIENT) components (for each of the RGBA color components), which specifies the fraction of light reflected. A surface may also emit light (GL_EMISSION). A surface has a shininess parameter (GL_SHININESS) - the higher the value, the more concentration of reflected-light in the small area around the perfect reflector and the surface appears to be shinier. Furthermore, a surface has two faces: front and back, that may have the same or different parameters.

You can use glMaterial() function to specify these parameters for the front (GL_FRONT), back (GL_BACK), or both (GL_FRONT_AND_BACK) surfaces. The front face is determined by the surface normal (implicitly defined by the vertices with right-hand rule, or glNormal() function).

The default material has a gray surface (under white light), with a small amount of ambient reflection (0.2, 0.2, 0.2, 1.0), high diffuse reflection (0.8, 0.8, 0.8, 1.0), and no specular reflection (0.0, 0.0, 0.0, 1.0).

Magnification

The commonly used methods are:

Nearest Point Filtering: the texture color-value of the fragment is taken from the nearest texel. This filter leads to "blockiness" as many fragments are using the same texel.

Bilinear Interpolation: the texture color-value of the fragment is formed via bilinear interpolation of the four nearest texels. This yields smoother result.

Minification

Minification is an operation that is used when applying a texture to an object, when the texture has to be shrunk to fit the object. Minification is needed if the resolution of the texture image is larger than the fragment. For an image texture, a minification filter is applied to compute the color of a pixel when that pixel covers several pixels in the image. Again, you can use the "nearest-point sampling" or "bilinear interpolation" methods.

However, these sampling methods often give rise to the aliasing artefact, due the low sampling frequency compared with the signal. For example, a far-away object in perspective projection will look strange due to its high signal frequency.

Minmaping

A minimap is one of a series of reduced-size copies of a texture image, of decreasing width and height. Starting from the original image, each mipmap is obtained by dividing the width and height of the previous image by two (unless it is already 1). The final mimpap is a single pixel. Mipmaps are used for more efficient mapping of the texture image to a surface, when the image has to be shrunk to fit the surface.
For example, suppose the original image is 64x64 (Level 0), we can create lower resolution images at 32x32, 16x16, 8x8, 4x4, 2x2, 1x1. The highest resolution is referred to as level 0; the next is level 1; and so on. We can then use the nearest matched-resolution texture image; or perform linear interpolation between the two nearest matched-resolution texture images.

N

Normal vector

A normal vector to a surface at a point on that surface is a vector that is perpendicular to the surface at that point. Normal vectors to curves are defined similarly. Normal vectors are important for lighting calculations.

Normalized vector

The result of dividing a non-zero vector by its length, giving a unit vector, that is, a vector of length one. (Note that "normalized vector" and "normal vector" are, confusingly, unrelated terms!)

O

Object Co-ordinates

Each object (or model or avatar) in a 3D scene is typically drawn in its own coordinate system, known as its model space (or local space, or object space). As we assemble the objects, we need to transform the vertices from their local spaces to the world space, which is common to all the objects.

OpenGL

OpenGL A family of computer graphics Application Program Interfaces (APIs) s that is implemented in many graphics hardware devices. There are several versions of the API, and there are implementations, or "bindings" for several different programming languages. Versions of OpenGL for embedded systems such as mobile phones are known as OpenGL ES. WebGL is a version for use on Web pages. OpenGL can be used for 2D as well as for 3D graphics, but it is most commonly associated with 3D.

OpenGL Perspective Projection
In OpenGL, there are two functions for choosing the perspective projection and setting its clipping volume:
   More commonly-used GLU function gluPerspective():
gluPerspective(fovy, aspectRatio, zNear, zFar)
where:
fovy is the angle between the bottom and top of the projectors;
      aspectRatio is the ratio of width and height of the front (and also back) clipping plane;
      zNear and zFar specify the front and back clipping planes.

OpenGL's Model-View Matrix and Projection Matrix
OpenGL manages the transforms via two matrices: a model-view matrix (GL_MODELVIEW for handling model and view transforms) and a projection matrix (GL_PROJECTION for handling projection transform). These two matrices can be manipulated independently.
We need to first select the matrix for manipulation via:
void glMatrixMode(GLenum matrix)　// Select matrix for manipulating, e.g., GL_PROJECTION, GL_MODELVIEW.
We can reset the currently selected matrix via:
void glLoadIdentity()
We can save the value of the currently selected matrix onto the stack and restore it back via:
void glPushMatrix()
void glPopMatrix()
Push and pop use a stack and operate in a last-in-first-out manner, and can be nested.

OpenGL Viewport
In OpenGL, by default, the viewport is set to cover the entire application window. We can use the glViewport() function to choose a smaller area (e.g., for split-screen or multi-screen application).
glViewport(xTopLeft, yTopLeft, width, height)
We can also set the z-range of viewport via glDepthRange():
glDepthRange(minZ, maxZ)

Orthographic Projection
A projection from 3D to 2D that simply discards the z-coordinate. It projects objects along lines that are orthogonal (perpendicular) to the xy-plane. In OpenGL the view volume for an orthographic projection is a rectangular solid.
Orthographic projection (or parallel projection), is the special case where the camera is placed very far away from the world (analogous to using telescopic lens). The view volume for orthographic projection is a parallelepiped (a box with parallel sides). This

is different from the pyramid-like shape of a frustum in perspective projection.
In OpenGL, we can use glOrtho() function to choose the orthographic projection mode
and specify its clipping volume:
glOrtho(xLeft, xRight, yBottom, e yTop, zNear, zFar)

The default 3D projection in OpenGL is the orthographic (instead of perspective) with
parameters (-1.0, 1.0, -1.0, 1.0, -1.0, 1.0), i.e., a cube with sides of 2.0, centered at
origin.

OpenGL face culling

In OpenGL, face culling is disabled by default, and both front-face and back-faces are
rendered. We can use function glCullFace() to specify whether the back-face
(GL_BACK) or front-face (GL_FRONT) or both (GL_FRONT_AND_BACK) shall be
culled.

OpenGL Depth buffering

In OpenGL, to use z-buffer for hidden-surface removal via depth testing, we need to do
three things: request that a depth-buffer be made available and also enable it.

So first instruct a depth-buffer be made available via glutInitDisplayMode():
glutInitDisplayMode(GLUT_RGBA | GLUT_DOUBLE | GLUT_DEPTH)

then we enable depth testing on depth-buffer via:
glEnable(GL_DEPTH_TEST)

and thirdly clear the z-buffer (to 1 denoting the farthest) and the color buffer (to the
background color):
glClear(GL_COLOR_BUFFER_BIT | GL_DEPTH_BUFFER_BIT)

OpenGL Alpha blending

In OpenGL, to perform alpha blending, we need to enable blending and disable depth-
test (which performs hidden-surface removal).

Source and Destination Blending Factors
In OpenGL, the glBlendFunc() function can be used to specify the so-called source and
destination blending factors:
glBlendFunc(sourceBlendingFactor, destinationBlendingFactor)

Suppose that a new object (called source) is to be blended with the existing objects in
the color buffer (called destination). The source's color is (Rs, Gs, Bs, As), and the
destination's color is (Rd, Gd, Bd, Ad). The source and destination color values will be
weighted with respective to the source blending factor and destination blending factor
and combined to produce the resultant value. Each of the RGB components will be
computed independently.

For example, suppose the source blending factor for G component is p and the destination blending factor for G component is q, the resultant G component is p×Gs + q×Gd.

There are many choices of the blending factors. For example, a popular choice is:
glBlendFunc(GL_SRC_ALPHA, GL_ONE_MINUS_SRC_ALPHA);

where each component of the source is weighted by source's alpha value (As), and each component of the destination is weighted by 1-As. In this case, if the original color component's value is within [0.0, 1.0], the resultant value is guaranteed to be within this range. The drawback is that the final color depends on the order of rendering if many surfaces are added one after another (because the destination alpha value is not considered).

Another example of blending factors is:
glBlendFunc(GL_SRC_ALPHA, GL_ONE);
where each component of source is weighted by source's alpha value (As), and each component of the destination is weight by 1. The value may overflow/underflow. But the final color does not depends on the order of rendering when many objects are added.

Other values for the blending factors include GL_ZERO, GL_ONE, GL_SRC_COLOR, GL_ONE_MINUS_SRC_COLOR, GL_DST_COLOR, GL_ONE_MINUS_DST_COLOR, GL_SRC_ALPHA, GL_ONE_MINUS_SRC_ALPHA, GL_DST_ALPHA, GL_ONE_MINUS_DST_ALPHA, GL_CONSTANT_COLOR, GL_ONE_MINUS_CONSTANT_COLOR, GL_CONSTANT_ALPHA, and GL_ONE_MINUS_CONSTANT_ALPHA.

The default for source blending factor is GL_ONE, and the default for destination blending factor is GL_ZERO. That is, opaque (totally non-transparent) surfaces.

The computations also explain why depth-testing shall be disabled when alpha-blending is enabled. This is because the final color will be determined by blending between source and destination colors for translucent surfaces, instead of relative depth (the color of the nearer surface) for opaque surfaces.]

OpenGL's Lighting and Material

OpenGL provides point sources (omni-directional), spotlights (directional with cone-shaped), and ambient light (a constant factor). Light source may be located at a fixed position or infinitely far away. Each source has separate ambient, diffuse, and specular components. Each source has RGB components. The lighting calculation is performed on each of the components independently (local illumination without considering the indirect lighting).

Materials are modeled in the same manner. Each type of material has a separate ambient, diffuse, and specular components, with parameters specifying the fraction that is reflected for each corresponding component of the light sources. Material may also have a emissive component.

In OpenGL, you need to enable the lighting state, and each of the light sources, identified via GL_LIGHT0 to GL_LIGHT8.
glEnable(GL_LIGHTING)   # Enable lighting in general
glEnable(GL_LIGHT0)   # Enable light source 0
glEnable(GL_LIGHT1)   # Enable light source 1

Once lighting is enabled, color assigned by glColor() are no longer used. Instead, the color depends on the light-material interaction and the viewer's position.

P

Painter's Algorithm

A solution to the hidden surface algorithm that involves drawing the objects in a scene in order from back to front, that is, in decreasing order of distance from the viewer. A disadvantage is that the order is usually not well-defined unless some objects are decomposed into smaller sub-objects. Another issue is that the order of drawing has to change when objects move or when the point of view changes.

Perspective Projection

Once the camera is positioned and oriented, we need to decide what it can see (analogous to choosing the camera's field of view by adjusting the focus length and zoom factor), and how the objects are projected onto the screen. This is done by selecting a projection mode (perspective or orthographic) and specifying a viewing volume or clipping volume. Objects outside the clipping volume are clipped out of the scene and cannot be seen.

Perspective Projection Matrix

The Fourth component of vertex vectors
The last row of the matrix is no longer [0 0 0 1]. With input vertex of (x, y, z, 1), the resultant w-component would not be 1. We need to normalize the resultant homogeneous coordinates (x, y, z, w) to (x/w, y/w, z/w, 1) to obtain position in 3D space. (It is amazing that homogeneous coordinates can be used for translation, as well as the perspective projection.)
After the flip, the coordinate system is no longer a Right-Hand System (RHS), but becomes a Left-hand System (LHS).

Phong Lighting Model for Light-Material Interaction

Phong shading is a technique for computing pixel colors on a primitive using a lighting equation that takes into account ambient, diffuse, and specular reflection. In Phong shading, the lighting equation is applied at each pixel. Normal vectors are specified only at the vertices of the primitive. The normal vector that is used in the lighting equation at a pixel is obtained by interpolating the normal vectors for the vertices. Phong shading is named after Bui Tuong Phong, who developed the theory in the 1970s.

The Phong lighting model is quick and does not slow down image processing It considers four types of lightings: diffuse, specular, ambient and emissive.

Pipeline or Programmable Pipeline

A graphics processing pipeline is the image processing sequence in which some of the processing stages can or must be implemented by programs. Data for an image is passed through a sequence of processing stages, with the image as the end product. The sequence is called a "pipeline." Programmable pipelines are used in modern GPUs to provide more flexibility and control to the programmer. The programs for a programmable pipeline are known as shaders and are written in a shader programming language such as GLSL.

Pixels and Frame

All modern displays are raster-based. A raster is a 2D rectangular grid of pixels (or picture elements). A pixel has two properties: a color and a position. Color is expressed in RGB (Red-Green-Blue) components - typically 8 bits per component or 24 bits per pixel (or true color).

Pixel versus Fragment

Pixel. Pixels refers to the dots on the display, which are aligned in a 2-dimensional grid of a certain rows and columns corresponding to the display's resolution. A pixel is 2-dimensional, with a (x, y) position and a RGB color value (there is no alpha value for pixels). The purpose of the Graphics Rendering Pipeline is to produce the color-value for all the pixels for displaying on the screen, given the input primitives.

Fragment – see definition of Fragment above

In order to produce the grid-aligned pixels for the display, the rasterizer of the graphics rendering pipeline, as its name implied, takes each input primitive and perform raster-scan to produce a set of grid-aligned fragments enclosed within the primitive.

Position of pixels on the Display Screen

The position is expressed in terms of (x, y) coordinates. The origin (0, 0) is located at the top-left corner, with x-axis pointing right and y-axis pointing down. This is different from the conventional 2D Cartesian coordinates, where y-axis is pointing upwards.

Positioning the Camera

In 3D graphics, we position the camera onto the world space by specifying three view parameters: EYE, AT and UP, in world space.

The point EYE (ex, ey, ez) defines the location of the camera.

The vector AT (ax, ay, az) denotes the direction where the camera is aiming at, usually at the center of the world or an object.

The vector UP (ux, uy, uz) denotes the upward orientation of the camera roughly. UP is typically coincided with the y-axis of the world space. UP is roughly orthogonal to AT, but not necessary. As UP and AT define a plane, we can construct an orthogonal vector to AT in the camera space.

Primitives

The inputs to the Graphics Rendering Pipeline are geometric primitives (such as triangle, point, line or quad), which is formed by one or more vertices. OpenGL uses triangles as the fundamental primitive for its basic operations. However OpenGL has instructions which supports three classes of geometric primitives: points, line segments, and closed polygons. They are specified via vertices. Each vertex is associated with its attributes such as the position, color, normal and texture. OpenGL provides 10 primitives as shown. Sphere, 3D box and pyramid are not primitives. They are typically assembled using primitive triangles or quads.

Q

Quad

A quadrilateral, that is a four-sided figure in the plane.

R

Raster scan

The display reads the color values from the frame buffer row-by-row, from left-to-right, top-to-bottom, and puts each of the values onto the screen. This is known as raster-scan.

Rasterization

In the previous vertex processing stage, the vertices, which are floating-point value, are not necessarily aligned with the pixel-grid (integers) of the display. The relationship of vertices, in term of primitives, are also not considered.

In the rasterization stage, each primitive (such as triangle, quad, point and line), which is defined by one or more vertices, are raster-scan to obtain a set of fragments enclosed within the primitive. Fragments can be treated as 3D pixels, which are now aligned with the pixel-grid. The 2D pixels have a position and a RGB color value. The 3D fragments, which are interpolated from the vertices, have the same set of attributes as the vertices, such as position, color, normal, texture.

Refresh Rate

The display refreshes its screen several dozen times per second, typically 60Hz for LCD monitors and higher for CRT (Cathode Ray Tubes, as found in old TV sets). This is known as the refresh rate. Other refresh rates in use are 30, 90 and 120 frames persecond.

Rendering

In computer graphics, rendering is the process of producing image on the display from the model description. It is the process of producing a 2D image from a 3D scene description.

The 3D Graphics Rendering Pipeline accepts description of 3D objects in terms of vertices of primitives (such as triangle, point, line and quad), and produces the color-value for the pixels on the display.

The 3D graphics rendering pipeline consists of the following main stages:
1.   Vertex Processing: Process and transform individual vertices.
2.   Rasterization: Convert each primitive (connected vertices) into a set of fragments. A fragment can be treated as a pixel in 3D spaces, which is aligned with the pixel grid, with attributes such as position, color, normal and texture.
3.   Fragment Processing: Process individual fragments.
4.   Output Merging: Combine the fragments of all primitives (in 3D space) into 2D color-pixel for the display.

In modern GPUs, the vertex processing stage and fragment processing stage are programmable. You can write programs, known as vertex shader and fragment shader to perform your custom transform for vertices and fragments. The shader programs are written in C-like high level languages such as GLSL (OpenGL Shading Language), HLSL (High-Level Shading Language for Microsoft Direct3D), or Cg (C for Graphics by NVIDIA).

On the other hand, the rasterization and output merging stages are not programmable, but configurable - via configuration commands issued to the GPU.

Resultant Color

The resultant color is the sum of the contribution in all the four components of Diffuse, Specular, Ambient and Emissive:

S

Specular Light
The reflected light is concentrated along the direction of perfect reflector R. What a viewer sees depends on the angle (cosine) between V and R.

As the shininess factor increases, the light cone becomes narrower, and the highlighted spot becomes smaller.

Successive Transforms

A series of successive affine transforms (T1, T2, T3, ...) operating on a vertex V can be computed via concatenated matrix multiplications V' = ...T3T2T1V. The matrices can be combined before applying to the vertex because matrix multiplication is associative, i.e., T3 (T2 (T1 V)) = (T3T2T1) V.

SVG Scaled Vector Graphics.
An XML language for specifying 2D vector graphics. SVG is a scene description language. It is designed to integrate into web pages.

T

Texture
In computer graphics, we often overlay (or paste or wrap) 2D images, called textures, over the graphical objects to make them realistic.
An texture is typically a 2D image. Each element of the texture is called a texel (texture element), similar to pixel (picture element).

Texture Wrapping
The 2D texture coordinate T=(s, t) is typically normalized to [0.0, 1.0], with origin at the top-left corner, s-axis pointing right and t-axis pointing down.
Although the 2D texture coordinates is normalized to [0.0, 1.0], we can configure the behavior if the coordinates are outside the range.

Texture Filtering
In general, the resolution of the texture image is different from the displayed fragment (or pixel). If the resolution of the texture image is smaller, we need to perform so-called magnification to magnify the texture image to match the display. On the other hand, if the resolution of texture image is larger, we perform minification.

Transform
A transform converts a vertex V from one space (or coordinate system) to another space V'. In computer graphics, transform is carried by multiplying the vector with a transformation matrix, i.e., V' = M V.

Transforming from World Space to Camera Space
Now, the world space is represented by standard orthonormal bases (e1, e2, e3), where e1=(1, 0, 0), e2=(0, 1, 0) and e3=(0, 0, 1), with origin at O=(0, 0, 0). The camera space has orthonormal bases (xc, yc, zc) with origin at EYE=(ex, ey, ez).

U

Uniform Scaling
A scaling transformation in which the scaling factors in all directions are the same. Uniform scaling changes the size of an object without distorting its shape.

Unit Normal
A normal vector of length one; that is, a unit vector that is perpendicular to a curve or surface at some point on the curve or surface.

V

VSync (Vertical synchronization)
Double buffering alone does not solve the entire problem of frame tearing, as the buffer swap might occur at an inappropriate time, for example, while the display is in the middle of displaying the old frame. This is resolved via the so-called vertical synchronization (or VSync) at the end of the raster-scan. When we signal to the GPU to do a buffer swap, the GPU will wait till the next VSync to perform the actual swap, after the entire current frame is displayed.

The most important point is: When the VSync buffer-swap is enabled, you cannot refresh the display faster than the refresh rate of the display!!! For the LCD/LED displays, the refresh rate is typically locked at 60Hz or 60 frames per second, or 16.7 milliseconds for each frame. Furthermore, if you application refreshes at a fixed rate, the resultant refresh rate is likely to be an integral factor of the display's refresh rate, i.e., 1/2, 1/3, 1/4, etc.

Vertices
A primitive is made up of one or more vertices. A vertex, in computer graphics, has these attributes:

Position in 3D space V=(x, y, z): typically expressed in floating point numbers.
Color which is expressed in RGB (Red-Green-Blue) or RGBA (Red-Green-Blue-Alpha) components. The component values are typically normalized to the range of 0.0 and 1.0 (or 8-bit unsigned integer between 0 and 255). Alpha is used to specify the transparency, with alpha of 0 for totally transparent and alpha of 1 for opaque.

Vertex-Normal N=(nx, ny, nz):
A surface normal is a vector at right angles (perpendicular) to a polygon surface. In computer graphics we need to attach a normal vector to each vertex, known as vertex-normal. Normals are used to differentiate the front- and back-face, and for other processing such as lighting. Right-hand rule (or counter-clockwise) is used in OpenGL. The normal is pointing outwards, indicating the outer surface (or front-face).

Vertex Processing Stage
Each vertex is transformed and positioned in the clipping-volume cuboid space, together with their vertex-normal. The x and y coordinates (in the range of -1 to +1) represent its position on the screen, and the z value (in the range of 0 to 1) represents its depth, i.e., how far away from the near plane.

The vertex processing stage transform individual vertices. The relationships between vertices (i.e., primitives) are not considered in this stage.

View Transform

It is much more convenience to express all the coordinates in the camera space. This is done via view transform. After the world transform, all the objects are assembled into the world space. The next step is to place the camera to capture the view.

The view transform consists of two operations: a translation (for moving EYE to the origin), followed by a rotation (to axis the axes):

View Frustum in Perspective View

The camera has a limited field of view, which exhibits a view frustum (truncated pyramid), and is specified by four parameters: fovy, aspect, zNear and zFar.

Fovy: specify the total vertical angle of view in degrees.

Aspect: the ratio of width vs. height. For a particular z, we can get the height from the fovy, and then get the width from the aspect.

zNear: the near plane.

zFar: the far plane.

The camera space (xc, yc, zc) is renamed to the familiar (x, y, z) for convenience. The projection with view frustum is known as perspective projection, where objects nearer to the COP (Center of Projection) appear larger than objects further to the COP of the same size.

An object outside the view frustum is not visible to the camera. It does not contribute to the final image and shall be discarded to improve the performance. This is known as view-frustum culling. If an object partially overlaps with the view frustum, it will be clipped in the later stage.

Viewport

Viewport is a rectangular display area on the application window, which is measured in screen's coordinates (in pixels, with origin at the top-left corner). A viewport defines the size and shape of the display area to map the projected scene captured by the camera onto the application window. It may or may not occupy the entire screen.

In 3D graphics, a viewport is 3-dimensional to support z-ordering (depth), which is needed for situations such as placement of spatial sequence (ordering) of overlapping triangles.

Viewport Transform

Our final transform, viewport transform, maps the clipping-volume (2x2x1 cuboid) to the 3D viewport.

Viewport transform is made up of a series of reflection (of y-axis), scaling (of x, y and z axes), and translation (of the origin from the center of the near plane of clipping volume to the top-left corner of the 3D viewport).

W

World Space
The common position reference co-ordinate system that we place all our objects in our graphics model world. The matrix multiplations that transport the vertices of each object from their local space to the world space is known as the world transform. The world transform consists of a series of scaling (scale the object to match the dimensions of the world), rotation (align the axes), and translation (move the origin).

X

XML
eXtensible Markup Language. Not a single language as such, but a class of languages that follow certain syntax rules. For example, SVG is an XML language because it follows those rules, but it also has further restrictions on it syntax that make it appropriate for specifying 2D graphics. XML documents, like HTML documents, have a tree-like structure defined by "elements." However, HTML is not an XML language since it does not follow all the syntax rules. XHTML is an alternative language for web pages that is similar to HTML but follows XML syntax rules.

Y
No entry for "Y" yet.

Z

Z-Buffer and Hidden-Surface Removal
z-buffer (or depth-buffer) can be used to remove hidden surfaces (surfaces blocked by other surfaces and cannot be seen from the camera). The z-buffer of the screen is initialized to 1 (farthest) and color-buffer initialized to the background color. For each fragment (of each primitive) processed, its z-value is checked against the buffer value. If its z-value is smaller than the z-buffer, its color and z-value are copied into the buffer. Otherwise, this fragment would be occluded by another object and is therefore discarded. The fragments can be processed in any order, in this algorithm.

2. Graphics Software and Hardware

This appendix offers hints and pointers on how to discover if our graphics hardware and software is working properly. It is not comprehensive. It is merely a collection of hints to get us going.

Skill Acquisition
Crafting graphics software forces us to grow our knowledge and skills
in the direction of hardware behavior which means probing and discovering that uncertain frontier where hardware and software are difficult to separate. It becomes unclear where the distinction between hardware and software lies. Good hardware can do many things that software does and good software, like OpenGL, can do many things that hardware does, only slower. One approach in dealing with this uncertainty is develop the know-how to test performance. In chapter 8 we looked at ways to measure graphic rendering times and that is the basic type of test that is needed in order to be able to compare the results of writing software in different ways. Therefore a prerequisite to effective graphics programming is to have methods to acquire, install and test software tools.

We can get advice and assistance on how to do things through questions and keywords posed to the Google search engine. Google will present us with long and confusing lists of forums that handle questions and answers. A lot of this material is useless. We are likely to encounter more bad advice than good advice. The internet seems to have an abundance of people who are inexperienced but eager to help. Youtube has hundreds of recorded video instructions on how to do difficult things, made by well meaning but unskilled novices. But some of those videos are pure gold – made by people who are good at what they do. We have to develop the ability to find the valuable gems in amongst the pile of flotsam.

Here is the author's personal philosophy regarding the acquisition of software expertise, based on hundreds of hours of trial, error, success and failure:
1. Keep written notes and sketches of what you are doing in a notebook. Your memory is NOT photographic – you will not remember everything you do. It is very useful to have a record of what did not work because we tend to repeat the same habits of thought that caused us to make the mistake.
2. In general there is some extremely valuable tutorial material on Youtube. There is also a lot of material of little value and some material that is downright misleading. Take note of the name or nickname of the person who made a Youtube video that you found useful because that same 'teacher' is likely to have made other, similar material that is also useful.
3. There are also useful Blogs (articles published on privately owned websites). The same rules apply as for Youtube tutorials – when you find a good article then the same author is likely to have written other articles of similar value.

That author often refers to articles written by other people who have also written material that is valuable.

4. Old fashioned books, printed on paper or in electronic format, are very valuable because a lot of thought and energy goes into writing a book and this naturally filters out o lot of irrelevant material.
5. Experiment often. Nothing is nearly as valuable as personal experience. It is the ONLY way to acquire real skill. The more mistakes you make, the fewer mistakes you will make in the future. Humans are perfect trial-and-error mechanisms.

http://www.ntu.edu.sg/home/ehchua/programming/opengl/cg_basicstheory.html
(Nottingham Trent University?)
http://www.nvidia.com/content/cudazone/cudau/courses/ucdavis/lectures/intro.pdf

Do we have the Software Tools and are they in Working Order?

What follows are brief recipes for acquiring and installing the software used in this book. The author uses the Linux operating system. One of the irritations of being held in the thrall of the Microsoft operating systems is that that we are vulnerable to the whims of companies whose chief objective is to discover ways of increasing revenue rather that increasing the usefulness of software tools. We also become the natural prey of malware aimed at the operating system. Microsoft is everywhere but has lost some proportion of market share. This trend is likely to continue into the far future. However Windows 7 methods have been included.

For Linux Users

For developing and testing software Linux is arguably the best platform because it is Open Source. This means there is technically no hidden behaviour. If a flaw is discovered it is typically a matter of hours before it is fixed. The operating system is based on UNIX which is the oldest and most stable operating system. The Android cellphone and tablet operating system is a stripped-down version of Linux. Because Linux has been going so long most flaws have already been discovered and fixed in Linux. Linux comes essentially in two parts: the kernel and then a bunch of extra tools and utilities. The Kernel is like the engine, gearbox and chassis of a motor car and the extras are the body, upholstery, media players, air conditioners and the other add-ons.

There are mainly four user variations of linux:
1. Ubuntu
2. Red Hat
3. Gentoo
4. Light varieties.

Tools for Hardware Discovery

Which hardware chip sets are installed in our computer? Can our computer benefit from an additional graphics card? Is more memory going to help?

Graphics capability of our Motherboard

We use the terminal command *lspci -vnn | grep VGA -A 12*

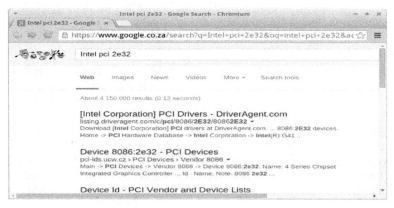

The first line:

00:02.0 VGA compatible controller [0300]: Intel Corporation 4 Series Chipset Integrated Graphics Controller [8086:2e32] (rev 03) (prog-if 00 [VGA controller])

This tells us we have some Graphics controller chips made by Intel, which does not seem very specific. The real information is in the yellow highlighted codes *8086:2e32*
The first part (8086) indicates the vendor identifier (which is Intel here) and the second number (2e32) indicates the pci identifier, which indicates the model of the graphics unit. See below for an explanation of what pci is.

Now you can now search google for more details using the Vendor name and the pci id.

Which CPU have we got?

The command-line *cpuid* gives complete information about our CPU.
For example:
Vendor ID: "GenuineIntel"; CPUID level 13

Intel-specific functions:
Version 0001067a:
Type 0 - Original OEM
Family 6 - Pentium Pro
Model 7 - Pentium III / Pentium III Xeon - external L2 cache
Stepping 10
Reserved 4

Extended brand string: "Intel(R) Celeron(R) CPU   E3400 @ 2.60GHz"
CLFLUSH instruction cache line size: 8
Hyper threading siblings: 2

Comprehensive Hardware Inventory

The command-line *hwinfo* gives complete and detalied information about the hardware on our motherboard.

Both *hwinfo* and *cpuid* are not normally included as system tools. We need to download and install them. For Ubuntu/Debian based Linux use:
sudo aptget install hwinfo
and
sudo aptget install cpuid

Install OpenGL for use with Python

For Ubuntu/Debian based Linux install:
sudo aptget install python-opengl

Which version of OpenGL is on your Computer?

Type the following command into a terminal:
glxinfo | grep "OpenGL version"

and you should a response similar to:
OpenGL version string: 2.1 Mesa 8.0.4

Mesa is a 3-D graphics library with an API that is identical to OpenGL for Python.
glxinfo is a command-line tool that can help you diagnose problems with your 3D acceleration setup. It can also provide additional helpful information for developers.
Use ***man glxinf***o to get an overview of its options.
It issues a lengthy list of results that gives information on both hardware and software rendering. For example:

mikeodf@mikeodf-HP-500B-Microtower:~$ glxinfo
name of display: :0.0
display: :0 screen: 0
direct rendering: Yes
server glx vendor string: SGI

server glx version string: 1.4

...

...

client glx vendor string: Mesa Project and SGI

client glx version string: 1.4

client glx extensions:

...

...

OpenGL vendor string: Tungsten Graphics, Inc

OpenGL renderer string: Mesa DRI Intel(R) G41

OpenGL version string: 2.1 Mesa 8.0.4

OpenGL shading language version string: 1.20

...

The first line, highlighted in yellow, tells you whether direct rendering is used. In this example, direct rendering is enabled, which means that all 3D rendering commands are handled by the client application. If indirect rendering is used, all rendering commands are sent to the server, and the server may use either software or hardware rendering. Software rendering is relatively slow.

In the line *OpenGL renderer string: Mesa DRI Intel(R) G41*. The "Mesa" tells us that OpenGL uses software functions from the Mesa library to do graphic rendering. MESA is purely a software library for OpenGL. It implements the opengl functions entirely inside software. It does not make use of any drivers. So it is possible to render graphics using opengl without actually having an opengl compatible gpu. In fact the hardware on which the above *glxinfo* command was run has no graphics card installed.

Test that OpenGL is working on our Operating system

We use a utility program that is part of Mesa called **glxgears** that displays an animation of three gears turning.

Ensure it is installed with:

sudo apt-get install mesa-utils

Then execute **glxgears** in a command-line terminal:

This graphic animation will be accompanied by a continuous renning measurement of the number of frames rendered by our OpenGL implementation. For example:

mikeodf@mikeodf-HP-500B-Microtower:~$ glxgears
Running synchronized to the vertical refresh. The framerate should be
approximately the same as the monitor refresh rate.
301 frames in 5.0 seconds = 60.184 FPS
300 frames in 5.0 seconds = 59.921 FPS
301 frames in 5.0 seconds = 60.123 FPS
301 frames in 5.0 seconds = 60.114 FPS
301 frames in 5.0 seconds = 60.129 FPS
301 frames in 5.0 seconds = 60.120 FPS
...

The hardware on which the above *glxgears* command was run has no graphics card installed so what we are seeing is base-line, no graphics acceleration, performance of the Pentium III CPU chip (*Pentium III / Pentium III Xeon - external L2 cache*).

Globs Benchmarking Utility

GL O.B.S. is based around a PyGTK interface that launches OpenGL programs. It feeds OpenGL with various selectable graphic intensive 3D animation tasks like stacks of dots, rotaing textures cubes, arrays of small images, and simulatd smoke and gathers statistics on the resulting framerates. It is simple and easy to use.
Install it with **sudo apt-get install globs** .

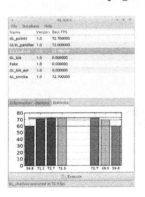

To execute globs simply type **globs** into a command-line, set options like screen resolution and duration of test. When the test finishes click on the "statistics" button and see the distribution graph of frame rates.

Heavyweight Benchmarking with phoronix-test-suite

This a general purpose collection of test for benchmarking (performance testing and measurement) on practically everything that Linux can do. On Ubuntu systems you simply download it using the Ubuntu Software Center GUI (Graphic User Interface). It has a list of 175 separate tests it can perform. 53 of these test are for graphics capabilities. Type in **phoronix-test-suite list-tests** into a command line to see what is available. The tests are to compare different systems with each other. They difficult to run because they often require lengthy downloads and ofter have external dependencies. They are also difficult to interpret.

A Brief Overview of PCI.

Here is a brief overwiew and the URL of two good in-depth, articles that pretty useful. PCI stands for *Peripheral Component Interconnect,* an Intel standard for a 64 and 32 bit connection bus used by graphics acceleration hardware. A bus is a channel or path between the components on the computer. Special hardware, usually on a graphics card, is needed to control the process of rapid transport of the millions of pixels per second that make up the moving images on the screen. The graphics card talks to the processor using the computer's bus as a communication path. Modern computers have PCI graphics chips integrated into the motherboard as well as PCI slots that can take extra cards. The graphics card can be changed by plugging a different graphics card into the PCI bus slots. If two monitors are required then two graphics cards can be plugged into the bus.
The PCI-Express (a.k.a PCI e) is much faster than PCI for two reasons. Firstly is just works at a higher clock speed (that is, processor speed) and, in addition, it makes dedicated serial point-to-point electrical connections using special hardware circuits called switches. These switches are designed to change data flow connections as needed rather than allowing all devices to send all their data traffic over the same bus. Old PCI is a parallel fixed width bus of 32 bits and can handle only 5 devices at a time. The new PCI Express paradoxically is based on many serial connections rather than one parallel bus. As speeds get higher the signals from adjacent conductors on a parallel bus interfere with each other and thus limit the maximum data transmission rates that will work reliably. Every device has its own dedicated connection, so devices no longer share bandwidth. The PCI Express bus comes in several versions (1X, 2X, 4X, 8X, 12X, 16X and 32X), which provide throughputs of between 250 Mb/s and 8 Gb/s.

The following articles, with good illustrations, explain about PIC quite well:
http://computer.howstuffworks.com/pci-express1.htm
http://arstechnica.com/features/2004/07/pcie/

3. The Matrix Transfomation Module used in this Book

```
"""
Program name: matrix_transforms.py
Objective: Provide Matrix Transform module in Python for 2D and 3D transformations.
A Perspective transformation is included,

Keywords: 3d matrix, geometric transformations, perspective transform.
================================================================79
Comments: Rudimentary examples are appended below.

Tested on: Python 2.6, Python 2.7.3, Python 3.2.3
Author:  Mike Ohlson de Fine
===================================
"""
import math
import numpy as np

#%%%%%        3D LINEAR TRANSFORMATIONS        %%%%%%%%%%%
#%%%%%                                         %%%%%%%%%%%%
# STANDARD TRANSFORMATION MATRICES FOR 3D GEOMETRIC SHAPES:
#  Transformations: Translation, rotation, shear, scaling, perspective.

def T_reflect_xy():
    """ Reflection through the X-Y plane
    """
    T = np.matrix( [ [1.0,   0.0,   0.0,   0.0],
                     [0.0,   1.0,   0.0,   0.0],
                     [0.0,   0.0,  -1.0,   0.0],
                     [0.0,   0.0 ,  0.0,   1.0] ])
    return T

def T_reflect_yz():
    """ Reflection through the Y-Z plane
    """
    T = np.matrix( [ [-1.0,   0.0,   0.0,   0.0],
                     [ 0.0,   1.0,   0.0,   0.0],
                     [ 0.0,   0.0,   1.0,   0.0],
                     [ 0.0,   0.0,   0.0,   1.0] ])
    return T

def T_reflect_zx():
    """ Reflection through the Z-X plane
    """
    T = np.matrix ( [ [1.0,    0.0,   0.0,   0.0],
                      [0.0,   -1.0,   0.0,   0.0],
                      [0.0,    0.0,   1.0,   0.0],
                      [0.0,    0.0,   0.0,   1.0] ] )
    return T
```

```python
def T_translate(tx, ty, tz):
    """ Shift points tx in the X-direction,
                ty in the Y-direction and
                tz in the Z direction.
    The apparent direction of Z increasing seems intuitively negative.
    """
    T = np.matrix( [ [1.0,   0.0,   0.0,   0.0],
                     [0.0,   1.0,   0.0,   0.0],
                     [0.0,   0.0,   1.0,   0.0],
                     [tx,    ty ,   tz,    1.0] ] )
    return T


def T_scaling(sx, sy, sz):
    """ Expand points sx in the X-direction,
                sy in the Y-direction and
                sz in the Z direction.
    """
    T = np.matrix( [ [ sx,   0.0,   0.0,   0.0],
                     [0.0,   sy,    0.0,   0.0],
                     [0.0,   0.0,   sz,    0.0],
                     [0.0,   0.0,   0.0,   1.0] ])
    return T


def T_rotx(theta):
    """ Rotate points theta (radians)around the X-axis.
    """
    T = np.matrix( [ [1.0,              0.0,               0.0,   0.0],
                     [0.0,   math.cos(theta),   -math.sin(theta),   0.0],
                     [0.0,   math.sin(theta),    math.cos(theta),   0.0],
                     [0.0,              0.0,               0.0,   1.0] ])
    return T


def T_roty(theta):
    """ Rotate points theta (radians)around the Y-axis.
    """
    T = np.matrix( [ [ math.cos(theta),   0.0,   math.sin(theta),   0.0],
                     [            0.0,   1.0,              0.0,   0.0],
                     [ -math.sin(theta),   0.0,   math.cos(theta),   0.0],
                     [            0.0,   0.0,              0.0,   1.0] ])
    return T


def T_rotz(theta):
    """ Rotate points theta (radians)around the Z-axis.
    """
    T = np.matrix( [ [math.cos(theta),   -math.sin(theta),   0.0,   0.0],
                     [math.sin(theta),    math.cos(theta),   0.0,   0.0],
                     [            0.0,               0.0,   1.0,   0.0],
                     [            0.0,               0.0,   0.0,   1.0] ])
    return T
```

```python
def T_shear(sh_x, sh_y, sh_z):
    """ Shear or skew points points by sh_x in the X-direction,
                    sh_y in the Y-direction,
                    sh_z in the Z-direction.
    """
    T = np.matrix( [ [ 1.0,    sh_x,   sh_z,   0.0],
                     [sh_x,     1.0,   sh_y,   0.0],
                     [sh_z,    sh_y,    1.0,   0.0],
                     [ 0.0,     0.0,    0.0,   1.0] ])

    return T


def T_Z_perspective(xyz_numpy_point, kz):
    """
    Using matrix multiplication, convert a 3D homogeneous matrix (numpy form)
    to an equivalent perspective matrix.
    z_component is the z-component of the point being transformed to perspective coordinates.
    kz is the distance to the projection plane.
    The returned matrix is the plane projection of the object, correctly scaled.
    """
    z_component = xyz_numpy_point.item(2)
    fz = 1/(z_component/kz + 1)

    Pz = np.matrix( [ [fz,    0.0,    0.0,    0.0],
                      [0.0,    fz,    0.0,    0.0],
                      [0.0,   0.0,    0.0,    0.0],
                      [0.0,   0.0,    0.0,    1.0] ])
    return Pz

def T_Y_perspective(xyz_numpy_point, ky):
    """
    Using matrix multiplication, convert a 3D homogeneous matrix (numpy form)
    to an equivalent perspective matrix.
    y_component is the z-component of the point being transformed to perspective coordinates.
    ky is that distance to the projection plane.
    The returned matrix is the plane projection of the object, correctly scaled.
    """
    y_component = xyz_numpy_point.item(1)
    fy = 1/(y_component/ky + 1)

    Py = np.matrix([ [fy,    0.0,  0.0,   0.0],
                     [0.0,    fy,  0.0,   0.0],
                     [0.0,   0.0,  0.0,   0.0],
                     [0.0,   0.0,  0.0,   1.0] ])

    return Py
```

```python
def T_X_perspective(xyz_numpy_point, kx):
    """
    Using matrix multiplication, convert a 3D homogeneous matrix (numpy form)
    to an equivalent perspective matrix.
    x_component is the z-component of the point being transformed to perspective coordinates.
    kx is that distance to the projection plane.
    The returned matrix is the plane projection of the object, correctly scaled.
    """
    x_component = xyz_numpy_point.item(0)
    fx = 1/(x_component/kx + 1)

    Px = np.matrix ([ [fx,   0.0,   0.0,   0.0],
                      [0.0,   fx,   0.0,   0.0],
                      [0.0,  0.0,   0.0,   0.0],
                      [0.0,  0.0,   0.0,   1.0] ] )
    return Px


# A functional form of the above.
def map_2_perspective(numpy_threed_matrix, f):
    """ Convert a 3D homogeneous matrix (numpy form) to an equivalent perspective matrix.
    The view plane is the xy-plaze at z=0. The eye position is at z = -f.
    The view plane is between the object and the eye, always.
    For values of f < -2 the perspective distortion is excessive.

    "numpy_threed_matrix" is an array of 3D faces belonging to an object.

    Note: This is not a transformation matrix. It is a mapping function.
    This means you do not obtain the pespective transformed matrix by matrix post multiplication.
    Instead you pass the matrix and view distance to the "Map_2_perspective()" function,
    and the required perspective matrix is returned.
    """
    bbb = numpy_threed_matrix.tolist()
    twod_line = []
    perspective_3d_array =[]
    perspective_3d_mat =[]
    for i in range(0, len(bbb)):
        divisor = (bbb[i][2]/f + 1)
        new_x = bbb[i][0]/divisor
        new_y = bbb[i][1]/divisor
        new_z = bbb[i][2]
        new_w = 1
        new_vertex = [new_x, new_y, new_z, new_w]
        perspective_3d_array.append(new_vertex)
    perspective_3d_mat = np.matrix(perspective_3d_array)
    return perspective_3d_mat


def T_ortho_xy():
    """ Orthogonal projection onto XY-plane.
    """
```

```python
    C = np.matrix( [ [1.0,   0.0,   0.0,   0.0],
                     [0.0,   1.0,   0.0,   0.0],
                     [0.0,   0.0,   0.0,   0.0],
                     [0.0,   0.0,   0.0,   1.0] ] )
    return C

def T_ortho_xz():
    """ Orthogonal projection onto XZ-plane
    """
    C = np.matrix( [ [1.0,   0.0,   0.0,   0.0],
                     [0.0,   0.0,   0.0,   0.0],
                     [0.0,   0.0,   1.0,   0.0],
                     [0.0,   0.0,   0.0,   1.0] ])
    return C

def T_ortho_zy():
    """ Orthogonal projection onto ZY-plane .
    """
    C = np.matrix( [ [0.0,   0.0,   0.0,   0.0],
                     [0.0,   1.0,   0.0,   0.0],
                     [0.0,   0.0,   1.0,   0.0],
                     [0.0,   0.0,   0.0,   1.0] ] )
    return C

#================================================================
```

4. The Vector Operation Module used in this Book

```
"""
Program name: vector_2d3d_ops.py
Objective: Basic vector operations addition, subtraction,
dot product, cross product, intersection of lines
centroids, normal vectors.

Keywords: vectors, dot product, cross product, intersection, normal, centroid
==========================================================79
Comment: Two dimensional cases (2D) in the x-y plane can be treated as 3D
problems with the z-component set tp zero.

Tested on: Python 2.6, Python 2.7.3, Python 3.2.3
Author:  Mike Ohlson de Fine
================================
"""
import math
import itertools
#-------------------------------------------------------------------
# Vector 3D operations
#=========================

def intersect(p1,p2, q1, q2):
    """ Intersection of 2 lines in 3D cartesian space. Lines are coplanar.
    Inputs are the position vectors of two points on each line.
    There should be a test to confirm the the the two lines are co-planar,
    prior to any solution being computed. For the time being
    we will assume the lines are coplanar.
    """

    px1 = p1[0]
    py1 = p1[1]
    pz1 = p1[2]

    px2 = p2[0]
    py2 = p2[1]
    pz2 = p2[2]

    qx1 = q1[0]
    qy1 = q1[1]
    qz1 = q1[2]

    qx2 = q2[0]
    qy2 = q2[1]
    qz2 = q2[2]

    # Slopes
```

```python
# Q1: Are any divisors zero? ie. are lines paralell?
if (px2 - px1) == 0:
    divsr_mp_xy = 0.000000001
else: divsr_mp_xy = (px2 - px1)

if (pz2 - pz1) == 0:
    divsr_mp_zy = 0.000000001

else: divsr_mp_zy = (pz2 - pz1)

if (qx2 - qx1) == 0:
    divsr_mq_xy = 0.000000001
else: divsr_mq_xy = (qx2 - qx1)

if (qz2 - qz1) == 0:
    divsr_mq_zy = 0.000000001
else: divsr_mq_zy = (qz2 - qz1)

mp_xy = (py2 - py1)/divsr_mp_xy
mp_zy = (py2 - py1)/divsr_mp_zy

mq_xy = (qy2 - qy1)/divsr_mq_xy
mq_zy = (qy2 - qy1)/divsr_mq_zy

# Intercepts - constants.
cp_xy = py1 -mp_xy*px1
cp_zy = py1 -mp_zy*pz1

cq_xy = qy1 -mq_xy*qx1
cq_zy = qy1 -mq_zy*qz1

# Intersection in the x-y plane.
if (mp_xy - mq_xy) == 0:
    divsr_m = 0.000000001
else: divsr_m = (mp_xy - mq_xy)

xi = (cq_xy - cp_xy)/divsr_m

yi = xi*mp_xy +cp_xy

if (mp_zy - mq_zy) == 0:
    divsr_m = 0.000000001
else: divsr_m = (mp_zy - mq_zy)
zi = (cq_zy - cp_zy)/divsr_m

return xi, yi, zi

def unit_normals(p,q,r):
    """ Compute the vector cross-product of vectors drawn between three points.
        Three points are given by their position vectors p, q, and r.
```

```python
    Compute the vector cross product from three vertices of a triangle.
    The result returned: The position vector of the unit normal
    to the plane containing the three points given.
    """

    vx1 = p[0] - r[0]  # x1 - x3.
    vy1 = p[1] - r[1]  # y1 - y3.
    vz1 = p[2] - r[2]  # z1 - z3.

    vx2 = q[0] - r[0]  # x2 - x3.
    vy2 = q[1] - r[1]  # y2 - y3.
    vz2 = q[2] - r[2]  # z2 - z3.

    vnx = vy1*vz2 - vz1*vy2
    vny = vz1*vx2 - vx1*vz2
    vnz = vx1*vy2 - vy1*vx2

    len_vn = math.sqrt(vnx*vnx + vny*vny + vnz*vnz)
    if len_vn == 0:
        vnx = 0
        vny = 0
        vnz = 0
    else:
        vnx = vnx/len_vn
        vny = vny/len_vn
        vnz = vnz/len_vn

    return vnx, vny, vnz

def half_unit_normals(p,q,r):
    """ Compute the vector cross-product of vectors drawn between three points.
    Three points are given by their position vectors p, q, and r.

    Compute the vector cross product from three vertices of a triangle.
    The result returned: The position vector of the unit normal
    to the plane containing the three points given.
    """

    vx1 = p[0] - r[0]  # x1 - x3.
    vy1 = p[1] - r[1]  # y1 - y3.
    vz1 = p[2] - r[2]  # z1 - z3.

    vx2 = q[0] - r[0]  # x2 - x3.
    vy2 = q[1] - r[1]  # y2 - y3.
    vz2 = q[2] - r[2]  # z2 - z3.

    vnx = vy1*vz2 - vz1*vy2
    vny = vz1*vx2 - vx1*vz2
    vnz = vx1*vy2 - vy1*vx2

    len_vn = math.sqrt(vnx*vnx + vny*vny + vnz*vnz)
```

```
    if len_vn == 0:
        vnx = 0
        vny = 0
        vnz = 0
    else:
        vnx = 0.5*vnx/len_vn
        vny = 0.5*vny/len_vn
        vnz = 0.5*vnz/len_vn

    return vnx, vny, vnz


def array_triangle_normals(vertex_array):
    """" Calculate the vertex normal for each face, repeat it three times to furnish a Normal for each
        vertex of the triangle in the vertex array. The output is the target glNormaArray.
    """"
    #print 'vertex_array:', vertex_array
    norm_array = []
    for i in range (0, len(vertex_array), 9): # Number of triangles .
        # Each sequence of 9 floats from vertex_array supplies three vertices v1, v2, v3
        a1 = vertex_array[i]        # first vertex.
        a2 = vertex_array[i+1]
        a3 = vertex_array[i+2]
        v1 = [ a1,a2,a3]

        b1 = vertex_array[i+3]      # second vertex.
        b2 = vertex_array[i+4]
        b3 = vertex_array[i+5]
        v2 = [ b1,b2,b3]

        c1 = vertex_array[i+6]      # third vertex.
        c2 = vertex_array[i+7]
        c3 = vertex_array[i+8]
        v3 = [ c1,c2,c3]

        vec_norm = unit_normals(v1, v2, v3)
        norm_array.append(vec_norm) # Set stride to 0 to match each face to a normal..
        norm_array.append(vec_norm)
        norm_array.append(vec_norm)
    norm_array = list(itertools.chain(*norm_array))    # Ensure the array has been flattened.
    return norm_array
#================================================================
# Test for array_triangle_normals(vertex_array)
'''
octet4tri = [
-0.0, 0.7, 0.7,   -0.0, 1.0, 0.0,   -0.7, 0.7, 0.0,  # 1st triangle
-0.7, 0.0, 0.7,   -0.0, 0.7, 0.7,   -0.7, 0.7, 0.0,  # 2nd triangle
-0.0, 0.7, 0.7,   -0.7, 0.0, 0.7,   -0.0, 0.0, 1.0,  # 3rd triangle
-1.0, 0.0, 0.0,   -0.7, 0.0, 0.7,   -0.7, 0.7, 0.0 ] # 4th triangle
```

```
get_normals = array_triangle_normals(octet4tri)
print 'get_normals:', get_normals
```

Answer: get_normals: [-0.36650, 0.85518, 0.36650,   -0.36650, 0.85518, 0.36650,   -0.36650, 0.85518, 0.36650,

　　　　　　-0.57735, 0.57735, 0.57735,   -0.57735, 0.57735, 0.57735,   -0.57735, 0.57735,
0.57735,

　　　　　　-0.36650, 0.36650, 0.85518,   -0.36650, 0.36650, 0.85518,   -0.36650, 0.36650,
0.85518,

　　　　　　-0.85518, 0.36650, 0.36650,   -0.85518, 0.36650, 0.36650,   -0.85518, 0.366508,
0.36650]
'''

#==

```
def tri_centroid(p,q,r):
    """ Locate the centroid of a triangle.
        The intersection of the lines joining a vertex
        with the mid-point of the opposite side is computed.
        Arguments: three vertices of a triangle.
    """
    # Mid-points of p-q and p-r.
    # Distances point-to-point.
    vx1 = r[0] - p[0]  # x1 - x3.
    vy1 = r[1] - p[1]  # y1 - y3.
    vz1 = r[2] - p[2]  # z1 - z3.

    vx2 = q[0] - p[0]  # x2 - x1.
    vy2 = q[1] - p[1]  # y2 - y1.
    vz2 = q[2] - p[2]  # z2 - z1.

    # Mid-points of p-q (position vector).
    pqx_mp = p[0] + vx2/2.0
    pqy_mp = p[1] + vy2/2.0
    pqz_mp = p[2] + vz2/2.0
    pq_mp = [pqx_mp, pqy_mp, pqz_mp ]

    # Mid-points of p-r (position vector).
    prx_mp = p[0] + vx1/2.0
    pry_mp = p[1] + vy1/2.0
    prz_mp = p[2] + vz1/2.0

    pr_mp = [prx_mp, pry_mp, prz_mp ]

    # Intersection.
    xi, yi, zi = intersect(r,pq_mp, q, pr_mp)
    return xi, yi, zi

def centroid_normals(vertex_array, dxy):
    """ For OpenGL triangle normals.
        Calculate the vertex normal for each face, repeat it three times to furnish a Normal for each
```

vertex of the triangle in the vertex array. The output is the target glNormalArray.
"""

```python
norm_arrows = []
for i in range (0, len(vertex_array), 9): # Number of triangles
    # Each sequence of 9 floats from vertex_array supplies three vertices v1, v2, v3
    a1 = vertex_array[i]        # first vertex.
    a2 = vertex_array[i+1]
    a3 = vertex_array[i+2]
    v1 = [ a1,a2,a3]

    b1 = vertex_array[i+3]      # second vertex.
    b2 = vertex_array[i+4]
    b3 = vertex_array[i+5]
    v2 = [ b1,b2,b3]

    c1 = vertex_array[i+6]      # third vertex.
    c2 = vertex_array[i+7]
    c3 = vertex_array[i+8]
    v3 = [ c1,c2,c3]

    vnor = half_unit_normals(v1, v2, v3)
    vcen = tri_centroid(v1, v2, v3)
    vsum  = [vnor[0]+vcen[0], vnor[1]+vcen[1], vnor[2]+vcen[2] ]
    # Now we produce the triangles that point in the direction of the normal.
    # Each must be added to an array of normal spikes - which are visible normals.

    tris = [ vcen[0], vcen[1], vcen[2],   vcen[0]+dxy, vcen[1], vcen[2],   vsum[0], vsum[1], vsum[2],
            vcen[0], vcen[1], vcen[2],   vcen[0], vcen[1]+dxy, vcen[2],   vsum[0], vsum[1], vsum[2 ]
]
    norm_arrows.append(tris)
norm_arrows = list(itertools.chain(*norm_arrows))    # Ensure the array has been flattened.

return norm_arrows

def vec_sum(p,q):
    """ Sum of two vectors -  3D.
       Sum the components of two vectors.
       The difference is obtained by negating one of the vectors.
    """
    xs = p[0] + q[0]
    ys = p[1] + q[1]
    zs = p[2] + q[2]

    return xs, ys, zs

def vec_difference(p,q):
    """ Difference of two vectors.
       Subtract the components of two vectors.
    """
```

```
    xs = p[0] - q[0]
    ys = p[1] - q[1]
    zs = p[2] - q[2]

    return xs, ys, zs
#=================================================================
# Vector 2D operations
#=========================
def plot_vector(origin, vector, scale, kula, width):
    """ Plot a 2D vector.
    """

    chart_1.create_line(org[0], org[1], org[0] + vector[0]* scale, org[1] - vector[1]* scale, width =
width, fill = kula)

def vec_add(vec_a, vec_b):
    """ Sum of 2D vectors.
    """

    vec_sum = [vec_a[0] + vec_b[0], vec_a[1] + vec_b[1]]
    return vec_sum

def vec_sub(vec_a, vec_b):
    """ Difference of 2D vectors.
    """

    vec_sum = [vec_a[0] - vec_b[0], vec_a[1] - vec_b[1]]
    return vec_sum

def vec_dot_product(vec_a, vec_b):
    """ Dot (scalar) product of 2D vectors.
    Vector dot product is product of magnitudes x cosine of angle between the vectors.
    Result is a scalar quantity.
    """

    magn_a = math.sqrt(vec_a[0]*vec_a[0] + vec_a[1]*vec_a[1])
    magn_b = math.sqrt(vec_b[0]*vec_b[0] + vec_b[1]*vec_b[1])
    theta = math.atan2(vec_a[0], vec_a[1]) - math.atan2(vec_b[0], vec_b[1])
    vec_dot_product = magn_a * magn_b * math.cos(theta)
    return vec_dot_product

def vec_cross_product(vec_a, vec_b):
    """ Vector product of 2D vectors.
    Vector cross product is product of magnitudes x sine of angle between the vectors.
    Result is a vector whose direction is mutually at right angles to the plane
    containing the two vectors. The direction given by the right-hand screw rule.
    Alternate method: Used in the "unit_normals(p,q,r)" function above it uses the determinant
    derived formula, with values from three points in a triangle.
    vx1 = p[0] - r[0]  # x1 - x3.
    vy1 = p[1] - r[1]  # y1 - y3.
    vz1 = p[2] - r[2]  # z1 - z3.

    vx2 = q[0] - r[0]  # x2 - x3.
    vy2 = q[1] - r[1]  # y2 - y3.
```

```
    vz2 = q[2] - r[2]  # z2 - z3.

    vnx = vy1*vz2 - vz1*vy2
    vny = vz1*vx2 - vx1*vz2
    vnz = vx1*vy2 - vy1*vx2
    """
    magn_a = math.sqrt(vec_a[0]*vec_a[0] + vec_a[1]*vec_a[1])
    magn_b = math.sqrt(vec_b[0]*vec_b[0] + vec_b[1]*vec_b[1])
    theta = math.atan2(vec_a[0], vec_a[1]) - math.atan2(vec_b[0], vec_b[1])
    vec_cross_product = magn_a * magn_b * math.sin(theta)
    ''' This answer is merely the magnitude of the cross product. We need three a
        three dimensional coordinate system to be able to provide the vector.
        For this case it is directed parallel to the negative z-axis.
    '''

    return vec_cross_product
#-----------------------------------------------------------------
```

5. OpenGL and Python 3.2 Problems.

How do our Python programs find modules?

When the python interpreter comes across instructions like

import math

import numpy

import OpenGL

import kittykat

import my_home_grown_python_thingy,

where does it find, *math, OpenGL, kittykat* and *my_home_grown_python_thingy?*
Often they are in different places, like different operating system directories or our
own created directories. If we delve into the directory containing these python modules
we discover that there is no standard agreed place to keep them. To make matters
worse if we are testing our code on different versions of Python such as version 2.7 and
version 3.2 then then modules like OpenGL are kept in places seemingly accessible to
Python 2.7 but Python 3.2 cannot find them! What gives?

Many versions of Linux have Python installed as necessary components of the
operating system because some of the operating system programs are actually written
Python. Ubuntu and its offshoots is an example of one. Current versions of Ubuntu
come with Python 2.7 and it is set up to be able to find all standard modules inside a
library created for the purpose. Any time Python runs and an *import* instruction is
encountered, then Python will look in the following directories:
the current directory from which our program is being run,
/usr/local/lib/python2.7/dist-packages/PyOpenGL-3.1.0-py2.7.egg,
/usr/lib/python2.7,
/usr/lib/python2.7/plat-linux2,
 /usr/lib/python2.7/lib-tk,
'/usr/lib/python2.7/lib-old,
/usr/lib/python2.7/lib-dynload,
/usr/local/lib/python2.7/dist-packages,
/usr/lib/python2.7/dist-packages,
'/usr/lib/python2.7/dist-packages/PIL,
'/usr/lib/python2.7/dist-packages/gst-0.10,
'/usr/lib/python2.7/dist-packages/gtk-2.0,
'/usr/lib/pymodules/python2.7,
/usr/lib/python2.7/dist-packages/ubuntu-sso-client,
'/usr/lib/python2.7/dist-packages/wx-2.8-gtk2-unicode

PYTHONPATH, the key to the module search path.

The directory addresses listed above are called paths. There is an *environment*
variable called PYTHONPATH, that is unique to each version of Python we have
installed that Python uses as the list of directories it must search through inorder to

find the modules it needs. Python 2.7 has it's own PYTHONPATH environment variable and unfortunately Python 3.2 has a different one of it's own. A consequence of this is that if we run a Python 3.2 program containing import OpenGl we get an error message like
ImportError: No module named OpenGL. This is because the line
'/usr/local/lib/python2.7/dist-packages/PyOpenGL-3.1.0-py2.7.egg' is non present in Python 3.2's PYTHONPATH variable. This can happen with any module that is not part of the standard Python library. Is there a general procedure to fix this problem? Fortunately there is.

How to Fix Incorrect PYTHONPATH variables.

The procedure is the following:
1. Test if the version of Python we are using is able to find a particular module we need to use.
2. Discover the correct path for any particular module.
3. Modify the PYTHONPATH environment variable to include a missing path which makes a needed module reachable.

The example we use is the OpenGL module.
It is not a standard module that is automatically part of Python. It is some thing we install separately by running the terminal command (for any Ubuntu type of operating system:
sudo apt-get install PyopenGL

When OpenGL for Python is installed in this way, the PYTHONPATH variable is updated to include the search path for OpenGL but only for Python 2.7. Not for Python 3.2

1. The test to determine if PYTHONPATH is correct for Python version x.x
Run the Python version in a command line terminal and attempt to *import OpenGL*
If the PYTHONPATH is good there will no error message. Here is a typical sucessful command line dialog:
mikeodf@mikeodf-HP-500B-Microtower:~$ python
Python 2.7.3 (default, Feb 27 2014, 19:58:35)
[GCC 4.6.3] on linux2
Type "help", "copyright", "credits" or "license" for more information.
>>> import OpenGL
>>>

An unsuccessful command line dialog looks like:
mikeodf@mikeodf-HP-500B-Microtower:~$ python
Python 2.7.3 (default, Feb 27 2014, 19:58:35)
[GCC 4.6.3] on linux2
Type "help", "copyright", "credits" or "license" for more information.

>>> *import OpenGL*
>>>
2. Examine the PYTHONPATH variable for any Python version
The command print (sys.path) reveals the contents of PAYTHONPATH.

For Python version 2.7 the command line dialog is:
mikeodf@mikeodf-HP-500B-Microtower:~$ python
Python 2.7.3 (default, Feb 27 2014, 19:58:35)
[GCC 4.6.3] on linux2
Type "help", "copyright", "credits" or "license" for more information.
>>> import sys
>>> print(sys.path)
['', '/usr/local/lib/python2.7/dist-packages/PyOpenGL-3.1.0-py2.7.egg',
'/usr/lib/python2.7', '/usr/lib/python2.7/plat-linux2', '/usr/lib/python2.7/lib-tk',
'/usr/lib/python2.7/lib-old', '/usr/lib/python2.7/lib-dynload',
'/usr/local/lib/python2.7/dist-packages', '/usr/lib/python2.7/dist-packages',
'/usr/lib/python2.7/dist-packages/PIL', '/usr/lib/python2.7/dist-packages/gst-
0.10', '/usr/lib/python2.7/dist-packages/gtk-2.0', '/usr/lib/pymodules/python2.7',
'/usr/lib/python2.7/dist-packages/ubuntu-sso-client', '/usr/lib/python2.7/dist-
packages/wx-2.8-gtk2-unicode']
>>>

For Python version 3.2 the command line dialog is:
mikeodf@mikeodf-HP-500B-Microtower:~$ python3
Python 3.2.3 (default, Feb 27 2014, 21:31:18)
[GCC 4.6.3] on linux2
Type "help", "copyright", "credits" or "license" for more information.
>>> import sys
>>> print(sys.path)
['', '/usr/lib/python3.2', '/usr/lib/python3.2/plat-linux2', '/usr/lib/python3.2/lib-
dynload', '/usr/local/lib/python3.2/dist-packages', '/usr/lib/python3/dist-
packages']
>>>

If we compare the PYTHONPATH variables for Python 2.7 and Python 3.2 we can
see that Python 3.2 has no entry using the word *PyOpenGL* anywhere. So we need a
method of modifying Python 3.2's PYTHONPATH.

3. Modify PYTHONPATH
We use the *append* command that is used so often in this book and we append the
entry *'/usr/local/lib/python2.7/dist-packages/PyOpenGL-3.1.0-py2.7.egg' that we*
saw in the Python 2.7 PYTHONPATH.
So the command line dialog is:
mikeodf@mikeodf-HP-500B-Microtower:~$ python3

Python 3.2.3 (default, Feb 27 2014, 21:31:18)
[GCC 4.6.3] on linux2
Type "help", "copyright", "credits" or "license" for more information.
>>> import sys
>>> sys.path.append("/usr/local/lib/python2.7/dist-packages/PyOpenGL-3.1.0-py2.7.egg/")
>>>

We can then test and verify that this was successful by typing *import OpenGL* into the terminal and we see with gladness that there was no error message.

However, Beware – The change to PYTHONPATH is not persistent.

The command *sys.path.append(" / usr / local / lib / python2.7 / dist-packages / PyOpenGL-3.1.0-py2.7.egg / ")* has to be run from within a python program and the PYTHONPATH variable modification only lasts until the program terminates. **The sys.path.append(...) must be run afresh every time the Python 3.2 program is executed.**

This why it is incorporated as part and parcel of the Python program code.

www.ingramcontent.com/pod-product-compliance
Lightning Source LLC
Chambersburg PA
CBHW071406050326
40689CB00010B/1772